VIXI

VIXI

Memoirs of a Non-Belonger

RICHARD PIPES

Yale University Press   New Haven & London

Copyright © 2003 by Richard Pipes.
All rights reserved.
This book may not be reproduced, in whole or in part, including illustrations, in any form (beyond that copying permitted by Sections 107 and 108 of the U.S. Copyright Law and except by reviewers for the public press), without written permission from the publishers.

Designed by James J. Johnson and set in Fairfield Medium type by Keystone Typesetting, Inc. Printed in the United States of America by R. R. Donnelley & Sons Co., Inc.

Library of Congress Cataloging-in-Publication Data

Pipes, Richard.
Vixi : memoirs of a non-belonger / Richard Pipes.
   p.   cm.
Includes bibliographical references and index.
ISBN 0-300-10165-1 (alk. paper)

1. Pipes, Richard. 2. Historians—United States—Biography. 3. Sovietologists—United States—Biography. 4. Soviet Union—Historiography. I. Title.
DK38.7.P5A3 2003
947.084′092—dc21
[B] 2003049705

A catalogue record for this book is available from the British Library.

The paper is this book meets the guidelines for permanence and durability of the Committee on Production Guidelines for Book Longevity of the Council on Library Resources.

10 9 8 7 6 5 4 3 2 1

I dedicate this book to the memory of my parents,

Mark and Sofia Pipes,

*in gratitude for giving me life and
then saving me from certain death at the
hands of the Nazis.*

But take the utmost care and watch yourselves scrupulously, so that you do not forget the things you saw with your own eyes and so they do not fade from your mind as long as you live. And make them known to your children and your children's children.

DEUTERONOMY 4:9

Contents

Illustrations

Irene in Celerina, Switzerland, 1957.
With the head of Central Asia's Muslims, Tashkent, April 1957.
With Alexander Kerensky in Stanford, California, summer 1959.
Freshly baked professor in his Widener study, c. 1960.
Our sons, Steven and Daniel, Paris, 1962.
Parents: last picture together, Chesham, N.H., 1971.
With my graduate students Dan Orlovsky and Nina Tumarkin, 1971.
Skating at the Evening with Champions at Harvard, 1972.
With Leszek Kołakowski, Franco Venturi, and Isaiah Berlin, Oxford, February 1974.
Isaiah Berlin.
Edmund Wilson.
With Andrei Amalrik, outside Moscow, July 1975.
China: with the 176th Division, spring 1978.
My portrait by *People* magazine, 1977.

FOLLOWING PAGE 230

Shaking hands with Ronald Reagan, July 1981.
Richard V. Allen, 1981.
At my desk in the Old Executive Office Building, 1982.
With the NSC staff, 1982.
Irene with President Reagan, January 1982.
Lunch for Soviet dissidents in the White House, May 1982.
Briefing Vice President George Bush, July 1983.
With Andrei Sakharov, Boston, 1988.
Family in Chesham, 1990.
The entrance to the old Central Committee headquarters, Moscow, September 1991.
World Economic Forum, Davos, January 1992.
Receiving honorary doctorate in Cieszyn, May 1994.
Lecturing on Struve in his birthplace, the Ural city of Perm, February 2003.

Preface

Vixi in Latin means "I have lived." I have chosen it as this book's title because any other that I could think of for my memoirs has already been used by someone or other. It also has the advantage of brevity.

The subtitle "Memoirs of a Non-Belonger" also requires explanation. In the British Virgin Islands, where my wife and I purchased a house in 1986, the law recognizes, besides residents and visitors, a third category, that of "non-belongers" who, like residents, can own property yet, like visitors, possess no residential rights. It struck me some time ago that the term has some application to my life. I have, of course, "belonged" to various institutions, notably Harvard, where I taught for nearly half a century, and the U.S. government, which I served for three years in the Air Corps and two years in the White House. But when I say that in some important respects I feel to have been a lifelong "non-belonger" I mean that I have always insisted on following my own thoughts and hence shied from joining any party or clique. I could never abide "group think." My views on the history of Russia estranged me from much of the profession, while my opinions of U.S.-Soviet relations alienated me from the Sovietological community. The subtitle of my memoirs is meant to emphasize this aspect of my personality and the life's experiences resulting from it.

The life of an academic is not commonly of general interest since it is rather repetitious where teaching is involved and esoteric where it concerns scholarship. However, there are three aspects of my past that, it seems to me, may be of wider interest. One is my experiences as a sixteen-year-old Jewish boy in 1939 Poland invaded by the Germans and my eventual escape with my parents to the United States. Another has to do with the fact that I was fortunate to be at Harvard, as both student and professor, during its golden age, between the end of World War II and the outbreak of full-scale war in Vietnam, when it was the world's unchallenged premier university. And third, I was personally involved in U.S.-Soviet relations at one of the high points of the Cold War in the 1970s and 1980s, especially during the two years (1981–82) when I served as President Reagan's specialist in East European and Soviet affairs.

There are various reasons for writing an autobiography, but for me the most important is to get to know oneself. For if one has lived to a ripe old age, as I have, one's life is a long story whose earlier chapters are clouded in darkness. Are we the same over these decades? Can we still understand what we have once said and done, and why? To write an autobiography is akin to doing an archaeological dig with the difference that the digger is also the site.

We are immensely complex creatures who know each other and even ourselves only approximately. In the words of the little-known but excellent nineteenth-century English essayist Alexander Smith, "The globe has been circumnavigated, but no man ever yet has; you may survey a kingdom and note the result in maps, but all the *savants* in the world could not produce a reliable map of the poorest human personality." We can get to know ourselves at all only by charting the course of our lives as best as we can. I found it an exhilarating experience, and I hope that the reader will develop some curiosity for a life that spanned eight decades and two continents and that was, at times, close to the center of historic events.

The writing of one's biography is a unique experience. When in my histories I am retelling the lives of others, I am always conscious that I have the choice of presenting the facts and interpreting them in various and different ways. But in recounting my own life, I felt that if I was to be honest, I had no alternative but to present them as they were engraved on my mind: there was a certain imperative driving the endeavor.

Having asked several persons close to me, beginning with my wife, to read the manuscript, I made a strange discovery: the closer people are to the author of memoirs, the more of a proprietary interest they develop in them. If they care for you, then they presume a right to contribute to and even touch up the portrait you paint of yourself because they feel that in some ways they know you better than you know yourself. I greatly appreciate these friendly readers' comments which I have given the most serious consideration, but ultimately my conscience was the arbiter of what to say and how to say it.

I have an additional reason for retracing my past in that I am, if not a survivor of the Holocaust, then a fortunate escapee from it. It may sound strange coming from a professional historian, but I have always had trouble dealing with the past. Not the past of others but my own and that of people close to me. I find it emotionally difficult to accept that the people I knew and the events I have experienced or witnessed have vanished as if they had never existed. I find it especially hard to cope with the fact that I am probably the only custodian of the memory of many people long dead: much of my family and nearly all my school friends who perished without trace in the Holocaust. I am depressed by this thought because it seems to make life meaningless, for which reason I feel an additional obligation to write these memoirs in order that their memory not be entirely lost.

VIXI

ONE

Poland, Italy, America

War

On Thursday, August 24, 1939, the Polish-Jewish daily *Nasz Przegląd (Our Review)*, which we read regularly, carried on the front page the startling news that the two archenemies, Nazi Germany and the Soviet Union, had signed a nonaggression treaty. The previous month, I had had my sixteenth birthday and had recently returned from a three-week course at a military preparatory camp (the Polish equivalent of ROTC) required of gymnasium students in their penultimate year. In the normal course of events I would have gone back to school in a few days for the final year of my studies. But it was not to be.

Father concluded that the news spelled war and decided that we would move from our apartment because the house in which we lived, being located next to Warsaw's central railroad terminal, was a likely target of aerial bombardment. We moved to Konstancin, a resort town south of Warsaw, where we rented a large room in a villa and awaited further developments. The authorities ordered the city to maintain a blackout. I recall in the evening a discussion by candlelight between father and one of my uncles about whether there would be war: uncle was of the opinion that all depended on Mussolini, which proved quite wrong since in fact Hitler's war machine, with Stalin's blessing, was already deployed north, west, and southwest of Poland, poised to attack.

The city government instructed residents living in the suburbs to dig trenches as protection from bombs. I tackled the task with great energy until the lady who owned the villa demanded I stop because I was damaging her flower beds.

At 6:30 in the morning on Friday, September 1, I was awakened by a sequence of booming sounds coming from a distance. My first thought was that I was hearing thunder. I dressed and ran out, but the weather was clear. High above I saw a formation of silvery planes heading for Warsaw: a solitary biplane—it looked as if it were constructed of wood—rose steeply to meet them. The sounds I heard were not thunder but bombs being dropped at the Warsaw airport, which quickly smashed what small air force the Poles had managed to assemble.

Despite the great disparity in military forces, the position of Poland was not entirely hopeless. For one, Poland had guarantees from both England and France that should Germany attack, they would declare war on her. The French furthermore promised the Poles that they would promptly counterattack on the Western Front so as to pin down German forces. Second, the Poles counted on Soviety neutrality which would enable their forces to regroup and make a stand in the eastern half of the country where the Wehrmacht would not be able to outflank them. They did not realize that the French would not keep their word and that the Russians had a secret clause in their nonaggression treaty with Berlin which awarded them the eastern half of Poland.

Before the morning was much advanced, we learned from the radio that Poland and Germany were at war and that enemy troops had crossed the frontier at multiple points.

My attitude toward the war was a blend of hope and fatalism. As a Pole and a Jew I despised the Nazis and expected that with the help of the Allies we would win. This fatalism stemmed from the belief, common to youths and those adults who never quite grow up, that whatever happens is bound to happen. In practice, it meant that one lived from day to day and hoped for the best. The attitude of fatalism was summarized in my favorite saying of Seneca's: *Ducunt volentem fata, nolentem trahunt*—"The fates guide the willing and drag the unwilling."

In the evening of this first day of what became World War II, father sat me down on a bench in the park that surrounded the villa and told me that if anything were to happen to him and mother, I should make my way to Stockholm and there contact a Mr. Ollson at the Skanska Banken, where he had an account. As I was to learn many years later, the money, in the form of a check, had been smuggled out, concealed in a typewriter, in 1937 by a close friend: it was initially deposited in London and then transferred to Stockholm. It was the first time ever that father addressed me as an adult. The money—a modest $ 3,348—was to save our lives.

The war, of course, came as no surprise: we had long anticipated it and contemplated leaving Poland. Following the Allies' capitulation at Munich in October 1938 I thought a general European war inevitable. But there were immense difficulties with obtaining visas. My parents applied for tourist visas to visit New York's World Fair, which the American consulate agreed to issue them provided they left me behind. It was arranged, therefore, through an uncle of mine who lived in Palestine and had good connections with the British mandate authorities, that I would join him, which is what I preferred in any event. I subsequently learned that had Hitler attacked Poland six days later, we would have been gone because my parents had received on August 28 tourist visas to the United States, while I had the necessary papers for Palestine.*

The day after war broke out I volunteered to help direct the traffic in Konstancin. My instructions were to wave cars off the road at the sound of the air alarm sirens. I did this dutifully for several days but then realized the futility of it since the cars, some loaded with officers in uniform and their families, ignored my signals as they sped south and east to get out of the country.

European civilians in the late 1930s had been repeatedly warned of the dangers of chemical warfare from the air. I happened to own a gas mask which I had brought from the ROTC camp, but it had no filter, which rendered it useless. A Jewish girl I had met in Konstancin told me that she had such a filter and offered to give it to me if I came to her villa. I turned up in the evening and knocked on the door of the darkened frame house. When it opened I saw a roomful of young people dancing sensuously to phonograph music. The girl had no idea what I wanted and, dismissing me, returned to her partner.

The war was barely six days old when we heard stunning rumors that the Germans were drawing near: I recorded this in the diary I began to keep. In fact (although this was not known to us at the time), the Polish government already on September 4–5 had carried out a partial evacuation of its personnel from Warsaw: the following night (September 6–7) the commander in chief of the Polish armed forces, General Rydz-Śmigły, secretly abandoned the capital. Father secured a car and we headed back to Warsaw. En route we were stopped by a picket, but after father showed his documents, including papers proving him a War World I veteran of the Polish Legions, we were allowed to proceed. In

---

*Years later mother told me that the Swedish consul in Warsaw, whom my parents knew socially, had offered them visas to Sweden, but when he learned that my mother's legal first name was "Sarah" informed her that unfortunately he was unable to honor the offer.

the city the situation was very tense. The Germans were dropping leaflets from the air urging surrender. I tried to pick one up but a passerby warned me that they were "poisoned." The radio kept our spirits up with appeals from the city president, Stefan Starzyński (subsequently interned and four years later executed in Dachau), and round-the-clock broadcasts of Chopin's "Military" Polonaise (no. 3). Into the city straggled on foot, on horse, and by cart the remnants of the defeated Polish army—some wounded, all ragged and despondent.

On September 8, the Germans began the assault on Warsaw but they ran into stiff resistance. I saw long lines of civilian men, presumably reservists, responding to a government appeal, carrying small bags, marching out of the city eastward where they were to be inducted into the armed services. My parents discussed leaving Warsaw: we had a car at our disposal, and father wanted us to flee to Lublin, some one hundred miles southeast of Warsaw because the government was evacuating to that city. The idea came from the Polish foreign minister, Joseph Beck, whom father knew and who urged him to follow the government. Mother firmly refused, convinced that the proposal was inspired by the belief that father had money; as soon as it ran out, we would be abandoned. I heard a furious shouting argument in the bedroom on this subject. Fortunately, mother prevailed.

By mid-September, Warsaw was encircled and we were trapped. We left our lodgings for the second time, moving in with friends who lived in a solid apartment house away from city center. Parents settled with them while I was put up in a small room on the top floor, the residence of a Jewish scholar. He had a sizeable library, and I borrowed a history of Byzantium, part of Wilhelm Oncken's multivolume World History series, which he asked me please to return in the same shape in which I had found it. I also had some books of my own. As bombs were raining on the city, mother time and again came up to ask me to take refuge in the cellar, but I refused until the bombardment got too fierce. After Warsaw had surrendered, I found that a huge artillery shell had ripped through the ceiling of my room and crashed through the wall a foot over my bed, settling without exploding on the landing.*

---

*Years later I learned that Pliny the Younger behaved in a similar manner during the terrible earthquake that destroyed Pompeii. In a letter to Tacitus, he described how, staying at nearby Misenum, he felt violent tremors. His mother urged him to leave, but he—whether "from courage or folly"—asked that a volume of Livy be brought to him and "went on reading as if [he] had nothing else to do." He left only after his house was in danger of tottering. He was seventeen at the time. *The Letters of the Younger Pliny* (Hammondsworth, 1969), 170–71.

Beginning with the night of September 22, after the diplomatic corps had been evacuated, Warsaw was subjected to round-the-clock bombardment: by day Stuka bombers circled over the defenseless city, diving with a screeching noise and dropping explosives on civilian targets; at night we came under artillery fire. The bombardment was indiscriminate, except on September 23, the day of Yom Kippur, when the German fliers amused themselves by concentrating on Warsaw's Jewish quarter.

Among my papers, I have found a diary written eight months after these events, and I can do no better than to quote from it:

Around the 23rd the radio [transmitter] fell silent, having been destroyed by bombs. The next day we had no water (gas had been lacking for some time). We slept fully dressed with all our things on hand, ready to run. I slept alone on the sixth floor reading Nietzsche's *Will to Power* and the poetry of [Leopold] Staff or writing notes for my essay on Giotto. Artillery reverberated throughout the 24th, day and night, and on the 25th in the morning we were awakened by the sound of bombs. There were no longer any antiaircraft defenses or [Polish] planes, only here and there a machine gun resounded. There began day-long bombardment by 450 planes, which exceeded anything seen in the annals of history. Bomb after bomb fell on the defenseless city like a rainstorm. Houses collapsed, burying thousands of people or else spreading fire along the streets. Mobs of nearly crazed people, carrying children and bundles, ran along the streets that were covered with rubble. German pilots, the worst beasts in the world, deliberately flew low to rake [the streets] with machine-gun fire. By evening, Warsaw was in flames resembling Dante's Inferno. From one end of the city to the other all one could see were the glows of fire reddening the sky. Then German artillery went to work, blanketing the city with a hail of shells. . . . Our [temporary] home miraculously escaped being hit and bore the traces of "only" two artillery shells.

But we were not to be spared anything. Around 1 A.M. we were awakened by a loud explosion—a shell had struck the floor below, killing a woman. We jumped up and ran down the darkened stairwell crowded with people. Screams, desperate calls, and moans mingled with the harsh echoes of detonating shells. Our house began to burn. We fled to the courtyard, I with a briefcase containing my most precious writings and books, carrying in my arms our trembling dog. The instant I crossed the courtyard, a shrapnel exploded nearby, but it caused no harm. We took refuge in the cellar, but at 5 A.M. we had to abandon it because it was no longer safe—one of the stairwells was on fire.

We ran into town. On Sienkiewicz Street we found refuge in an immense but very dirty and crowded basement. Artillery was pounding without letup. At 7 in the evening this building began to burn. We ran out into the street again, this time on Marszałkowska Street, where we settled down on a narrow stairwell. . . . The second night came around. Artillery kept on pounding—the entire city stood in flames. I shall never forget the sight that met our eyes on the corner of Marszałkowska and Zielna: horses freely roaming on the streets or else sprawled dead on the pavement, lit up by the glow of houses burning like boxes; people running from house to house in search of secure shelter. During the night the artillery fire subsided somewhat, and so, resting my head on the knees of a waitress, I fell asleep. I was hungry: we barely saved our dog by giving it sugar and some miraculously obtained water.

Suddenly the door opened and four badly wounded soldiers were brought in. They were bandaged by the light of candles, without water and medicines. Women began to faint and lose their reason; children cried. I too was near collapse. Finally I calmed down and listened indifferently to arguments whether, for example, to put out the candles or not, etc. Crowds of people stormed our door trying to enter. Artillery fire weakened appreciably. It became quieter. . . . Warsaw, and Poland along with it, has lived through its last day.

I may add something that I did not record in my diary, namely, that as we were running along the burning streets, mother ran alongside holding a pillow over my head to protect me from falling debris.

In the cellars, the wildest rumors circulated. I noted them in my pocket diary: the Poles were repulsing German attacks and recapturing cities; the French had broken through the Siegfried Line; and the British had landed in East Prussia. One of the irregular news sheets that appeared during these days under the chipper title *Dzień dobry!* (*Good Day!*) announced in its headlines: "Siegfried Line broken. French enter the Rhineland. Polish bombers raid Berlin," all of which was pure fiction. Finally the truth dawned: on September 17 the Soviet army had crossed into Poland and occupied her eastern provinces. In my diary I noted under Sunday, September 24: "Warsaw defends itself. The Soviets have occupied Borysław, Drohobycz, Wilno, Grodno. On the Western Front—silence. Poland is lost. For how long?"

On the twenty-sixth, the Polish authorities and the German military opened negotiations. Warsaw capitulated the next day. The terms agreed upon provided for forty-two hours of armistice. At 2 P.M. of the twenty-seventh the guns fell silent and the planes disappeared from the sky: between them, they had destroyed one in eight of the city's buildings. An eerie silence ensued. On September 30, the Germans entered the city. I happened to run into their vanguard unit, a convertible military car which stopped at the corner of Marszałkowska and Aleje Jerozolimskie, the heart of Warsaw. A young officer sitting next to the chauffeur got up and photographed the crowd that had surrounded the car: I glared at him with hatred.

During the two-day armistice we returned to our apartment, which except for some broken windows had escaped damage. The houses on both sides of ours and across the street, however, lay in ruins. Coco, our year-old cocker spaniel, who had accompanied us on our wanderings, went mad with joy, running wildly around the dining room and jumping on and off the sofa. She must have thought that our tribulations were over.

There exists a great deal of misinformation about the Polish campaign of 1939: the Poles are ridiculed for trying to stop German tanks with cavalry and depicted as collapsing after offering token resistance. In fact, they fought very bravely and effectively. Declassified German archives reveal that they inflicted heavy casualties on the Wehrmacht in the four weeks of war: 91,000 dead and 63,000 seriously wounded.[1] These were the heaviest losses it would suffer until the battles of Stalingrad and the siege of Leningrad two years later—two years during which the Germans conquered virtually all Europe.

We had something to eat and drink because just before the outbreak of the war mother had bought a large bag of rice which she stored under her bed: this would be our staple food for the next month. It was served in a variety of ways, even spiced up with marmalade. We had also filled the bathtub with water.

On October 1, German units began to roll into the city. They drove in trucks, and I noticed with surprise that their soldiers were not the blond supermen of Nazi propaganda: many were short and swarthy and quite unheroic in appearance. The occupying power soon restored the utilities. Bakeries opened. Polish stores sold, or rather gave away their goods for next to nothing: I bought what I could, including sardine cans and chocolate bars. The behavior of the occupying troops during the first month of occupation was quite correct. I witnessed no acts of violence. One image that sticks in my mind is that of a German soldier on a motorcycle with a bearded Jew in the sidecar directing him through the Warsaw streets. On another occasion, I saw two young Jewish women flirting with an embarrassed German guard at the entrance to a building, tickling his nose with flowers. The only overtly anti-Semitic incident I observed was a truckload of Germans barreling down a street in the Jewish quarter, the soldiers roaring with laughter as the Jews, some of them elderly, scattered to avoid being run down. Soon posters appeared on the walls issued by the German commander. One listed Poles who had been executed for various "crimes," such as uttering in the presence of a German the word *psiakrew,* literally "dog's blood," a rough equivalent of the English "damn." There was also a picture plastered all over town depicting a wounded Polish soldier, his arm in a sling, angrily pointing to the ruins of Warsaw and shouting to Chamberlain: "This is your work!" We studied these posters in silence.

Father was once stopped on the street by a German who walked up to him, put an arm on his shoulder, and asked *"Pole?"* Father responded angrily in flawless German: "No! Get your hands off me." The flustered soldier thinking he had annoyed a fellow-German apologized and walked away.

On October 6, Hitler came to survey in triumph the conquered capital of Poland. I watched him from our window on the fourth floor: there were German soldiers with guns posted every few feet along the route on Marszałkowska, the city's main thoroughfare, and below our house. He rode in an open Mercedes, standing up in the familiar pose, giving the Nazi salute. I thought how easy it would be to assassinate him.

The Poles initially bore the foreign occupation with sullen fatalism. After all, their country had been independent for only 21 years, following 120 years of foreign rule. Their patriotism centered more on the nation with its culture and on their religion than on statehood. They had no doubt that they would outlast this occupation as well and see Poland reborn once again.

For the Jews the situation was, of course, very different. The majority of Polish Jews—Orthodox and living in compact settlements—probably knew little of Nazi attitudes toward them. The Jews of Eastern Europe were the most pro-German group of the population (apart from those among them who sympathized with communism and the Russians).* They remembered the years during World War I (1915—18) when the Germans, having conquered Poland from the Russians, brought law and order: my mother's family had nothing but good recollections of that period. I believe that the majority of Jews were not terribly frightened by what had happened in September 1939 and counted on resuming more

---

*Which, unfortunately, many did. Jews, who for centuries had been isolated by the Christians among whom they lived, were very realistic, indeed hard-bitten, about their private affairs but remarkably naive about politics from which traditionally they had been excluded. Some of the assimilated among them tended to believe in socialism as their Orthodox brethren believed in the coming of the Messiah.

or less normal lives. Israel Zangwill in his *Chidren of the Ghetto* rightly says that "the Jew has rarely been embittered by persecution. He knows that he is in the *Goluth*, in exile, and that the days of the Messiah are not yet, and he looks upon the persecutor merely as the stupid instrument of an all-wise Providence."[2]

The assimilated Jews were more worried: they knew of the Nuremberg laws and Kristallnacht. But even they believed they would manage somehow under German rule: after all, the Germans would need physicians, tailors, and bakers. Jews had learned over two millennia how to survive in hostile environments. They achieved this not with appeals to honor and sympathy or claims to human rights but by making themselves useful to the powers that be: by lending money to kings and aristocrats, by marketing their commodities, by collecting their rents and taxes. True, once in a while they were robbed of their belongings and expelled, but by and large they had managed. They thought this time they would do likewise. They were deeply mistaken. For the people they had to deal with now were motivated not by economic self-interest but by an insane racial hatred—a hatred that could not be appeased.

I came to understand this attitude better half a century later as I observed the naïveté of many Israelis in dealing with the Palestinians. Having beaten back three Arab invasions intended to destroy Israel and massacre or at least expel its Jewish population, the Israelis settled into a comfortable existence, inclined to make almost any concession to the Arabs in order to enjoy peace and prosperity. A good part of the Israeli population simply ignored the unmistakable evidence of the unappeasable, destructive passions of their Palestinian neighbors, convinced that they could be bought off with concessions. Because they did not hate, they found it difficult to believe they could be hated.

Life in occupied Poland returned with surprising rapidity to normal: it is amazing how quickly the everyday overwhelms the "historic." This experience left me with the abiding conviction that the population at large plays only a marginal role in history, or at any rate in political and military history, which is the preserve of small elites: people do not make history—they make a living. I found this insight confirmed in Arnold Bennett's introduction to his *Old Wives' Tale*, where he recalls interviewing an aged railroad employee and his wife about Paris during the Prussian siege of 1870–71. The "most useful thing which I gained from them," Bennett writes, "was the perception, startling at first, that ordinary people went on living very ordinary lives in Paris during the siege."

If I may revert to my recollections of these days as I recorded them in

May 1940, this is what I wrote of the time we spent under German occupation:

> There began the saddest month in my life so far, which was to have such a fine end: October 1939. It is difficult for me to describe what I did during this time and how I spent my time. The apartment was beastly cold; I slept under the comforter almost fully clothed. It was dangerous to go out because the Germans nabbed people for work. I could read and study only at daytime because in the evening there was no electric light and candles had to be used sparingly. We ate day after day rice, macaroni, and various soups—later cabbage and bread were added. I rose from bed around 10 and with great revulsion but equal hunger ate breakfast, following which I went to visit [my friends] Olek or Wanda, or else stayed home. . . . I was in despair when I thought of my predicament—how all my ambitions, plans and dreams lay shattered.

I do not know precisely why father found intolerable the prospect of mere survival under German occupation, to which most Jews resigned themselves. It probably was pride: he was a dignified man who found unbearable the thought of being treated like a pariah. He shared none of the prevailing illusions and anticipated correctly what lay ahead. In a letter he wrote a month later, before overt persecution began, he warned, "Polish Jews face a fate worse than German Jews."

Sometime during the first half of October we began to hold family consultations in the kitchen, which we had all to ourselves, our maid, Andzia, having vanished at the outbreak of the war. The possibility had arisen of leaving Poland for the West on forged papers as citizens of a Latin American country. Father knew the honorary consul of that country, whom I shall call Mr. X, who had in his possession a single blank passport although no consular stamp: the latter had been taken by the consul general when he left Warsaw with the diplomatic corps. Mr. X offered to place this passport at our disposal. But we faced the question: dare we uproot ourselves and go into the unknown? Although we were not rich, money was never discussed in our household (in general, money was not a topic of conversation in Jewish middle-class families), and I had no inkling that it was necessary for survival. While father pondered aloud the pros and cons of such a venture, I saw only the pros. I wanted to enroll at a university and knowing that this was unthinkable in German-occupied Poland, urged that we leave. As for money, we would somehow manage: after all, father did have a bank account in Stockholm to tide us over.

According to mother, the decision to leave was made after the Germans posted billboards announcing that bread ration cards would be issued to residents who registered with them. Father concluded that this was their way of determining who was Jewish.

My arguments and my (unwarranted) self-confidence undoubtedly helped sway father: in retrospect, I am still amazed at the sheer audacity of his decision. Mother located a Jewish engraver who in less than an hour forged the missing consular seal. Father then began negotiations with the German Command for permission to leave. The Gestapo had moved into Warsaw on October 15, but he dealt exclusively with the military. He told me that while negotiating our departure at German headquarters he ran into Mayor Starzyński who, suspecting him to be a German agent or collaborator, gave him an angry look, but there was no opportunity to explain.

While this was happening, I visited my friends, all of whom, fortunately, had survived the siege. Entering the courtyard of the apartment house of a school friend who passionately loved music, I heard the sounds of Beethoven's *Eroica*. The mother of another schoolmate was so frightened that she refused to open the door to me. My best friend, Olek Dyzenhaus, was in fine shape. As we walked on Marszałkowska, we noticed a queue for bread: we took our place in it, talking and laughing. A man behind us, shaking his head, murmured, "Ah, youth, youth!" We thought this queer, but I now understand his reaction.

Finally all the papers were ready, including a transit visa to Italy. We were to depart at 5:49 A.M. on Friday, October 27, on the first train to leave Warsaw since the Germans had occupied the city. It was a military train carrying troops on home leave. Our destination was Breslau (today's Wrocław).

Father had made arrangements with a Pole of German origin—they were known as *Volksdeutsche*—to move into our apartment, presumably to protect it until we returned. The man signed a detailed inventory of the apartment's possessions. I gathered some of my treasures, mostly books on music and art history and photographs. I bade good-bye to the rest of my small library, consisting mostly of volumes on philosophy and art history. Its centerpiece was Meyer's multivolume *Konversationslexicon,* an encyclopedia published in the late nineteenth century from which I learned most of what I knew of art history. The Russian censor had blacked out with India ink all passages deemed offensive; the covers had been carefully torn off to serve—so my uncle had informed me—as fuel during the freezing winters of World War I. I trembled uncontrollably throughout the night.

It was still dark when I went to the railroad terminal to fetch two porters: we traveled first class with a lot of baggage, as befitted foreigners of some standing. The terminal was crowded with uniformed Germans. For safety's sake, father persuaded Consul X to accompany us as far as Breslau from where we were to proceed by way of Munich to Rome. One of mother's brothers, Max, who came to the station to bid us good-bye, held Coco, whom we felt we had no choice but to leave behind. She whined and tugged at the leash. As the train gathered steam, she tore loose and jumped up the steps straight into my arms. I would not let go of her. Inside, she slunk under the seat and stayed there for the entire journey, as if aware that she was not meant to be on the train and not wanting to cause trouble. She remained with us until her death some ten years later.

In our compartment sat a German physician in uniform, a sergeant, and a stout lady with a swastika pinned to her suit. The doctor engaged me in conversation: when he learned that I was from Latin America he told me that Spanish oranges were superior to American ones (or was it the other way around?), that the Radio City Rockettes were outstanding, and that his son had asked him to bring back a Polish gardener, adding with a chuckle that he would not allow him into the house because Poles "stank." The sergeant took a side of lard out of his satchel, cut off a thick slice, and chewed on it in silence. Mother, who sat next to me, kicked me gently from time to time to warn me not to say anything that could get us into trouble. When she tried to go to the lavatory, a German soldier standing in the corridor, apparently properly race-conscious, barred her way, saying she was fortunate to be on the train.

With Poland conquered by Germany, there were no borders separating the two countries and we arrived in Breslau without trouble. To deflect suspicion from us, father had chosen one of the best hotels in the city, Vier Jahreszeiten, close to the railroad terminal. After unpacking and washing up, I went into town and bought a couple of books: the city's neatness and prosperity astonished me. In the evening we visited the elegant hotel restaurant on the second floor, which was filled with uniformed officers and well-dressed ladies. We ordered roast duck. The waiter politely inquired whether we had meat coupons. We did not: he advised us how we could obtain them the next day.

I revisited this hotel sixty years later when it was renamed Polonia. It now provided third-rate accommodations. But the dining room on the second floor was still there, though a quarter as large as it loomed in my memory.

We spent a second night in Breslau before departing for Munich on Sunday, October 29. Father had no German money to purchase a ticket to Munich and from there to Rome. He circled the Breslau terminal looking for an officer with an honest face. It was another risky operation. He settled on someone and asked him—under what pretext I do not know—whether he would be so good as to exchange Polish złotys in his possession for Deutsche marks, which German military returning from Poland were entitled to do. The officer obliged.

We traveled to Munich by way of Dresden and arrived there in the afternoon. We had a wait of several hours before boarding the night train to Rome. I was determined to use that time to visit the great Munich museum, the old Pinakotek. I ignored my parents' objections, promising to avoid trouble. I walked from the railroad terminal to the Karolinen-platz where, at that time, stood a mausoleum to Nazi thugs who had fallen in some brawls for the Führer: guards stood at attention and the whole square was bedecked with swastika flags. The distance to the Pinakotek was no more than one kilometer, and I soon reached the eastern side entrance. At the top of the stairs stood a uniformed Nazi.

"Is this the entrance to the Pinakotek?" I asked.

"The Pinakotek is closed. Don't you know there's a war on?"

I returned to the terminal. Later mother said that she had discreetly followed me just in case. I retraced this route in 1951 and felt enormous satisfaction that the Nazi was no longer there but I was.

In the evening we arrived at Innsbruck which, since the Anschluss, served as a border with Italy. A Gestapo official entered our compart-ment—we were now its sole occupants—to collect our passport: we had one for the three of us. He soon reappeared saying that regrettably we could not proceed into Italy because we lacked the Gestapo's permit to leave Germany.

"What must we do?" father asked.

"You should proceed to Berlin where your embassy will procure for you the necessary documents." With these words he saluted and re-turned the passport.

We removed our luggage from the train and piled it on the platform. Father disappeared somewhere. Mother and I stood helplessly while all around us young Germans and Austrians with skis over their shoulders chattered gaily. Suddenly father returned. He told us to load the luggage back onto the train. We did so in great haste for the train was about to leave. We had barely placed our bags in the compartment which we had vacated when the Gestapo official reappeared.

"I asked you to leave the train," he said sternly. But he was a little man and did not sound very frightening.

Father, whose German was native (he had spent his youth in Vienna), did his best to butcher it in both grammar and pronunciation so as to play the role of a Spanish-speaking South American. (In fact, none of us spoke a word of Spanish.) He explained that he had seen the Innsbruck station master and told him of our need to return to our native country as soon as possible. The stationmaster, probably an easygoing Austrian who had no authority in the matter, heard him out and said something like *"von mir aus,"* which roughly translates as "as far as I am concerned," or, perhaps, more colloquially, *"das ist mir Schnuppe"*—"much do I care."

The Gestapo man requested the passport and left. The train by this time was slowly wending its way to the Italian border at Brennero, some twenty-five miles away. Through the window loomed the massive Alps. It was the most critical moment of our lives for if taken off the train at Brennero and compelled to travel to Berlin, we would surely perish since "our" embassy there would at once determine that the passport we carried was invalid and possibly turn us over to the Germans.

I do not recall how long we had to wait for the decision. It was probably minutes but time stretched unbearably. Before we reached the border, the Gestapo man was back. He said:

"You can proceed on one condition."

"What condition?" father asked.

"That you not come back to Germany."

"Aber NEIN?"—"But NO!"—father responded, almost shouting, as if the very notion of ever again setting foot in Germany filled him with horror.

The German handed us the passport and withdrew. Mother burst into tears; father offered me a cigarette, the first ever.

Early in the morning we reached Bolzano, where, during a brief stop, we bought fresh sandwiches. The sun shone brightly. Shortly before noon on Monday, October 30, we arrived in Rome.

We were saved.

My Origins

At this point I shall turn back the clock and tell who I was and from whence I came.

I was born on July 11, 1923, into an assimilated Jewish family in the small town of Cieszyn (Teschen), in Polish Silesia, on the Czech border, fifty kilometers from what would become the Auschwitz extermination camp. My father, Mark, born in Lwów (Lemberg, Lviv) in 1893, spent his youth in Vienna. His ancestors, whose name was originally spelled "Piepes," were since the early nineteenth century prominent in the reform-minded Jewish citizenry of his native city. In the 1840s, one of our forebears by the name of Bernard, who served as secretary of the Jewish community, took the initiative of bringing to Lwów a reform rabbi to head the "Progressive Temple," whose membership consisted mostly of professional men. Even though by modern standards "progressive" Judaism at that time was quite conservative, the Orthodox Jews felt such outrage that one of them murdered the new rabbi and one of his daughters by sneaking into his kitchen and pouring poison into their food.

In 1914, father enrolled in the Polish Legions, which Joseph Piłsudski was organizing under German-Austrian auspices to fight for the independence of Poland. He remained on active service until 1918, fighting under the assumed name of "Marian Olszewski" against the Russians in Galicia. What he experienced I do not know because like most men who had seen war at close quarters, he did not like to talk about it. During this time he made friends with some of the officers who subsequently would run the Polish republic, friendships which stood him in good stead during the interwar period and our escape from Poland.

My mother, Sarah Sophia Haskelberg, known to family and friends as "Zosia," was the ninth of eleven children of a well-to-do Hasidic Warsaw businessman. Mother recalled him as a jolly person, a bon vivant who liked to eat, drink, and sing loudly in a bad voice. He had extensive dealings with the Russian government, selling uniforms and weapons to its army; he acquired considerable real estate in Warsaw and its suburbs. Several of her brothers were sent before the war to Belgium to attend either technical institutes or boarding schools. The family spent the summers at a resort town near Warsaw where grandfather owned a villa: the family moved there around Passover, before school ended, and remained there until after school had started in September. In Warsaw, they lived in an apartment house owned by grandfather: as late as 1939, it had a toilet but no bathroom and one had to wash in the kitchen sink.

When the Russians evacuated Warsaw in summer 1915, they compelled mother's father to come with them, very likely to prevent him from betraying to the Germans what he knew of the Russian military. He spent the next three years in Russia, one of them under Communist rule. Through connections with the Germans, it was arranged in 1918 that he would return home and his place be taken by two of his sons, Henry and Herman. Both married Russian women and spent the rest of their lives in the Soviet Union. Herman perished in Stalin's purges: he was arrested in November 1937 and promptly executed.

We accepted Christmas Eve, 1902, as the date of mother's birth, but it was by no means certain because Jewish families under Russian rule commonly "traded" the birthdays of their sons and daughters to enable the boys to evade military service. (In fact, her brother Leon, who emigrated to Palestine in the 1920s, gave his date of birth as December 28, 1902). My maternal grandfather died of cancer the year I was born. Mother's mother, whom I recall well, spoke almost no Polish, so we had minimal communication. She perished in the Holocaust at the age of seventy-three, being deported and gassed at the Nazi death camp of Treblinka. From time to time, after school, I used to drop into her apartment, where I was always generously fed, but I do not recall her ever visiting us.

My parents met in 1920 when father was living in Warsaw. Mother told me that she first learned of him from a friend who complained that Marek Pipes paid no attention to her when he visited her father on business. Mother said she was confident she could get him to invite her on a date. She called him at his office and pretended to have seen him at a restaurant which she had heard he frequented. Intrigued, he bit the bait, asked her out, and thus began the romance which two years later ended in marriage. The wedding took place in September 1922, following which my parents moved to Cieszyn where, two years earlier, father with three partners—one of them his future brother-in-law—had opened a chocolate factory called "Dea." It exists to this day under the name "Olza" and produces a popular wafer bar called "Marco Polo." The city was (and remains) divided by a river: the eastern part was Polish, the western half belonged to Czechoslovakia. Jews had been living there since at least the beginning of the sixteenth century.

We spent only four years in Cieszyn, and I have few recollections of my hometown. I was born in a two-story house, which still stands. When, seventy years later, the mayor of Cieszyn bestowed on me the city's honorary citizenship, I mentioned during the ceremony three childhood incidents that stuck in my memory. I remembered mother giving me a sandwich of rye bread covered with a thick layer of butter and radishes. As I was eating it in front of the house, the radishes slid off. Thus I learned about loss. Next door lived a boy my age who had a rocking horse covered with a glossy hide. I badly wanted one like it. Thus

I became acquainted with envy. And finally, my parents told me that I had once invited several of my friends to a grocery store and gave each an orange. Asked by the proprietor who would pay, I replied, "parents. " Thus, I concluded, I learned what communism was, namely, that someone else pays.

I visited Cieszyn several times after we had moved away: once during the winter vacations of 1937–38 and then again in February 1939, after the Polish government had forced the Czechs, abandoned by their allies at Munich, to surrender their half of Cieszyn. Walking its deserted streets, I felt sick with shame for my country.

The population used Polish, German, and Czech interchangeably. At home, my parents spoke alternatively Polish and German. With me they spoke exclusively in German; they also engaged German-speaking nannies. But the children I played with spoke Polish and so I picked up the language. As a result, at the age of three or four I was bilingual.

It must be difficult for an American to visualize the cultural crosscurrents that met in the geographic heart of Europe,* for although the United States has many ethnic groups, the English language and heritage have always dominated its culture. Where I was born, cultures met on an equal footing. This environment gave one a keen sense for foreign ways of thinking.

In 1928, having sold Dea, father moved our small family briefly to Cracow where his sister lived with her husband and two sons, as well as father's parents. His father, Clemens (or Kaleb), born in 1843 during the age of Metternich, I recall as a dignified tall gentleman who let me kiss his bearded face but never uttered a word to me. He died in 1935. In Cracow, father founded with his brother-in-law and another partner another chocolate factory, a branch of the Viennese firm of Pischinger & Co., which specialized in manufacturing chocolate wafers. (It operates today under the name Wawel.) We lived in Cracow less than a year. Entrusting the management of the factory to his brother-in-law and his partner, father moved us to Warsaw with the intention of opening retail outlets there. But soon the depression struck. Father disengaged from Pischinger and went into the import business, purchasing fruits, mainly from Spain and Portugal, with hard currency funds allocated to him by friends in the government. The profits, supplemented by mother's income from her family's real estate sufficed for a modest existence. I

---

*Lines drawn from Nordcape to Sicily and from Moscow to the eastern coast of Spain intersect in the vicinity of Cieszyn.

might add that father was really not suited for business. Although he had good ideas, he lacked the perseverance to see them through, quickly growing bored with day-to-day management. My parents led an easy life: later, when things got harder, father recalled nostalgically how the main problem mother had faced each morning was in which café to spend the day. He had the reputation of being one of the best dressed men in Warsaw. He always had a maid who cooked, cleaned, and stoked the tiled furnaces early in the morning. She slept in the kitchen and her wages came to five or six dollars a month plus room and board.

On moving to Warsaw, we first settled in one room in a pension run by a lady from Vienna. There we met a Viennese couple, Oscar and Emmy Burger, who were destined to become our closest lifelong friends. Oscar Burger was the representative for Poland of the Austrian car manufacturer Steyr-Daimler-Puch, which produced compact, low-priced cars that anticipated the Volkswagen. They had a son, Hans, a year younger than me. Soon we leased separate apartments in the same house in another part of town, but when we had to vacate our apartment we moved in with them and for the next five years we shared the same living quarters. Our parents were inseparable and Hans became my surrogate brother.

Tolstoy wrote to a friend that "children are always—and the younger they are, the more so—in a state which physicians call the first state of hypnosis." I remember my childhood that way. I lived in a world of my own, disrupted by occasional contacts with the "real" world. Until adolescence, everything I experienced other than my own thoughts and feelings seemed to lie outside of me and to be not quite real. It was as if I lived in a hypnotic trance, occasionally waking up from it and then promptly reverting to it.

When I was eight or nine, mother taught me a brief prayer in German. I later learned that its author was a poetess of the romantic era, Luise Hensel:

> Müde bin ich, geh' zur Ruh,
> Schliesse beide Äuglein zu;
> Vater, lass die Augen dein
> Über meinem Bette sein.*

Neither then nor since have I experienced any doubts about God's existence or benevolent guidance. Nor did I ever feel the need to prove either. Indeed, God's existence is all that I was absolutely certain of for

---

*Roughly: "I am tired and lay down to rest, shutting my eyes. Father, let your eyes hover over my bed."

His presence was everywhere; all else seemed and still seems to me conditional and problematic.

Perhaps this explains why I led a happy childhood. On the family photographs we managed to save from the war, I usually appear smiling—at any rate, until afflicted by adolescence. The external world was there to be sporadically enjoyed, but when it turned threatening, I could always withdraw into my inner world. That sense outlasted childhood and in some measure accompanied me throughout life. Even the events of World War II, which could have cost me my life, seemed outside of me and hence not really relevant. I was quite confident of a happy ending.

All the same, I had one problem with religion. If, I reflected as a boy of thirteen or fourteen, all that existed emanated from an eternal God, then everything—every creature no matter how small, every event no matter how insignificant—should have an eternal existence. And yet things constantly perished without trace. Peering into a microscope in biology class, I wondered whether God really could account for every amoeba that ever lived. Looking at old photographs, I asked myself whether God remembered this person in a crowd or that horse pulling a cart, all long dead. I never resolved this problem in my mind. My love for history in some ways derived from this quandary. By dealing with events that were past and seemingly dead, in a sense I brought them back to life and so cheated time.

The reputation of interwar Poland as a "fascist" and anti-Semitic country is such that one may wonder how a Jewish youth could have lived there in any state other than one of desperate misery. The term "fascism" has been subjected to such verbal manipulation by the Soviet communists since the 1920s as to have lost all meaning. Italian Fascism—"fascism" in the original and precise meaning of the word—was the outgrowth of an extreme radical socialist movement, headed before 1914 by Benito Mussolini. With the outbreak of World War I, Mussolini, impressed by the patriotic frenzy that had seized Europe and the ease with which national loyalties overwhelmed class loyalties, grafted nationalism onto socialism, proclaiming that the class struggle in the modern world pitted not the citizens of one and the same country against each other, as taught by the socialists, but countries and nations, some of which were rich and exploitative while others were poor and exploited. Gradually, Mussolini abolished rival parties, introduced comprehensive censorship, and forced business enterprises to collaborate with trade unions under overall state supervision. This was a mild version of what had taken place in the Soviet Union.

Nothing of the kind occurred in prewar Poland. Until 1926, Poland tried to follow the democratic path but the difficulties proved insurmountable as communists and socialists battled nationalists, and the rights of the minorities, which made up one-third of the population, were violated. In May 1926, Piłsudski, who during the preceding years had stayed out of politics, staged a coup d'état. But it was limited in scope. Political parties, including the Communist Party, continued to function in the open, press freedom was respected, and the courts retained their independence. Although the military played a prominent role in government and Piłsudski was able to overrule the legislature, his dictatorship was benign and nonviolent. Until his death in 1935, Poland was a traditional authoritarian government which bore little resemblance to Fascist Italy and none to Nazi Germany.

The general perception of Polish anti-Semitism also requires a certain correction. Unquestionably, for Poles the defining criterion of Polishness was adherence to the Catholic Church: thus Orthodox Ukrainians or Jews were not regarded as truly Poles no matter how Polish they might have been in their culture and loyalty. This was the result of 120 years of foreign occupation during which the Catholic Church had held the nation together. The population at large was imbued with a hostility toward Jews, instilled in it over centuries by the Catholic Church. It was not racial anti-Semitism but it was only slightly less painful since it could be averted only by renouncing one's religion and one's people, and even then, in Polish eyes, one never quite got rid of one's Jewishness. But there was no overt discrimination against Jews (except in government and the military) and there were no pogroms. The majority of Orthodox Jews lived, of their own choice, in compact communities because such a lifestyle facilitated the observance of their religion. Assimilated Jews, such as we were, lived outside these communities in an in-between world, but I must say that I felt more in common with educated Poles than with Orthodox Jews who treated the likes of us as apostates.

For all these reasons, a Polish-Jewish middle-class child could be quite happy in pre-1935 Poland. To be sure, there were ugly incidents. In the early 1930s we lived in a residential compound where we were the only overt Jews. This led to occasional name-calling. Once a Jewish youth from a converted family called me a "Jew." I shouted back, "You are a Jew yourself!" whereupon he struck me on the head with a penknife, drawing some blood. His parents apologized profusely. But I cannot say that my childhood years were much disturbed by such rare incidents. We led normal lives: skating and skiing in the winter, driving out of town for picnics and swimming in the big "Legia" pool in the summer, going to the movies.

I was not in any way an outstanding child. I showed no early talents in any direction. I did not read much. I was, however, regarded as a very attractive boy: my olive complexion and raven-black hair which my mother insisted on keeping in bangs, attracted much admiration, and I was often thought to be a Persian or Indian. One of the more traumatic side effects of adolescence was that this admiration quite suddenly ceased.

Surprisingly for someone who would become a professional writer, as a youth I experienced great difficulty putting my thoughts down on paper. I spoke, however, with great facility. As a teenager I entertained my classmates with improvised stories in which they figured as heroes, a talent that many years later enabled me to keep both my children and grandchildren in suspense night after night with bedtime tales. But composing the routine school exercises was for me sheer agony. I learned to write decently only later on, when subjects sprung from my own mind and expressed my own feelings.

Intellectual and Artistic Stirrings

The year 1935 was a watershed in my young life. Three events occurred that year: Marshal Piłsudski died; the Nazis passed the Nuremberg laws which deprived German Jews of citizenship and, indeed, human status; and I experienced the turmoils of puberty.

Although a military dictator in the last decade of his life, Piłsudski had a socialist background: in 1887 he had been arrested and exiled to Siberia for joining a conspiracy to assassinate Tsar Alexander III, the same conspiracy that cost Lenin's elder brother his life. One abiding legacy of socialism was an aversion to all forms of ethnic and religious bigotry, which socialists regarded as a diversion from the class struggle. As long as he was at the helm, Poland did not tolerate overt anti-Semitism. But almost immediately after his death, power passed to generals and colonels who had served under him in the Legions. The worldwide trend was toward authoritarian rule and the creation of single political blocs. Poland could hardly escape the fate of a Europe mired in depression. The situation of Jews deteriorated rapidly, the more so that the Nazis fanned abroad the flames of anti-Semitism. Talk was heard of "solving" the Jewish question (although the only thing that needed "solving" was anti-Semitic paranoia). Jewish enterprises were boycotted; some non-Jewish stores displayed prominently signs proclaiming them "Christian"; Poles were urged to "buy from your own kind." In my school, where previously Catholics and Jews had led separate but amicable lives, students debated the "Jewish question," by which was meant the allegedly harmful influence of Jews on Poland's economy and culture. The term *zażydzenie* or "Judaization" of Poland gained currency. Jewish university students suffered physical assaults, and in 1937, the minister of education, bowing to the demands of the fascist National-Democrats, ordered them to sit on separate benches on the left side of the lecture rooms. All this created an intolerable atmosphere.

Soon after Piłsudski's death, pogroms began. In March 1936, in the small town of Przytyk near Radom, Jews were robbed by local peasants and two of them killed; other incidents of violence followed. Although I was only twelve at the time, I experienced a sense of burning outrage when the authorities condemned to prison Przytyk Jews who had defended themselves while acquitting their murderers and robbers.

All this was occurring against the background of state-sponsored anti-Semitism in Germany, which helped legitimize and encourage this hate-filled ideology throughout the rest of Europe. Father would rush home to listen on the radio to Hitler's latest ravings. Although my German was almost native, I could understand next to nothing of these hysterical screams punctuated by the inhuman braying of the audience. It was not so much frightening as bewildering.

My Jewishness, which until then I treated as a fact, now became a problem. We were trapped. I sympathized with Zionism. Yet the British mandatory power, anxious to pacify the Palestinian Arabs who in 1936 has perpetrated massive violence against Jewish settlers, severely restricted immigration to Palestine. We talked of my being sent to boarding school in England or even Cuba but nothing came of it, partly for reasons of inertia, partly for lack of money.

For all our pride in Jewishness and our commitment to it, like most assimilated Polish Jews—estimated at 5 to 10 percent of Poland's Jewish population, or between 150,000 and 300,000 individuals—we did not observe Jewish rituals. Once in a rare while father would take me to the synagogue, where I would watch, without being able to follow, the congregation's prayers. It struck me how much more informal synagogues were than churches: Catholics seemed to behave in their house of prayer like guests, whereas Jews acted as if they were at home. Worried that the lovely Christmas holidays which the Burgers staged would confuse me about my religion, mother once or twice made me light Hanukkah candles, but it was a colorless affair compared to Christmas with its shimmering evergreen tree, mounds of presents, and the singing of "Holy Night."

Mother worried needlessly about my religious proclivities. Sometime in my thirteenth year I realized that I was not being prepared for my Bar Mitzvah. I told parents that I wished to have one, and they hired an elderly Jew to tutor me. The poor man taught me things that in his eyes I should have learned when I was six, with a resignation that conveyed he thought it futile work. I was fourteen when Bar Mitzvah'ed in the neighborhood synagogue of my mother's family. Compared to the sumptuous Bar Mitzvahs I would later attend in the United States, it was a very modest affair. I was called to read the day's passage in the Torah, following which we repaired with other members of the congregation to a room where mother had laid out cakes and wine. That was all. My only present was a tefillin, the phylecteries worn on the forehead during prayers, a gift from grandmother.

Then, as well as subsequently, I felt awkward praying in public. Thus, although as an adult I would attend services during High Holidays, observe the fast on Yom Kippur, and refrain from eating bread during the eight days of Passover, I never felt at home at any communal observances. Like Harry Wolfson, the eminent Jewish scholar at Harvard, I was a "nonobservant Orthodox Jew." I found and still find the Jewish faith exceptional because it combines idealism with realism. Granted that the Christian ideal of poverty and sacrifice may be theoretically nobler, it never was nor could be practiced except by extraordinary individuals. Rather than urge Jews to give up their wealth, our religion advises them to acquire possessions so as not to be a burden on the community and then practice charity. This strikes me as far more realistic an ethical doctrine than that preached by Jesus.

My commitment to the Jewish faith and Jewish nation rests on several grounds. One, Judaism is totally devoid of pagan accretions; it is an uncompromisingly spiritual religion. Second, I have always admired the mood of resigned idealism that pervades Jewish culture: the preservation of moral ideals in a world that is harsh, especially to Jews, and the sense of humor that makes life under these conditions more bearable. Like Orthodox Jews, I have always viewed every human action in ethical terms, both in my daily life and in my work as a historian. *Sittlicher Ernst*—moral earnestness—was and remains for me a luminous ideal.

And finally, I feel boundless admiration for the ability of my ancestors to survive in a hostile world for two thousand years and still remain true to their faith.

In the poisonous atmosphere that came to prevail following Piłsudski's death, father had to take on a Catholic partner, a colleague from the Legions, who, as far as I could tell, served merely as a front man. In 1936, father opened an office in Gdynia, Poland's main seaport. We visited him during this and the following summer but otherwise we had no contact: I do not recall father calling or writing to me even once during the two years of his absence.

The deterioration in the political and social atmosphere after 1935 coincided with my crossing the border from childhood to adolescence, with all the accompanying physical and psychic turmoil. Things began to happen to me of which I knew nothing but which transformed me, as it were, into a different human being. Initially it found expression not in interest in girls but in a profound intellectual and aesthetic metamorphosis.

It began with music. Once while spending the night with mother's younger sister Regina, I fiddled with the radio set, a so-called superheterodyne model which was supposed to pick up stations throughout Europe but in fact produced mostly wheezing noises. Suddenly I heard riveting music. It was the last movement of Beethoven's Seventh Symphony; judging by the fast tempo with which it was performed it was probably a Toscanini recording. I had never heard anything like it. It was not simply "beautiful"; rather, it spoke to me in a language which I felt I had known long ago but forgotten, a language articulated not in words but sounds. It penetrated my innermost being. That night I tossed incessantly as the music, running through my head, would not let me sleep.

I was determined to relearn that language. I began to frequent concerts at the Philharmonic, usually on Sunday mornings, where I heard outstanding soloists like the pianists Joseph Hoffman and Wilhelm Backhaus. I started piano lessons. In November 1938, I enrolled for private tutoring in harmony with a musician who bore the fitting name of Joachim Mendelson. A dwarf, he treated me very kindly and made me feel that I was destined to be a composer. When the war broke out, I was preparing to start counterpoint. I also took piano lessons with Poland's leading accompanist, whose name I believe was Rosenberg. He habitually wore a jaundiced expression which my playing did nothing to mellow. Father encouraged my musical interests and took me to the opera and my first concert, although when I began to admire Wagner's orchestral music he merely shook his head in incomprehension. He altogether had difficulty understanding my evolution past childhood, and by the time I entered adolescence he gave up trying to fathom me.

Young people can be quite realistic about themselves, if anything, tending toward excessive self-deprecation. I realized quickly enough that despite my love of music, my talents, whether for piano playing or composition, were mediocre at best. I observed with chagrin how effortlessly some of my contemporaries learned to play the piano and how much better they were at it. I concluded with regret that while I could understand the mysterious language of music, I would never learn to speak it. Although I continued with my lessons to the outbreak of the war, I knew by then that I was not destined to be a musician and gave up the effort altogether after leaving Poland.

But I found a substitute in art: not in drawing, sculpting, or painting, but in art history. One afternoon sometime in the winter of 1937–38 (I was fourteen then), while I was at the Warsaw Public Library, I was turning the leaves of an illustrated German history of medieval art, when, passing over the delicate but conventional paintings of the Byzantine era my eyes fell on Giotto's *Descent from the Cross* from the Arena Chapel in Padua. This early fourteenth-century fresco, one of a series in the life of Jesus which inaugurated European painting, affected me as much as Beethoven's Seventh Symphony. The grief of the bystanders, amplified by the crying of the little angels dispersed in the sky, was so convincing that I virtually could hear the sounds of lamentation. It was an overwhelming aesthetic experience, what Kenneth Clark would have called "a moment of vision," that aroused my passion for art. I began to study assiduously histories of every branch of the visual arts—painting, architecture, sculpture—taking copious notes. I translated from the German half of a history of music by O. Keller. During the summer of 1938, which I spent on a private estate in western Poland, I rose early every morning, sat myself down at a table in the ancient park, and read through several pages of manuals on the history of European art. I had no guidance in the matter and my studies concentrated on the names of the artists of the various schools, their dates and principal works, without any historical or aesthetic background. My interest in the subject continued as my musical ambitions waned, and when I went to college in 1940 I thought of devoting my life to it. This passion explains why I insisted—quite foolishly—on visiting the Munich Pinakotek as we were fleeing Poland.

After Beethoven and Giotto came Nietzsche. I discovered the German philosopher quite by chance one day in the early fall of 1938 when the book I wanted from the lending library was checked out and I borrowed instead Henri Lichtenberger's biography of a man whose name had a familiar ring but of whom I knew nothing. When I came home and opened it, I was transfixed for I read my own vague though intense feelings rendered into words. "Nietzsche's philosophy is strictly individualistic," I read. "What does your conscience tell you?" he asks. "You must be what you are." He continues:

> Man, then, must above all know thoroughly himself, his body, his instincts, his faculties; then he must draw up his rules of life to suit his personality, gauge his striving in accord with his hereditary or acquired aptitudes . . . there are no general and universal rules for finding oneself . . . everyone should create his own truth and morals for himself; what is good or bad, useful or harmful for one man is not necessarily so for another.

These words acted like a narcotic on an adolescent groping for identity: while everyone else was telling me to conform, Nietzsche urged me to rebel. Today his advice strikes me as irresponsible and inflammatory prattle. Nietzsche's morality for "free spirits"—"Nothing is true, everything is permitted"—appalls me.[3] It may have sounded like a clever bon mot in Victorian Europe, but in the twentieth century it provided a rationale for mass murders. My disenchantment with such ideas is a result of the experiences of World War II and the Holocaust. In my diary in August 1945 I wrote:

> I have always had a tendency to be attracted by subjects and ideas which I thought to be the least common. When I was younger and more naive, this inclination made me an avid follower of Nietzsche's philosophy: his attacks on the common concepts of "good," "sympathy," "happiness," appealed to me because I thought [the latter concepts] prevalent and vulgar. Since then I have learned that they are among the rarest encountered in the world. I was misled by books that praised them into thinking that they are widely accepted—they were, moreover, so logical and self-evident! Now I know they are most difficult to find.*

Still, Nietzsche was the first intellectual influence on me, and the notion that I was entitled to be myself—to think as I chose if not always to act as I chose—has remained with me ever since.

---

*But I had experienced my first doubts about Nietzsche much earlier when my friend, Olek, translated *Thus Spake Zarathustra* into Yiddish—*Azoy sugt Zaratustra*—which instantly punctured it. Yiddish deflates all pomposity.

I scoured the secondhand book stores on Holy Cross Street where I would buy for pennies the works of Schopenhauer, Kant, and other philosophers in the original German or in Polish translation. I had no philosophical preparation so I only dimly understood what I read: but something remained and the passion to know burned undiminished. Father was not very happy with my philosophical interests. On one occasion when he saw me reading Kant's *Prolegomena* he said that I was "burdening" my mind and should study more practical things.

As far back as I can remember, I felt that the reality we perceive with our senses is merely a veneer behind which lies concealed ultimate reality. As a small boy playing with my cousins on their street in Cracow I was attracted by the sound of running water coming from below a sewer grate: it was a most ordinary sewer outlet and the most ordinary waste-water, but the sound from an invisible source reinforced in me the belief that we move in a world of shadows. (Needless to say, I had not even heard of Plato then.) I had the same experience at a country fair where, equipped with a fishing rod, I was to pick up a present hidden behind a screen: what else lay behind that wall, I wondered. On another occasion it struck me that the ideas we have of objects do not render them as they really are but serve as mere "symbols" for reality that enable us to deal with it without ever understanding it. This sense has remained with me throughout my life: my studies were always driven by the compulsion to seek out the "real" behind the apparent.

Although I did not become a musician or even an art historian, my early passion for music and painting had a lasting effect on me in that in all my scholarly work I would consciously strive to satisfy aesthetic canons. Many years later I read with approval the words of Trevelyan: "Truth is the criterion of historical study; but its impelling motive is poetic."[4] The difficulty in being a historian lies in the fact that it calls for two incompatible qualities: those of a poet and those of a laboratory technician—the first lets one soar, the other constrains. I have tried to present everything I write in an aesthetically satisfying way, as concerns both language and structure, while being meticulous about the evidence. This compensates in some measure for my disappointment at not being a creative artist. But it means more than that. It means also that I view scholarship as an aesthetic experience and hence a highly personal one: I simply cannot conceive collaborating with someone on an article or book. I was always more interested in wisdom than knowledge. Everything that I wrote reflected, as is the case with a work of art, my private vision. Hence I never participated in any collective scholarly endeavors and never felt obligated to accommodate my own work to the consensus.

This attitude made me from an early age controversial. Many years later, I was asked by a graduate student at Harvard why my writings constantly provoked controversy, and I did not know how to reply until I found the answer in a letter of Samuel Butler: "I never write on any subject unless I believe the opinion of those who have the ear of the public to be mistaken, and this involves, as a necessary consequence, that every book I write runs counter to the men who are in possession of the field; hence I am always in hot water . . . "[5]

My early passion for art had another beneficial and lasting effect in that it immunized me against every kind of ideology. All ideologies contain a kernel of truth to which their creators attribute universal validity. During the occasional discussions I had had as a teenager with Marxists, I could do little to counter their arguments, for I was utterly ignorant of the Marxist canon. But I knew with absolute certainty that no formula could explain everything. Some people yearn to have the world neatly ordered, to have everything "fall into place"—they are the raw material for Marxism and other totalitarian doctrines. Others delight in what Tolstoy called "the infinite, eternally inexhaustible manifestations" of life, a delight that is ultimately rooted in aesthetics. I belong to the latter category.

I was extremely shy with girls. On the way to school, I would often pass and admire an exquisite dark-haired, dark-eyed beauty my age: I would look at her, she at me, but we never exchanged a word. Once when I was in the public library leafing through books on the shelf, she walked up and placed herself nearby: it was an invitation, but I did not dare to approach her. Later on, in Rome, I found out who she was from a young man who had befriended her in Warsaw. She undoubtedly perished in the Holocaust.

In July 1938, on my fifteenth birthday, I began to keep an occasional diary. It miraculously survived. Before leaving Warsaw, I made a bundle of my most precious papers for which we had no room for in our luggage. A Mrs. Lola De Spuches, a lady of Polish-Jewish origin but Italian citizenship (of whom more below), traveled frequently to Warsaw during the war to visit her family, and on one such trip Olek, who had kept it, gave her the packet. By the time she returned to Rome we were gone, and so she saved it throughout the war and handed it to me in the summer of 1948 on my first return trip to Europe.

My diary of the prewar year makes for quite depressing reading. Allowing that perhaps I confided to it mainly in unhappy moments, there runs through it a constant strain of rage. It was in part directed at my surroundings: Polish nationalism, anti-Semitism, and the looming war. But external causes were not the only source of my anger. I discovered then, as I have confirmed many times since, that unless I engage in meaningful intellectual work I easily fall into depression. At fifteen I had no meaningful intellectual work to pursue: I dabbled in music and art history, on my own and without guidance, unclear what would come of my efforts. Hence those frequent moments of despondency that would vanish permanently as soon as I discovered my scholarly vocation.

School in the three or four years preceding the war was sheer agony. From the time we came to Warsaw, I attended a private gymnasium named after its founder, Michael Kreczmar, located in the center of town, half of whose students were Catholics and half Jews. In 1935 or so, the atmosphere, which until then had been quite agreeable, changed noticeably for the worse. The director, a kindly classicist, was pushed aside by a new breed of nationalistic teachers who took over, headed by an instructor of Polish literature, one Tadeusz Radoński, who became deputy director of the school and my nemesis. There were no overt manifestations of anti-Semitism but it was an ever-present undercurrent. The stress of the curriculum was on national subjects—Polish history, Polish literature, Polish geography—in which my interest was quite limited and which interfered with my passion for music, art, and philosophy. The Jews who constituted 10 percent of Poland's population and allegedly dominated the Polish economy and culture were treated as if they did not exist for they were never mentioned: it is astonishing how little they impinged on Polish consciousness. Poland, past and present, was at the core of the curriculum. The world was in deep depression, to the east of us Stalin was murdering millions, to the west Hitler was getting ready to murder millions more, yet we were studying the intricacies of the *ablativus absolutus* and made to trace the course of Africa's Limpopo River.

Little wonder that I did no homework and misbehaved in class, for which I was either temporarily expelled from the classroom or, when my behavior became especially egregious, sent home for the day or more. I would read Nietzsche under the desk, oblivious of what went on around me. Mathematics was my weakest subject: I understood nothing of it and passed from year to year to the higher grade only thanks to the intercession of my mother and the fact that I was a paying student.

(Many if not most of the Catholic students, I believe, were on scholarships.) Except for ancient history and world geography, my record was a dismal accumulation of the lowest passing grades. Even in "conduct" I earned only a "good." Yet I do not recall a single occasion when a teacher took me aside and talked to me to learn the causes of my misbehavior and poor grades and to appeal to my self-respect: the only didactic tool used was punishment and humiliation. In retrospect, I believe that my poor performance in school was a blessing because by not doing the required homework I gained time to learn more valuable things than those taught as well as to test my abilities and discover what I was good at.

When treated like a human being I could do very good work. In the spring of 1937 our history teacher, Marian Małowist, asked me to read during the summer a German translation of Prescott's *Conquest of Peru,* which at the time was not available in Polish. I was to report on it in the fall. I wrote the requested report but when I returned to school, Małowist, the only Jew on the faculty, was gone: he had left because he could no longer stand Radoński's anti-Semitic chicaneries. I filed my report away and it reached me after the war together with my diary and other papers. Małowist, although crippled by polio, miraculously survived the Holocaust and was appointed a professor of economic history at the University of Warsaw. He visited Harvard in 1975 and I finally had the opportunity to hand him, with a delay of nearly forty years, my report on Prescott. I thought this set some sort of a record. He wrote me from Poland that it brought tears to his eyes to think that a fourteen-year-old youth before the war could write a historical essay beyond the capacity of most postwar university students.

In June 1938 I graduated from gymnasium and was to enroll in the same school's two-year Lyceum. The graduation was witnessed by an inspector from the ministry of education. The teacher would call each of us to her desk and ask a question or two meant to display our maturity. When my turn came, she asked me where I was born. "Cieszyn," I replied. "What is special about Cieszyn?" "The city is divided in two, one part belonging to the Czechoslovakia, the other to Poland." "And to whom should both parts belong?" she pressed. "To Czechoslovakia," I responded without hesitation. "Why?" she asked, startled, "Wasn't there a plebiscite there which showed that the majority of the population wanted to be Polish?" "True" I responded, "but the plebiscite was rigged." "Thank you, you may sit down." Now, in fact, I knew nothing about the plebiscite; I was just being contrary because I did not want to say what was expected of me and wanted to express my disapproval of Polish nationalism. Sixty years later I learned that there never was a plebiscite in Cieszyn and that, in fairness, the city should have been alloted to the Poles because they constituted the majority of the population. Father was horrified when I told him what had transpired, and either he or mother went to the teacher to patch things up: I think they excused me on the grounds that I had heard such heretical views on a foreign radio broadcast.

Hardly any of my schoolmates shared my artistic and intellectual interests so I was in large measure alone. I had two friends, however, one of whom, Alexander (Olek) Dyzenhaus, remained loyal to me for the rest of his life (he survived the war in Poland and died in South Africa). The other, Peter Blaufuks, was something of a brilliant neurotic. He, unfortunately, perished.

I also acquired a female friend. We met in the winter of 1938–39 in the resort town of Krynica. Wanda Elelman was two years older than I and had already graduated from gymnasium. Judging by my diary I was passionately in love with her, but in retrospect I think this was not the case: once I had left Poland, I regret to say, I gave her little thought. But we spent many happy hours together, especially in the spring of 1939, in cafés and walking under the blooming chestnut trees along the Łazienki Park.

LWar was approaching. Mother and Emmy Burger took lessons in glove and hat making meant to prepare them for future contingencies. I attended English lessons at a Methodist evening school. It was my first contact with Americans and they made on me a strange impression. Before each class we assembled in a large hall to sing the latest hits, such as "I love you, yes I do, I lo-o-ove you," led by a toothy woman at the piano and a man whose hair was parted in the middle and slicked down with pomade. We did not normally associate popular love songs with learning. I acquired enough English, however, to be able to converse, which would stand me in good stead later on.

In June 1939 I lost John Burger who, with his family, emigrated to the United States. His mother, Emmy, was half Jewish, which made him quarter-Jewish; under the Nuremberg laws, both were non-Aryans. And since they had to exchange their citizenship when Germany annexed Austria in 1938, they thought it prudent to leave. I envied them greatly.

One of the banes of my existence in the last year of school before the war was military training, popularly known as "PW," which stood for "Military Preparation," a kind of ROTC, which required us to come to school every Monday dressed in a crumpled pea green uniform and go through some drills. Between the penultimate and final year of lyceum, the year before we were to graduate, we had to attend a three-week course of military training with students from other schools. Toward the end of June 1939 I left with my schoolmates for a camp in Kozienice, a wooded area some one-hundred kilometers southwest of Warsaw. It was an excruciating experience. We lived in crude barracks, sleeping on cots covered with straw mattresses. We had enough to eat but the food was primitive—thus our breakfast consisted of plain rye bread and a choice of black coffee or tea. But the worst was the pervasive anti-Semitism carried to the camp by students from the other Warsaw schools. The Jewish pupils were insulted and harassed, but being greatly outnumbered, they took it in stride. The only thing I enjoyed was standing guard duty in the woods, for though it meant a sleepless night, it was quiet and private.

I soon got into trouble. One day I was caught smoking in the ranks. Radoński, who served in the camp as a reserve officer, reprimanded me and ordered some kind of mild punishment. Next I was assigned a small team that was to stand in the open field and stare at the sky to report on overflights of foreign planes. It was an absurd assignment since there were no foreign planes in the sky and we would not have been able to identify them even if there were. I went to a nearby store to buy cigarettes. A sergeant who was there with some colleagues invited me to share some vodka with them. I had never drunk vodka before but flattered to be treated as an adult, I accepted the invitation. We were caught and once again I had to report to Radoński for disciplinary action. Were I allowed to defend myself, I would have placed the blame on the sergeant who was in charge of us. But by then I was so disgusted with the whole affair that, subconsciously, I wanted out. Not long after, we were assembled in a field for some activity or other. A bearded Jew drove by in a horse-drawn cart. The soldiers jeered; to make matters still more disgusting, he joined them, laughing at himself. My stomach churned. Shortly afterwards, three days before the camp was to have closed, I was caught smoking in the barracks. Radoński with ill-concealed glee informed me that I was expelled. I never saw him again: less than a year later, as a prisoner of war, he would be murdered by the Soviet security police.

I returned home. When they learned what had happened, my parents were dismayed. Through his connections, father quickly arranged for me to attend a second tour of camp training, for failure to complete the summer training would have barred me from finishing school. The second camp was much more pleasant than the first because the provincial

Maternal grandfather, S. Haskelberg.

Maternal grandmother, B. Haskelberg.

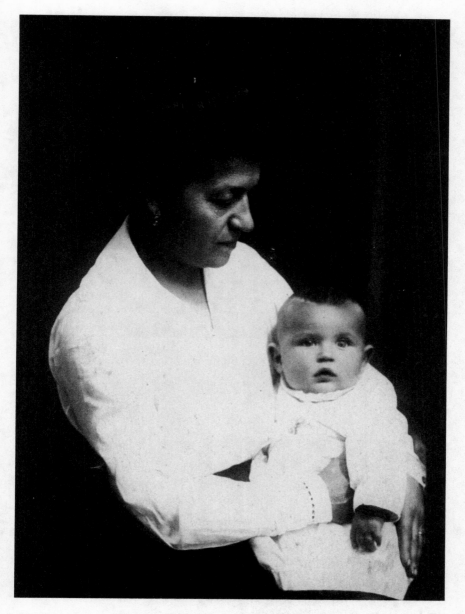

Grandmother B. Pipes, with my cousin Julius. Cracow, 1922.

Mother and her family, c. 1916. Second from left in the rear, with a bow in her hair, my mother.

Father, Vienna, 1919.

Parents' wedding picture. September 1922.

Me, eighteen months old.

On my fourth birthday, 1927.

With the Burgers, 1934.

Irene Roth, my future wife, aged ten. Warsaw, 1934.

In school, dressed in military uniforms: me on the left in front row,
P. Blaufuks in the center, Olek Dyzenhaus on the right, 1938.

Hans Burger. Warsaw, 1939.

The author. Warsaw, June 1939.

Marszałkowska, Warsaw's main street, after the German bombardment,
c. October 1, 1939. From Apoloniusz Zawilski, *Bitwy polskiego września*,
vol. 2, Nasza Księgarnia, Warsaw, 1972.

The passport photo on the bogus South American passport with which we left German-occupied Warsaw. October 1939.

Aboard the *Nea Hellas* in Lisbon, Portugal, about to sail for America, July 1940.

schools that took part in it were not saturated with the kind of Jude-ophobia so prevalent in Warsaw. I completed it without trouble and returned to Warsaw at the beginning of August, shortly before the out-break of war.

Italy

We arrived in Rome the morning of Monday, October 30. Depositing our luggage at the terminal, we walked into town: crossing Piazza Esedra with its splendid fountain, we turned left into Via Nazionale. It was a lovely fall day. Father said that although he had acquaintances in many European capitals, unfortunately he knew no one in Rome. Minutes after he had uttered these words someone shouted "Pipes!" We turned around. The shout came from an Italian businessman by the name of Roberto de Spuches who had lived in Warsaw before the war. It was a most fortuitous encounter for, as it turned out, de Spuches was the only Italian who knew father. It is difficult to believe that his appearance at this particular instance in this particular spot in Rome, a city of more than one million inhabitants, was mere coincidence. De Spuches helped to set us up at a modest pensione near the railroad terminal. We were penniless: I had to sell some postage stamps for thirty lire (approximately one U.S. dollar) to pay for our dinner that evening. The following day father wired to Stockholm for money and we breathed easier.

Although Poland had ceased to exist and Italy, as an ally of Germany, acknowledged that fact, the Polish embassy in Rome was allowed to function until June 1940 when Italy herself entered the war. This was a great boon for us because father knew the ambassador, cavalry general Bolesław Wieniawa Długoszowski, once an officer in the Legions, a loyal follower of Piłsudski, and in the interwar years a notorious Warsaw playboy. As I later learned from father's letters, it was Wieniawa's pres-ence in Rome that had made him choose Italy as our destination. The general, with whom father spent many hours in conversation at the embassy on via Beccaria, proved immensely helpful, issuing us Polish passports for future travel, smoothing relations with the Italian authori-ties, and introducing father to the U.S. consul in Rome and even some Roman socialites of whose aristrocratic titles father was immensely proud.

As foreigners, we were required to register with the police shortly after arriving. I accompanied father and Mr. de Spuches to the Ques-tura, the police headquarters located on Piazza del Collegio Romano, a dreary square near Mussolini's palace. A dour Fascist policeman, leafing through our Latin American passport, remarked on father's given name, Mark:

"*Marco e un nome ebreo*" (Mark is a Jewish name), he declared.

"How?" father protested, "What about Saint Mark?"

To this he had no answer. Of course, the policeman could have replied that St. Mark was a Jerusalem Jew, but he lacked the wit. He excused himself to consult with a colleague. Father took advantage of the interval to phone the Polish embassy. The matter was satisfactorily resolved, and we received permission to reside in Rome for three months, which was later extended.

Father believed the war would soon spread to the rest of Europe, and so he wanted us to leave for overseas as soon as possible. His first choice was Canada because we (mistakenly) thought Canada to be more "European" and hence easier to adjust to than the United States, which we knew, mainly from movies, as a country of frenetic activity and impetuous extremes. But Canada did not welcome immigrants unless they disposed of a considerable quantity of ready cash. The United States since the 1920s issued immigration visas in accord with country quotas, which discriminated against East Europeans. In December 1939, Consul X came to Rome carrying our Polish identity papers which we had had to leave behind. With them in hand and an affidavit from the Burgers, we applied for American visas and settled in for a wait. As it happened, the six months that followed were the period of *Sitzkrieg* or "phony war" during which the Allies and the Germans faced each other immobile on the Western Front. There was warfare on the high seas and the Germans occupied Denmark and Norway while the Russians fought the Finns; but in Italy it was easy to grow complacent. Its Fascist government hardly resembled that of Nazi Germany or the Soviet Union. The Italians are not prone to fanaticism and much of what passed for "totalitarianism" (a word Mussolini proudly applied to his regime) was an opera buffa which no one, the Fascists included, took seriously. Father pursued various business deals, of which I knew nothing but which apparently brought in enough money to enable us to live modestly on about $100 a month without drawing on our capital, now transferred to the safety of a New York bank.

After one month, we moved out of the pensione to a room on via Rasella 131, apartment 5, in the center of town—the street where in March 1944 Italian partisans would attack a detachment of German military police; in retaliation the Germans rounded up at random 335 civilians and massacred them in the Ardeantine Caves. It was a pretty miserable existence in near-slum conditions in an unheated building. In a January 1940 letter to the Burgers, father thus described our landlady:

> I could not write this letter at all if I did not have next to my feet an electric "sun." I tremble with fear what would happen if the landlady found out about this. My American bank account would not suffice to pay her compensation. . . . If I could box the Neapolitan witch's ear I would do so with the greatest pleasure. Her personality is not too bad, but she screams when she speaks; in the morning she is especially coarse; she has a toothless mug, drags, like a witch, one leg, and when she holds in one hand a broom and in the other a chamber pot, I quickly reach for my overcoat and run out into the cold Roman air. The apartment is the only thing that makes our life here difficult. We must save and for that reason live fairly modestly.

Fortunately, in March we were able to move to comfortable quarters on via Piemonte.

With the help of the Polish ambassador, father procured passports and transit visas for our family in Poland and even for my friend Olek. These were sent with various messengers to Warsaw.

Olek and I corresponded regularly, at least once and sometimes twice a week, sometimes in Polish but usually in German to expedite the censorship process. Reading his letters, all of which I saved, one would not know that anything unusual was happening in Poland. My friend mostly complained of boredom which he tried to assuage by studying Greek and Italian, reading Proust and Pirandello, and visiting friends. I gathered from his letters that my sudden, miraculous disappearance from German-occupied Poland made me appear in the eyes of my friends as something of a phantom: some came to doubt whether I had ever existed. In early April, Olek received through the Hungarian tourist agency Ibusz all the necessary papers to leave for Italy. He—or rather his mother—worked feverishly to secure the necessary German permits. It was a race against time because we made it no secret that as soon as we received our U.S. visas we would leave Italy. The German permit came, but by then the Italians had stopped issuing entry visas and the Germans had closed the Hungarian travel bureau which was processing his trip. And so Olek stayed in Warsaw to experience all the horrors of the Holocaust.

Despite our urgent pleas and frequent letters to our family back and forth, nothing came of father's efforts. For one reason or another, no one came: most perished, and the few who survived lived but a short time after the war, worn out physically and emotionally.

Father was especially anxious about his sister Rose, her two sons, and his widowed mother. When the war broke out, Rose's husband, Israel Pfeffer, left Cracow for eastern Poland but was persuaded by his partner to return home to watch over their common business, the Pischinger chocolate factory. His wife and two sons settled in a small town in Galicia. When the Russians occupied eastern Poland, Pfeffer found himself cut off from them, although he was able, every now and then, to send them some of the money he earned helping the Germans operate the Pischinger factory. Father desperately wanted to bring them to Italy. He pleaded with his brother-in-law to move them to the German zone from where they could travel abroad. In January 1940, father met in Rome a certain Mr. Stueckgold who told him he had a son in Lwów familiar with the ways of crossing the border between the Soviet zone and German-occupied Poland. Father telegraphically arranged for his sister to contact this young man, whom I happened to have known because as children we attended the same school. Had father consulted me in the matter I would have warned him against relying on Stueckgold because even as a child he was notoriously dishonest. The crook asked my aunt to turn over to him her jewels to pay for the crossing. The naive woman did so.

At the end of February, a telegram arrived from Lwów: it is testimony of the closeness between the Soviet Union and Fascist Italy that Soviet censorship permitted such communication. Having read it, mother asked me immediately to deliver it to father who was lunching at his favorite Hungarian restaurant near the Trevi Fountain. It read (in German): "Stueckgold disappeared with money. Has postponed trip for three weeks. Am helpless and without means. Cable Lwów what next." Father turned white as he read the cable and soon fell ill for several weeks. It was a death sentence for his sister, mother, and nephews. His mother died a natural death in May of the following year, but the Germans killed Rose and the two boys sometime in 1943. Until then they lived in concealment in a small town near Lwów; I suppose some Pole or Ukrainian betrayed them. Pfeffer stayed on in his position and even managed to provide father with chocolate recipes after we had come to America, but then, having done his job for the new German owners, he was deported to Auschwitz and never heard from again.

My father's correspondence from that period, which mother saved, is filled with letters from Poland, Romania, Lithuania, and the Soviet Union begging for help. They were written in a naive code, such as "Arnold longs to see Dick," which was meant to fool the censors. Father worked desperately hard to help, but little came of these efforts—why, I do not know. At a time when American citizens can travel to most countries of the world whenever they choose, it is difficult to imagine what the term "visa" meant for us, Jewish refugees during the war: it spelled life. Superhuman efforts were expended to secure entry permits to Cuba, Brazil, or Shanghai—or at the very least "transit visas" leading nowhere but providing temporary refuge.

I was neither consulted nor in any way involved in these tragic matters, and for me Italy was sheer paradise. There was no school or PW, no Radoński, no *ablativus absolutus,* no Limpopo! I spent my days leisurely visiting Rome's museums, frequenting concerts and the opera, going to the movies. I paid for these cheap pleasures by collecting at the Polish embassy postage stamps from all over the world and selling them to a German refugee philatelic dealer. I noticed that as they paid for their tickets, some moviegoers would utter a formula—"Dopolavoro"—which admitted them at half price, one lira instead of the standard two. Ignorant what the word meant but eager to save, I would casually say "Dopolavoro" as I put down the money for a movie ticket. Only later did I learn that Dopolavoro ("After Work") was a Fascist labor organization. It is testimony to the laxity of Mussolini's dictatorship that no one ever questioned my claim to membership.

Rome was virtually empty of foreign tourists. The Sistine Chapel, which nowadays is so crowded that one can barely see the frescoes, had perhaps a couple of visitors at any one time. I visited every museum and gallery, some more than once, taking ample notes. I spent hours in the German art library on the top of the Spanish Steps where I collected materials for the projected book on Giotto. Through my parents I met and befriended a young Polish Jewish woman who had come to Rome from Shanghai in the hope of bringing out her daughter from Poland. We spent much time visiting museums together. She was my only companion, and I was sorry to lose her when she suffered a nervous breakdown.

I had conflicts with father over my future. He worried that in the turbulent world in which we lived I would be lost without a solid profession or business. In the diary of this time, under the date December 21, 1939, I find the following entry: "I reject father's insistence that it is inconceivable I should become a scholar and that, in time, I will have to replace him in some "chocolate factory" in Canada. *"Es kommt ausser Frage"* (Out of the question), *"kommt nicht in Betracht"* (Not to be considered) is what he tells me. . . . But I know that I decide about myself, that I will do what *I* want."

Although today I retain nothing but pleasant memories of my seven months in Italy, judging by the diary I kept sporadically, I was far from happy, suffering from loneliness, homesickness, missing my friends, and worried about the future.

I learned that the University of Florence offered special courses on Italian art and culture for foreigners and persuaded my parents to let me attend. It was the first time I was to be entirely on my own. In mid-March, mother accompanied me to Florence and found me a room in the apartment of a Jewish lady on via dei Benci, close to the Santa Croce church with its magnificent Giotto frescoes. I had picked up enough Italian by then to understand the lectures. I did not make any close acquaintances, but when pressed I did tell some of the students that I was from Latin America. During a lecture dealing with the influence of Italian literature abroad, one of the students rose to tell the professor that he had a Latin American student in the audience. "Splendid," the professor addressed me when I was introduced to him after class, "You must visit me and tell me all about the literature of your country."

After this incident I stopped attending lectures. Henceforth I spent all my time alone, wandering among Florentine churches and museums and the hillsides surrounding the city. It was springtime and all was in bloom. I lived very modestly. My main midday meal consisted day after day of the same pasta sprinkled with slivers of different meats, a glass of wine, and an orange for desert, for which I paid 7 lire (25 U.S. cents), and which left me agreeably tipsy. My breakfast and dinner cost 5 lire per day and my rent was 120 lire a month. It gives some idea of the inflation which the world has experienced in the past sixty years that the 700 lire which enabled me to live for a whole month would not buy one cup of espresso today. I kept up with the war news by reading the *Osservatore Romano,* the official Vatican daily which was reasonably objective.

In my apartment lived a refugee family from Germany, a dentist with his wife and daughter. I never told them who I really was but they undoubtedly guessed. Nearly sixty years later I chanced on a directory of Jewish dentists from Berlin. I looked up my acquaintances and was relieved to learn that they had managed to make their way to Somalia and from there to Palestine.

The Italian government was under steady pressure from its German ally to implement its anti-Jewish laws, which had largely been ignored. In April 1940 the authorities began to enforce an ordnance that forbade Jews to rent properties. I had to move out and took a room in a small pensione at Lungarno delle Grazie 10. The two other tenants there were a French girl, a student, and an Italian reserve officer. We took our meals together. I recall on one occasion the officer saying that if his government were to order him to fight the French, he would lay down his arms and surrender. I was dumbfounded: in Poland, not to speak of Nazi Germany or Soviet Russia, such a statement, if reported, would have caused the officer to be arrested and executed. Here nothing happened.

Despite the relative calm that continued to prevail in Europe, father was determined to get us out as soon as possible. At the end of April he asked me to accompany him, as the family's semi-English speaker, to Naples to persuade the American consulate to issue us visas. Our request was rejected: we were told that our turn would come in June. "I am sorry," the American consular official said as we parted: it was the first time I heard this expression.

Events in Europe were coming to a head. On May 10, I rushed home to tell the French girl that the Germans had invaded Belgium and Holland. She packed up and immediately left for home. Two days later I received a cable from parents asking me to return to Rome. It seems they had been notified by the U.S. consulate in Naples that our immigration visas would be ready on June 1. I returned on May 13 and spent the remainder of the month on via Piemonte. The German armies were advancing once again at extraordinary speed. The Dutch capitulated on May 14, the Belgians on May 26; by the beginning of June, the Germans had penetrated deep inside France and the Allies were in general retreat. There was widespread expectation that Mussolini would soon join Hitler and declare war.

On June 3 mother departed for Naples to pick up our American visas. Some time earlier, father had gotten us Spanish transit visas. In the mounting war fever, transportation to Spain was very difficult to obtain, but father had somehow managed to secure two tickets on a small hydroplane for Las Palmas in the Spanish Balearic Islands. It was decided that he and I, being of military age and hence liable to be detained in case of war, would leave by air and mother would follow by ship.

On June 5 father and I left for Spain. It was in the nick of time, for, as we later learned, on that very day British and French nationals were forbidden to leave Italy in order to serve as hostages; there was no assurance we would be let go. We went to the airport by taxi, carrying both the Latin American and Polish passports (the latter of which bore both the Spanish and American visas, while the former had only the Spanish one) because we were uncertain whether the Italians had us registered as Latin Americans. Father asked me to sneak behind the clerk sitting at the departure gate and unobtrusively glance at his passenger list to see whether our citizenship was listed next to our names. When I gave a negative signal, friends who had accompanied us took from mother the bag of oranges where the false passport was concealed. After the war we were told by friends that a few days later, the Italian police came to via Piemonte to arrest us.

The plane took off and we soon landed in Las Palmas. As we stepped off the plane, father lifted his hat and shouted *"Viva Italia!"* The Italian pilot, apparently taking him for a Spaniard, responded *"Viva España!"* That night we took a boat to Barcelona. It was filled with recently released Republican prisoners of war, one of whom I engaged in conversation. We arrived in Barcelona on June 6.

Mother, in the meantime, made her way to Genoa with Coco and the baggage and boarded on June 6 a ship called *Franca Fassio* bound for Barcelona. Before sailing, she saved a Polish-Jewish acquaintance from being taken off the boat as a young man of military age by pretending to be his fiancée. The Italian officials wanted to know who could confirm their relationship. Mother referred them to the Polish ambassador in Rome. They actually telephoned him. Wieniawa caught on at once and expressed surprise that my mother and the young man were not already married, whereupon they let him go. Mother's ship docked the following night (June 7). Judging by the fond farewells, she befriended half the passengers aboard.

We spent two and a half weeks in Spain. Little remains in my memory of this period, except learning that France had capitulated and listening to a speech by Churchill, delivered in atrocious French, offering France union with Great Britain. We left Spain on June 24 for Portugal where we hoped to find a boat to take us to the United States. By the time we reached Lisbon, streams of refugees were pouring in from France, all with the same purpose in mind: to get to America. With U.S. passenger ships giving priority to U.S. citizens, it was most difficult to find a vessel to take us across the Atlantic. Finally we obtained berths on a small Greek ship, the *Nea Hellas*. It had come from New York and was en route to Athens when Italy entered the war and the Mediterranean turned into a war zone. So it was going back without a full complement of passengers. We boarded on July 2 and departed the next morning. We traveled third class, a sort of steerage: the food was barely edible (one dish is listed on the menu I had saved as "Chou ndolma Horientale") and the wine (retsina) undrinkable. Aboard were quite a few Greeks who had been expelled from the United States and were not at all unhappy to be returning. The most notable passenger was Maurice Maeterlinck, the celebrated author and dramatist of the late nineteenth century, now forgotten and unread. In good weather, he lounged on the first class deck, sporting a hair net. I obtained his autograph. Although there was a certain danger of a German submarine stopping and searching us, the trip passed uneventfully.

On July 11, 1940, we docked at Hoboken, New Jersey. It was my seventeenth birthday.

College

Our notions of the United States were so skewed that when, at the time of our disembarkation, father spotted on the dock a man leisurely leaning against a lamppost, he said with relief that perhaps the country was not as frenetic as he had thought. Ossi Burger picked us up at Hoboken and after a day in New York City we took a train to Troy, New York, near where the Burgers had a farm.

In a way I knew what to expect of New York, and what impressed me most was not the size of the buildings or the traffic, which I was familiar with from American films, but the fact that accompanied by a young man, the son of a friend of the Burgers, I could enter the lobby of the Waldorf Astoria or visit a music shop and in a private booth listen to any classical record I chose. At Grand Central, as we were leaving for Troy, I went up to the newsstand to get some literature on higher education. "College," I said. "Information about college." The vendor looked puzzled but after a moment's thought sold me a copy of *College Life,* which was a forerunner of *Playboy.*

We spent the rest of the summer on the farm. In the hayloft where John and I slept, I chanced on a copy of the 1914–15 *Who's Who in America.* In the back were more than one hundred pages of advertisements for prep schools and colleges. It gave me what I needed: the names and addresses of institutions of higher learning. I purchased one hundred penny postcards and with the help of a friend typed identical requests to as many colleges telling them that I was a war refugee eager to enroll but my financial means were very limited and I required both a scholarship and assurance of gainful employment. I did not know the difference between Harvard and a small rural college. Most of the institutions did not respond; several responded negatively. But four offered me what I wanted: Butler College in Indianapolis, the University of Tennessee, Erskine College in South Carolina, and Muskingum College in Ohio. I had no criteria for distinguishing among them: what swayed me in favor of Muskingum was a map on its full-page advertisement in *Who's Who* which contrived to make its seat in New Concord, Ohio, look like the geographic center of the United States.

Father was not happy about my leaving for college because he wanted me to help him out in his new business. I now understand him better than I did then, when any further delay in getting a higher education seemed to me perverse and unreasonable. I had grand if unfocused ambitions: I did not know at all what I wanted to do, but I knew with absolute certainty that it was not making money. I felt that God had saved me from the hell of German-ruled Poland for some higher purpose, for an existence beyond mere survival and self-gratification. This feeling has never left me. Had father taken me aside and explained that while he understood and approved of my desire to study, in our present economic situation my help was indispensable, at any rate, for a while, I might possibly have yielded for a year or so. But in our culture fathers did not treat teenage sons as adults.

On September 7, 1940, I left by bus for Ohio. I arrived in New Concord the following day, a Sunday morning. The campus was deserted because virtually all the denizens of the college as well as the village were in church. I checked in at the local hostelry and took a stroll. The buildings, all of red brick, some dating to the mid-nineteenth century, were situated on knolls in a hilly landscape. They made an agreeable impression although the rustic college in no way resembled the universities of Warsaw or Florence. My one shock came when I saw engraved over the entrance of a classroom building a passage from the book of Exodus where God addressed Moses: "Put off thy shoes from off thy feet, for the place whereon thou standest is holy ground." It occurred to me that perhaps I had inadvertently landed in a theological seminary. But later in the afternoon, the vice president of the college picked me up and drove me around the campus, and all seemed well.

As it turned out, I had made an excellent choice. Muskingum was not Harvard and did not pretend to be, but it was a far more suitable place for me and this for two reasons. The college was small—it had some 700 undergraduates and a faculty of proportionate size—which meant that I was not lost in a crowd. I was a curiosity because apart from a Polish girl who had enrolled before the war I was the only European on the campus. In no time I got to know most of the students by first name and they to know me. Second, I was very poor: my entire wardrobe consisted of two suits and four shirts, which would make me cut a miserable figure at a grander university. I was soon taken in tow by the students, faculty, and administrators and spent a happy two and a half years there.

For a European, coming to central Ohio in 1940 was to step back into the nineteenth century: the outlook of the people and their values pre-dated World War I. There was a reassuring stability about the place such as I had not previously experienced. How remote Europe was for the people there may be gathered from a remark made by one bright and pretty girl whom I dated. She said she was especially glad to have met me because although she knew that Europe existed, in her heart she had never quite believed it. Apart from the president and several professors, no one had ever been to Europe. (By contrast, when I revisited Mus-kingum in 1988 to receive an honorary doctorate, most of the faculty and many of the undergraduates had been to the Continent, some more than once). People listened to my stories of the war sympathetically but with skepticism. For one, they were overwhelmingly Republican and Republicans at that time favored isolationism. But beyond their politics, they trusted in human goodness and could not be persuaded that the Germans were as evil as I depicted them. On one occasion I was re-minded how (allegedly) false the stories of German atrocities in World War I Belgium had turned out to be. Word got around that I read Nietz-sche for I was not averse to flaunting this fact for the shock effect it produced. One day, the vice president of the college saw me walking on the campus and offered me a ride. When we reached my destination, he delivered himself of a brief lecture. He told me that despite my experi-ences I should not lose faith in mankind, that people were basically good and life fair. He ended by saying "So you see, you should not read Nietz-sche." In fact, I had stopped reading him.

During my five semesters at Muskingum I was able to observe the many differences between America and Europe.

One notable difference was that young Americans were planning their lives with the kind of confidence that a European of my generation found quixotic: they seemed to live in the future whereas we lived from day to day. Leafing through *Fortune* magazine, I was struck by an adver-tisement of the Maryland Casualty Company that read: "Unforeseen events . . . need not change and shape the course of man's affairs." Really? I thought to myself: then why did events carry me from Warsaw to New Concord, Ohio, thoroughly changing the course of *my* affairs? The tacit assumption behind these reassuring words was that money could avert undesirable changes in one's life: but money was not enough, as experience had taught me. Young Americans seemed set on their life's course while we swam with the tide, convinced that the alternative meant drowning.

Then there were vast differences in the relations between the sexes which, in a way, also resulted from the prevailing sense of security. These relations were regulated by strict rituals as to what was and was not permitted and invariably pointed toward engagement and marriage. By the third date girls would inquire more or less directly about my intentions. My reaction was one of panic: at eighteen or nineteen, marriage was the last thing on my mind. As a rule, if given an unsatisfactory answer, they would break off relations. Relations with girls in Poland were more comradely, and marriage did not enter into the picture until one was much older. One reason I later came to marry my future wife, who had the same background as me, was that she never hinted at marriage until we had known each other for some two years: we were friends long before we became lovers. Altogether, I found American women of all ages much less secure in their femininity than women in Europe, they were extremely eager to please men whereas European women expected men to please them. The absurdities of "feminism" which burgeoned in the 1960s merely emphasized these insecurities: for to treat all men as would-be rapists is to concede that one has no clue how to deal with them.

In the spring of my sophomore year I fell in love. The girl, a year or two older than me, was a pianist. But with her, too, the familiar happened: one evening she asked me what I thought of marriage. When I replied that I had not given the matter any thought, I saw a tear running down her cheek. That summer, her letters became scarcer and colder, and by the time I returned for my junior year, we had stopped seeing each other.

American life at the time was pervaded by a great deal of moralizing. What was proper, what could and could not be done, what one should think about important matters was prescribed and regulated. For all the freedom of speech, of which Americans were justly proud, there was a great deal of pressure to conform to accepted standards, and from this point of view, Americans enjoyed less personal freedom than Europeans. What later came to be known as "political correctness" was embedded in

American popular culture even then. I did not resent the vice president of my college urging me to abandon Nietzsche because I knew he meant well: but I could not imagine that any European educator would ever dream of exerting such pressure. With such pressure came a genuine concern for people, a sense that what happened to others mattered—something I had not known in Europe where the prevailing philosophy taught one to take care of oneself. This changed profoundly in the 1960s, as did relations between the sexes. I think I prefer the older American culture, before it became so self-indulgent. But then Nietzsche had predicted that puritanism would end in nihilism.

I had another surprise in terms of human relations. Where I came from, strangers, if they were not rude or hostile to you for some specific reason, such as ethnic or religious prejudice, treated you correctly but coldly. Friendliness was reserved for friends. In the United States the code of proper behavior called for friendliness toward all. A few hours after I had arrived in New Concord, an upperclassman offered to help me get settled. He showed me the campus, took me to the small frame house where I was to spend my freshman year, and answered the many questions I had about the college and college life. I was thrilled to have made a friend so quickly. Yet when I ran into him a few days later, he was cool and distant, and we never again had close contact. I now understand that he had been asked by the college authorities to assist me, a foreign boy, in the strange environment, and he did so graciously but without having any special feelings for me. But I misread the signals and felt hurt. Later I learned that being "nice" to all and sundry was regarded as a virtue because it made life more agreeable: I concluded in time that, indeed, a meaningless smile was preferable to a meaningful snarl. But I also had to conclude that displaying superficial kindness to all and sundry inhibited closer human relations, that the kind of intimacy we had had with one or two friends was virtually unattainable in a country where the model, among men at any rate, was being "pals" or "buddies," words which have no equivalent in Polish.

My "majors" were history and speech. Muskingum was known for its debating team: I joined and participated in a number of debates on current issues, which taught me to argue in public. I also joined the swimming team as a breast-stroke swimmer even though I was not strong enough to do the butterfly stroke. My grades were adequate, on the B level: I earned them with a minimum of exertion. The main thing I acquired at college was a command of English. By the end of the first semester I wrote quite decent essays: my mistakes occurred mainly in tenses of verbs, a deficiency I have not been fully able to overcome to this day.

The atmosphere at Muskingum was more social than intellectual. Young people came to college to acquire a profession, to find a spouse, and to pass four agreeable years before facing the task of making a living and raising a family. I was occasionally embarrassed by my bookishness and unworldly ideals. One semester I enrolled in a course on the history of European art taught by the curator of a nearby museum. As he flashed on the screen slides of paintings and invited us to identify the artist, I would call out almost every one: "Velasquez," "Vermeer," "Tiepolo," and so on. After one class the college beauty, on whom I had a mild crush, asked me with a sweet smile "Dick, do you really know all these artists?" I don't know what answer she expected but I responded, "Of course not, these are just lucky guesses."

I read Thomas Mann's *Tonio Kröger* and discovered an affinity with its protagonist and his sense of isolation from friends caused by his artistic temperament. In November 1940 I wrote Mann a letter (unfortunately, I kept no copy) asking what he had in mind writing this novella. He replied in a friendly and substantive manner. His response, dated Princeton, New Jersey, December 2, 1940, read in part:

> When I wrote the story I did not visualize Tonio as a person standing below his two friends, but in the main as being superior to them. He stood aloof from his friends' simple and normal life, certainly, but he was half envious of that very life in reality. However, though this envy was tinged with regret that he was a stranger to their way of living, he was profoundly conscious of the profundity and promise of his own life as an artist.

I found these remarks encouraging.

I earned my living by working, at first mowing grass and rolling tennis courts, later by getting a job in the library inscribing shelf marks on the spines of books with an electric stylus, at the then-minimum wage of 35 cents an hour. But these earnings did not suffice. Father sent me off with $300, a sizeable sum considering that he was about to launch his business and needed every cent of his small capital; he let me understand that I could expect no more. Muskingum gave me a stipend of $200. But as the second semester approached, I was in a desperate situation for I had to come up with another $200. Someone advised me to contact the International Student Service in New York. I wrote them a letter describing my predicament, and by return mail received a check for $100!

It was manna from heaven that enabled me to continue my studies. It descended again the following autumn, when I received $210 from the same source. Both summers I took on full-time jobs, in 1941 selling cigarettes and candies in a drug store in Elmira, New York, where my parents had opened a small chocolate factory ("Mark's Candy Kitchen"). I worked fifty hours a week for $17.50 plus occasional commissions. The following summer I drove a Kraft Company truck delivering cheese to grocery stores. It was a pleasanter job because I was on my own and could spend two nights a week on the road. During the school year I supplemented my income by lecturing about my wartime experiences in Poland to nearby churches, Rotary clubs, and so on, for which the typical honorarium was $5.00.

Judging by my letters to parents, I was absolutely overwhelmed by the warmth and the atmosphere of fun which I encountered at Muskingum. "It is so swell here that you can't imagine," I wrote my parents shortly after settling down.

The Army

In the evening of June 21, 1941—I was spending the summer at home in Elmira—the radio interrupted its program with the news of the German invasion of the Soviet Union. A year later, after Pearl Harbor, I was asked at Muskingum to contribute a regular weekly column of political and military analyses to the college paper. They were my first publications and on rereading them, I find that they stand up rather well.

I followed the Russian campaign with keen interest. I doubted that the Russians would win, and the initial months of the war on the Eastern Front confirmed my worst fears. Although I was to devote my life to the study and teaching of Russian affairs, at the time I had little interest in Russia and hardly any knowledge of her. While I had lived in Poland, Russia was separated from us by an impenetrable wall. I was aware that two of mother's brothers had married Russian women and settled in Leningrad. They communicated from time to time with grandmother, but I knew nothing of their lives. In the late 1930s I heard muffled sounds of appalling events taking place in the Soviet Union, but I had no idea what these were and I was not terribly interested in finding out. I did learn with disbelief, however, that the Russians marked their Polish border with a wide strip of ploughed and mined land guarded by policemen with dogs.

Following Pearl Harbor and Hitler's inane declaration of war on

America, the United States found itself an ally of the Soviet Union. Interest in the USSR grew immensely. In fall 1942 it dawned on me that given the closeness between the Polish and Russian languages, I could easily learn Russian. I bought a Russian grammar and dictionary and began to study on my own. I think that what I had vaguely in mind was that upon being inducted into military service, as seemed inevitable, I could put the knowledge of Russian to good use.

In the fall of 1942, at the beginning of the first semester of my junior year, I tried to enlist, for with the world in turmoil I was growing restless in college. But I was told that as a foreign citizen I could not volunteer: I had to await a draft call. This came in January, and the following month I was inducted, in Columbus, Ohio, in the Army Air Corps.

The first thing that struck me about the American military was the quality of the food: for breakfast we had a choice of grapefruit or orange juice, scrambled or fried eggs, toast or muffins! Later that year, at another camp, at Thanksgiving, the desert option included baked Alaska. After a brief stint in Columbus, I boarded a train with hundreds of other recruits for an unknown destination. The train chugged along day and night and finally came to a halt in an open field of what turned out to be northern Florida. There the Air Corps had constructed a huge Tent City, where I spent several weeks before being moved to the elegant Vinoy Hotel in St. Petersburg to undergo basic training. I was promptly granted U.S. citizenship. The training was easy and allowed me free time on the beach.

While others in my company were being shipped to various specialized schools, I was kept back, apparently because the military needed time to carry out security checks on me.

One day in May, I saw an announcement of the Army's Specialized Training Program (ASTP) which placed soldiers in colleges and universities for instruction in both foreign languages and engineering. Borrowing a daytime pass from a colleague, I went to the ASTP office in St. Petersburg to fill out the application forms. On the way back, for some inexplicable reason, since I did not frequent bars, I stopped for a beer. Out of the corner of my eye I saw two MPs enter the establishment. They asked for my pass, which I duly produced, but I had not memorized the serial number, so I was taken back to my hotel under guard. The sergeant there sentenced me to one week of nighttime "kitchen police" or KP. That night I reported to the mammoth hotel kitchen and was told to scrub the ovens with steel wool. In conversation with the cook I learned that he was Polish. When he found out that I, too, came from

Poland, he told me to forget the punishment. For the next week I spent my mornings holed up in the bathroom, reading: in this uncomfortable position I went through the major novels of Sinclair Lewis which I had borrowed from the local USO library.

Finally in July I received orders to ship out to the Citadel, a military school in Charleston, South Carolina, which served as a distribution center for ASTP personnel. I was assigned to learn Russian. Given the choice of several universities, I picked Cornell in Ithaca, New York, because of its proximity to Elmira, my parents' new home. I arrived at Cornell in September 1943 and spent there the next nine months.

We had an unusually distinguished group of teachers, most of them Russian émigrés, including Marc Vishniak who had served in 1918 as secretary to the Constituent Assembly and subsequently as editor of a leading Russian magazine in Paris. The physicist Dmitrii Gavronsky introduced me to Max Weber. ASTP pioneered the "total immersion" method of teaching foreign languages. Our instructors spoke to us only in Russian: the very first phrase we learned was *Gde ubornaia?*—"Where's the toilet?" This principle was enforced in the classroom, but I cannot say that in our living quarters, a converted fraternity house, we spoke Russian as we were supposed to do. Most students learned nothing but a few words and phrases. The language teaching staff was intensely anticommunist but kept its feelings under control. The teaching of history and politics, however, was entrusted to communists: the first was Vladimir Kazakevich, who after the war would emigrate to the USSR; the second, Joshua Kunitz. Neither made a secret of their sympathies. The students in the Russian program, some sixty in all, were mildly friendly to the Soviet Union, some for ideological reasons, most out of loyalty to an ally who was crushing the Wehrmacht. But even they could not swallow the propaganda which Kazakevich and Kunitz dished out to us: both were virtually booed out of the classroom.

I mastered the rudiments of the Russian language in three months— it was the first time in my life that I really worked conscientiously in school—and devoted the remaining time to other matters. A colleague taught me how to develop and print photographs, and I spent many hours in the darkroom. In the music room I listened to classical records. I spent much time in the library reading and translating Rainer Maria Rilke, my latest discovery and passion. And I dated.

The director of the Russian ASTP at Cornell was Charles Malamuth, a professional translator: it was he who had rendered into English Trotsky's biography of Stalin. One evening, Malamuth brought to our lodgings a portable phonograph and played for those of us who were of Polish background—we roomed together—a recording of a pleasant female voice reading passages from the national epic, *Pan Tadeusz* of Adam Mickiewicz. Who was the reader we asked. He told us there were two Polish girls at Cornell and gave us their names. My best friend at the time was Casimir Krol, a tall Pole, somewhat older than I, a great lady's man though otherwise of a melancholy disposition. He called one of the girls for a date and chose for himself the taller of the two, who happened to be Irene Roth, my future wife. I arranged for a date with the other girl, the one who had made the record. The four of us went to the movies and to a milk bar. Neither girl made a great impression on me. Nor did we make a great impression on them: Irene wrote in her diary that evening that if forced to choose between us, she preferred her own date.

But before long Irene and I began to drift toward each other. We had remarkably similar backgrounds: our mothers came from Warsaw, our fathers from Galicia, and the two families vaguely knew each other. We had both learned German before Polish. We had lived in Warsaw several streets apart and recalled birthday parties we had attended as children. She and her family had fled Poland in the first week of the war by making their way to Lithuania and then to Sweden from where, with the help of her father's elder brother in the United States, in January 1940 they migrated to Canada. Soon afterwards, they moved to New York City. At Cornell she was studying architecture. Our first date was to a Rudolf Serkin recital, throughout which she scribbled notes on the program and passed them on to me, a concert habit she retained for many years. We listened to classical records and printed photographs. One day I took her to Elmira to meet my parents. Both took an instant liking to her.

At the beginning of June 1944 we had our formal ASTP "graduation" where I delivered, in Russian, the valedictory address. We expected to be sent to Officer Candidate School to receive commissions. But it turned out otherwise. On June 6, Allied troops had landed in France, and the armed forces needed replacements. We learned that instead of going to Officer Candidate School as promised, we would be posted to various infantry divisions for basic training. I was assigned to the 310th Infantry Regiment of the 78th or "Lightning" Division stationed at Camp Pickett, Virginia, a vast military reservation near Richmond. It was a sad day when we departed.

The American army, I believe, committed great mistakes in its personnel policy by treating men in uniform as interchangeable entities, like parts of a machine. Men fight not for their country but for their

comrades, in units as small as a platoon with its twenty-five or so soldiers. The esprit de corps is an essential ingredient of every successful military force. All the enlisted men in the 78th Division had been
shipped to Britain three months earlier as replacements to units readied
for the invasion of France, while the officers and noncoms remained in
place. The division I joined had been, as it were, eviscerated: we were so
many individual bodies replacing coordinated teams. It bode ill.

We underwent arduous basic training for the next eight weeks, quite
different from what I had experienced in the Air Corps in Florida. The
summer temperature in Virginia often exceeds 90 degrees Fahrenheit.
We had to drill and march in this heat in full gear: I was assigned to carry
a Browning Automatic Rifle, a portable machine gun weighing nearly
twenty pounds. During nightly bivouacs we were attacked by chiggers,
beastly little insects that dug into the skin and caused intense irritation:
they had to be removed by the application of a lighted cigarette to their
posteriors, the heat of which caused them to crawl out backwards. The
troops in our company were a mixed lot—not the best, for the best had
been shipped off to Europe.

I felt very bitter, considering that five years after my unhappy experiences in the Polish ROTC camp I was back lugging a gun. In my diary I
complained that I was "an imprisoned animal who works like a mule,
obeys like a dog, and lives like a pig." I thought I could contribute more
to the war effort by making use of my linguistic skills, especially German
and Italian, the languages of the enemy, and contacted the head of
divisional intelligence, an elegant colonel who in civilian life had been
connected with Harvard Law School. He expressed an interest in having
me join the G-2 staff. But when I returned a few days later to ask about
my transfer, he told me he had learned I was soon to be shipped out.

Indeed, a few days later, while I was attending a meeting which instructed company representatives how to pack weapons for overseas
transport—it was the end of August 1944—I was called out and told that
I was being transferred to the Air Corps base in Kearns Field, Utah. My
division proceeded to Europe without me. It played a minor role in the
Battle of the Bulge.

In Utah, the Cornell students met with Russian-trained students
from two other universities, and in October we proceeded to Camp
Ritchie in Maryland. The camp was a country club converted into an
intelligence school. Every two months fresh groups would arrive for an
intensive course in intelligence training, following which graduates received commissions and left for the front. Our destiny was somewhat

different. We were kept as a group for a special mission the nature of which I learned only after the war.

Since the summit conference at Teheran in November 1943, the American and Soviet military had been discussing the construction of joint air bases on Soviet territory. Washington's main concern was to secure facilities against Japan, but the European command also had an interest in utilizing Soviet airfields against German targets in Eastern Europe which lay beyond the reach of bombers based in the United Kingdom and Italy. The idea emerged of "shuttle bombing": U.S. bombers would fly over Eastern Europe, drop their bombs on industrial facilities and oil fields, land on Soviet territory, refuel and rearm, and on their way back to the home base repeat their missions. The Russians gave reluctant consent to this proposal, and in spring 1944, just as we were completing our course at Cornell, placed three air bases in the Ukraine at the disposal of the U.S. Air Corps: the principal one was at Poltava, with two smaller ones at Mirgorod and Piriatin. The project received the code name Frantic. On June 2, 1944, U.S. bombers flew their first mission over German territory from these bases. The Germans, surprised by this air assault from the east, on June 22 launched a concerted attack with 200 planes on the Poltava base, which left it a virtual ruin: 43 B-17 bombers were either demolished or damaged beyond repair. Nevertheless, the U.S. raids resumed in July: in all, more than two thousand sorties were flown from Soviet bases. The effect was small and friction with the Russians was constant. At the end of the summer, the Russians ordered the closing of the three Ukrainian air bases. The final evacuation of the so-called Eastern Command, however, did not take place until June 1945.[6]

Our Russian group was to have been sent to the Ukrainian shuttle bases as interpreters, but as the enterprise wound down, the mission evaporated. And so on completing the Ritchie course we were dispatched to Scott Field in Illinois, ostensibly to train as radio operators but in fact to be held in reserve for future contingencies requiring Russian speakers. It was a boring life: mastering the Morse code and the intricacies of radio mechanics was not something I enjoyed.

My stay there did have one important intellectual by-product: it was then that I decided to become a full-fledged historian. I had always been attracted to history, in part because the past excited my imagination, in part because it is so boundless in scope. But it was only then that I chose it as a profession.

Scott Field was located near St. Louis, Missouri, where I spent most of my weekend passes at concerts, in the public library, or exploring used bookstores. One day I chanced on a copy of François Guizot's *History of Civilization in Europe,* translated by William Hazlitt, son of the well-known essayist. The book—a series of lectures that Guizot had delivered at the Sorbonne in 1828—was unlike any history I had ever read. An inquiring mind can develop an interest in virtually everything that has ever happened because nothing is ever crystal clear: there are always questions about motivations and effects, and, indeed, about the course of the events themselves. Thus one can become engrossed in the history of grain prices in medieval Hungary, in the life and works of Pope Innocent III, or in the politics of the principality of Zerbst-Anstalt simply because they present intellectual challenges. But such topics lack broader significance: they are exercises in problem solving, much like chess playing. The same applies to standard general histories of countries and epochs. They tell what happened and possibly why, but they do not indicate the reason such knowledge matters one way or another.

With the kind of history that Guizot wrote, and that I have ever since taken as a model, a link is established between the past and ourselves. It is philosophical history, knowledge of which teaches us about us—where we come from and why we think as we do. From the opening page, Guizot defines his philosophical approach to history:

> For some time past, there has been much talk of the necessity of limiting history to the narration of facts: nothing can be more just; but we must always bear in mind that there are far more facts to narrate and that the facts themselves are far more various in their nature, than people are at first disposed to believe. . . . The very portion of history which we are accustomed to call its philosophy, the relation of events to each other, the connection which unites them, their causes and their effects—these are all facts, these are all history, just as much as the narratives of battles, and of other material and visible events. . . . Civilization is one of those facts. . . . I will at once add, that this history is the greatest of all, that it includes all.

The fourteen lectures which follow these introductory remarks offer a majestic sweep of eras and countries, of institutions and religions, all presented in an urbane and elegant literary manner. The book won me over completely. It showed me that all the things that I was interested in—notably philosophy and art—could be accommodated under the spacious roof of the discipline of history.

The rest of my military career was anticlimactic. From Scott Field we returned to Cornell for a summer refresher course, then back to Ritchie, where I was assigned to work as nighttime switchboard operator. In late 1945 we were sent to California, preparatory to being assigned to Korea as interpreters. But now that Japan had surrendered, the war was over, and we wanted home. Our unit bore the mysterious letters FAH. It occurred to me that these probably stood for the initials of the officer in the War Department in charge of us. I consulted the directory of regular army officers and, indeed, found a Colonel Frank A. Hartmann whose name matched these initials. We took the chance of telephoning him at the Pentagon and informing him that we had served three and more years and hence deserved to be discharged. A few days later orders came to ship us back East. I could not wait to return to civilian life and resume my studies. I was discharged in March 1946 at Fort Meade, Maryland.

The Holocaust Strikes Home

Spring 1945, which witnessed the capitulation of Germany, also brought personal tragedy to us and all Jews. As the Red Army advanced into Poland and from there into Germany, the newspapers began to publish accounts and photographs of liberated concentration and "extermination" camps: human beings resembling skeletons, piles of shoes and eyeglasses taken from the murdered victims, and crematoria where the gassed bodies were reduced to ashes. We were totally unprepared for this systematic and wholesale murder: it seemed impossible not only because of its barbarism but also because of its irrationality since the Germans could well have used the Jews to assist their war effort. Allied governments had known what was happening to Jews in occupied Europe but preferred to keep silent for fear of helping Hitler's propaganda machine, which claimed that the war was run by and waged on behalf of "world Jewry." I have in my possession a pamphlet issued by the Polish government in exile, based in London, dated December 10, 1942, under the title *The Mass Extermination of Jews in German Occupied Poland*, and addressed to the governments of the members of the United Nations. It reported accurately and in detail on the hundreds of thousands of Jews being deported and equal numbers being starved to death or killed. The information was ignored. To their eternal shame, America's Jewish community leaders also preferred to maintain silence about the genocide of their kin.

At the end of April 1945, I received a letter from Olek who had survived the war, hiding on the "Aryan" side, first in Warsaw, then in

Łódź. Soon after, mother sent me a clipping from a Polish-Jewish newspaper that described, in Wanda's own words, how she had jumped out of a cattle train transporting her to the Treblinka gas chambers and ended up as a Polish forced laborer in Germany. These were miracles. But for the rest of our family, miracles were few. Two of mother's brothers managed to survive. As soon as postal communications were restored, they sent us letters that brought the Holocaust, as it came to be known, home. Neither of these uncles was well educated and neither had accomplished much before the war, having lived mainly off the rents brought in by grandmother's properties. This makes their letters the more poignant. Mother's youngest brother, Sigismund, who before the war had devoted his life to chasing women, wrote as follows:

> I wander like a madman, with only one thought in mind, that they will return. I await with a pounding heart our beloved Arnold who together with our beloved mother, Max, Esther, and [their daughter] Niusia were yanked out the ghetto by the Fascist thugs on September 9, 1942, and loaded into a giant transport. The German bandits said at first that this was only for resettlement, but as we learned this was ordinary murder because on arrival people were either burned alive or gassed. Millions of people, the entire ghetto, have been murdered in this manner and even a more cruel one.

And Max wrote:

> Sigismund and I were almost eyewitnesses of the deportation to Treblinka of Dr. Max [Gabrielew], [his wife] Esther and [daughter] Jasia. . . . Arnold whom we all loved so much and for whom we shall never cease to grieve, stood, as always, with a smile on his lips in the "death row" together with our dearest Mother—aged, worn out by life. And this 73-year-old woman stood bravely. . . . Alas, there was no possibility of saving them. No human power or wisdom could do anything even to ease [their lot]. There was no way of handing them poison.

There is little I can say about the Holocaust that has not been said already. This is even more the case because I have deliberately shied away from reading about or viewing films and photographs of it. My reason was that every incident of this carnage that I have read about and every picture of it that I have seen has etched itself permanently in my mind and lingers there as a morbid reminder of the monstrous crime. I have been troubled by my attitude but have stuck to it for the sake of my sanity and positive attitude to life.

The Holocaust did not shake my religious feelings. Both intellectually and emotionally I accepted the words of God as recorded in the Book of Job, chapter 38 and following that we humans are utterly incapable of understanding His purposes.* Many Jews—my father among them—lost their religious beliefs because of the Holocaust. Mine, if anything, were strengthened. The mass murder (including those that occurred simultaneously in the Soviet Union) demonstrated what happens when people renounce faith in God, deny that human beings were created in His image, and reduce them to soulless and therefore expendable material objects.

The main effect of the Holocaust on my psyche was to make me delight in every day of life that has been granted to me, for I was saved from certain death. I felt and feel to this day that I have been spared not to waste my life on self-indulgence or self-aggrandizement but to spread a moral message by showing, using examples from history, how evil ideas lead to evil consequences. Since scholars have written enough on the Holocaust, I thought it my mission to demonstrate this truth using the example of communism. Furthermore, I felt and feel that to defy Hitler, I have a duty to lead a full and happy life, to be content with whatever life brings, to be cheerful and not morose: sadness and complaints seem to me forms of blasphemy, as are lying and indifference to cruelty. These attitudes, affecting my personal and professional life, are the result of my youthful experiences, and it is natural that people who have had the good fortune to escape them look at life and their vocation more dispassionately. On the debit side, I admit to having little patience with the psychological problems of free people, especially if they involve a "search for identity" or some other form of self-seeking. They strike me as terribly trivial. I agree with the Germany essayist Johannes Gross that mankind can be divided into two categories: "those who have problems, and those who have conversation. It is an important element of self-preservation to leave the bearers of problems to themselves."[7]

I should add two comments on this inexhaustible subject. First, people who have not lived under a totalitarian regime cannot conceive what a powerful hold it has on people and how it can drive even the most normal among them to commit monstrous crimes by instilling in them intense, focused hatred: Orwell accurately described this phenomenon in *1984*. While in the grip of this emotion, ordinary human reactions are

---

*In so doing, I was unknowingly following the advice of Talmudic sages who who discouraged speculation about matters beyond human comprehension: "Seek not out the things that are too hard for thee, and into things that are hidden from thee inquire thou not." A. Cohen, *Everyman's Talmud* (New York, 1949), 27.

suppressed; as soon as the regime falls, the spell is broken. This evidence has persuaded me that one should never subordinate politics to ideology: for even if an ideology is morally sound, realizing it usually requires resorting to violence because society at large may not share it.

Second, a few words about the Germans. Traditionally, the German nation was not regarded as bloodthirsty: it was a nation of scientists, poets, and musicians. And yet they proved singularly adept at mass murder. In May 1982, I visited, on his invitation, the mayor of Frankfurt, Walter Wallman, whom I had first met in Washington. We had a private dinner in his home, conversing on a variety of subjects, sometimes in English, sometimes in German. At one point he asked me: "Do you think that Nazism could have occurred anywhere else than Germany?" After a moment of thought I replied that I did not think so. He buried his face in his hands with the words *"Mein Gott!"* I instantly regretted having inflicted pain on this decent man, but I felt no other answer was possible.

The quality that has always struck me about the Germans was that although without peer in handling inanimate things and animals, they lack competence in dealing with human beings whom they tend to treat as mere objects.* It is significant that in the letters German soldiers wrote home from conquered Poland in 1939 and subsequently published, the stress was on the "dirtiness" of the Poles and Jews: their culture held no interest for them, only their hygiene.† They were as upset by a dirty person or household as they would be by a dirty piece of equipment. They also have little sense of humor. (Of German humor, Mark Twain said that "it is no laughing matter.")‡ They lack, therefore, the kind of tolerance for human foibles that makes humor possible; they are mechanics—probably the best in the world—whereas humans are living organisms who require infinite understanding and forbearance; unlike machines, they are messy and unpredictable. Hence, when or-

---

*Some readers may object to my generalizations about nations, whether German here or Russian later. If so, they ought to bear in mind that I am referring not to genetic but to cultural characteristics. These allude to upbringing and have nothing in common with "race." Thus, I have learned from observation that German Jews raised in the same culture resembled more their Aryan compatriots than they did say, Polish Jews. Second, to say that members of a given nation are prone to behave in a certain way, of course, does not mean that all of them do so: it is a descriptive statement *grosso modo* and, by and large, one which is more likely to be true than false.

†The Polish novelist Andrzej Szczypiorski explains this mentality as follows: "Jews are lice, and lice have to be exterminated. Such opinions appeal to the German imagination, because the Germans are clean, they like hygiene and order." *Noc, Dzień i Noc* (Warsaw, 1995), 242.

‡But help is on its way. At the end of 2001, the English press reported that the Austrian alpine resort of Mieming had opened special courses for Germans to teach humor: they include "laughter lessons." *The Week*, December 22, 2001, page 7, citing the *Sunday Telegraph*.

dered to murder for a cause, they murder, feeling no more pity for their victims than for a discarded object.

I recall reading about one German SS officer who had served at Treblinka saying that when trainloads of Jews arrived to be gassed, he regarded them as nothing more than "cargo." Such people, under a spell, can mow down innocent and defenseless people with a machine gun as unemotionally as a construction worker crushes a pavement with his pneumatic drill. This dehumanization of human beings, combined with a high sense of *Pflicht* or "duty," made the Holocaust possible in Germany as it would not have been anywhere else. The Russians murdered even more people than the Germans, and they murdered their own, but they did it without the mechanical precision, the rational calculation of the Germans who "harvested" human hair and gold fillings. Nor were they proud of their murders. I have never seen a photograph of a Soviet atrocity. Although they were forbidden to do so, the Germans took countless photographs of theirs.

Once in Munich I visited Charles Malamuth, my onetime Russian teacher at Cornell. He was renting an apartment that apparently had been requisitioned from a German. On the coffee table lay an album the previous owners had left behind, the kind of album where normal people paste pictures of babies and family outings. In this one, made up of snapshots probably sent home by the head of the family or a son serving the Führer on the Eastern Front, neatly affixed, were pictures of a very different kind. The first that met my eyes showed a German soldier dragging an elderly Jewish woman by her hair to the place of execution. On another page were three photographs: one showed a group of women with babies in their arms standing under a tree; the next, the same group stripped naked; the third, their corpses sprawled in a bloody heap.

TWO

Harvard

Graduate School

As a youth, I had an absurdly exalted notion of the university. My model was the University of Berlin in the first half of the nineteenth century when its faculty numbered such luminaries as the philosophers Hegel, Fichte, and Schopenhauer, the historians von Ranke, Niebuhr, and Mommsen, the theologian Schleiermacher. I imagined a fellowship of men, old and young, wholly dedicated to the pursuit of knowledge, selflessly sharing their learning and wisdom: a "School of Athens" as depicted by Raphael. Envy and careerism had no place in this imaginary environment.

Needless to say, I soon learned reality to be very different. The university turned out to be a microcosm of society at large and the quest for knowledge by its faculty was closely tied to personal advancement and the craving for fame. With everyone pursuing his own research interests, I found very little collegiate spirit: professors rarely read each other's books, even those in their own field. If they shared their interests with anyone it was usually with scholars in the same field at other institutions. In the 1980s I was invited to join a Harvard dinner society called "the Shop Club." Founded at the turn of the century, it met once a month and, following a dinner, heard a colleague report on his work. The trouble was that the club attracted mostly the aged and retired. After a full meal, they usually dozed off.

To state this is to voice a certain disappointment but not regret at my life as an academic. Although the university fell far short of my exalted idea of it, it nevertheless proved a highly congenial place: the combination of research and teaching in an atmosphere of unrestrained freedom as well as security suited me ideally, and I consider myself extremely fortunate to have spent my adult life at one of the world's leading centers of learning.

While I was on active service, Irene and I kept in constant contact— not only by mail but also in person, for I had frequent weekend passes which I spent in New York City or in Elmira. The summer of 1945 I was back at Cornell for a refresher course in Russian. We grew ever closer. When my discharge seemed imminent, we discussed our future and in January 1946 decided to marry. We arrived at this conclusion naturally, inevitably: in my diary I wrote that no decision was really required. This rather surprised me for, remembering Rabelais and the agonizing deliberations of his protagonist Panurge on the advantages and drawbacks of marriage, I expected greater vacillation. Our parents had mixed feelings about the news: mine thought me too young for marriage, hers would have preferred a businessman for a son-in-law. But neither couple objected, and the Roths gave us a splendid wedding at the Delmonico Hotel in New York City, following which we left for a honeymoon in New England and Canada.

I do not believe my marriage, which is now in its sixth decade, is of interest to anyone but us, and I shall not dwell on it. We were fully committed to each other from the onset and determined to succeed: my mother said that we suited each other as the lid fits the kettle. Although not an academic, Irene adapted herself well to the rarified intellectual atmosphere in which she found herself and created for me a wonderful environment. We complemented each other perfectly: to paraphrase Voltaire, she assumed command of the earth, I of the clouds, and between us, kept our little universe in good order. Her charm, beauty, and joie de vivre have never faded for me. My marriage was for me a continuous source of joy and strength. In a book which I dedicated to her after we had celebrated our golden wedding anniversary I thanked her for "having created for me ideal conditions to pursue scholarship." Some feminists were outraged by this homage, interpreting it to mean that she sacrificed her own life to cook and do laundry for me. Apparently they were unaware that "conditions" in this context involve not only physical comforts but also, and above all, spiritual ones.

In late 1945, while I was still in uniform, time came to apply to graduate school. Earlier that year, Cornell had generously granted me a B.A. degree based on the work I had done both there and at Muskingum, which spared me having to go back to college. I had a vague notion of combining Russian affairs with general cultural history. This left me with three choices—Columbia, Yale, and Harvard—the major centers of

Russian studies in the United States at the time. I applied to each, although I preferred Harvard from the beginning. All three accepted me. Money, this time, presented no problem because the government, through the so-called G.I. Bill, paid veterans' tuition plus a modest stipend, which our parents liberally supplemented. Neither then nor afterwards did we ever face financial problems.

Columbia I eliminated quickly, in part because I did not want to live in New York, in part because the leading Russian historian there, Geroid Tanquary Robinson, judging by a brief interview he had granted me, seemed a cranky pedant. It transpired that he had his Ph.D. candidates write dissertations on preassigned topics, all of which had to do with conceptions of the revolution: thus, "Bukharin and the Revolution," "Zinoviev and the Revolution," and so on. The enterprise had about as much value for the understanding of Russia, past and present, as would requiring Ph.D. candidates in American history to write on "Fillmore and the Constitution" or "Harding and the Constitution."

In favor of Yale was the fact that George Vernadsky, who held the Russian history chair there, was probably the leading specialist on the subject in the country, the author of numerous books, some of them published before the revolution. I visited Yale but did not have the opportunity of meeting him. What struck me in New Haven, however, was the abundance of tailor establishments.

In Cambridge, by contrast, I found few tailors but no end of bookstores. This helped sway me definitely in favor in Harvard, especially since Michael Karpovich, the professor of Russian history there, turned out to be a friendly and supportive person. Karpovich published very little because he had an ill wife who required constant care and also because he was something of an unofficial head of the Russian community on the East Coast and editor of the leading émigré "thick journal," the quarterly Novyi Zhurnal. Unlike the other Russians on Harvard's faculty, most of them prickly and vain, he was even-tempered and modest.

Irene and I cut our honeymoon short and came to Boston in mid-September. We rented a comfortable two-room apartment in the Back Bay; we also had a new car, a wedding present from Irene's uncle. We thus lived considerably better than the other graduate students. The disadvantage of this arrangement was that I did not have the opportunity of getting to know better the other doctoral candidates in history, most of whom were single and lived in dormitories.

The Saturday before the opening of the fall term, the History Department traditionally held a meeting where its entire faculty made itself available to new and returning graduate students. Apparently I had so worded the statement of purpose on my application that the department decided my main field was intellectual and cultural history. For this reason it assigned me to Crane Brinton, one of the stars of our department and the author of numerous books, including *The Anatomy of Revolution*. Brinton asked me about my interests. As I recorded in my diary: "When I showed him my tentative schedule, composed mostly of courses in philosophy and law, he shouted at me: 'You've got to get more history—political history—as "Prime Minister John Jones fell because etc."' I inserted a course in English history, to some extent against my will."

Brinton promptly brought me down to earth, as I would incoming students in the years to come. "You have to prepare four fields for your General Examinations in two years. Some if not most of them must be in national fields. Have you any preferences as far as national histories are concerned?" I replied: "I suppose Russia would be my first choice." "Well, in that case you ought to have Professor Karpovich as your advisor. He is sitting over there." I went over to Karpovich and signed up with him. In this casual manner was decided my professional career.

At this point it may be appropriate to clarify how I feel about the country that was to preoccupy me professionally for my entire academic life. This is of some importance because Russian nationalists have repeatedly accused me of "Russophobia." I draw a sharp distinction between Russian governments and the Russian people, and further between educated Russians and the population at large. I have immense admiration and sympathy for Russian intellectuals (even as I criticize their politics). When I read the prose of Turgenev, Tolstoy, or Chekhov, the poetry of Pasternak and Akhmatova, when I listen to the songs of an Okudzhava or Vysotsky, when I observe the heroism of a Sakharov, I am at home. Indeed, I almost feel Russian. But things appear to me in a very different light when I study Russian politics, the focus of my interests as an historian, or meet with Russians who hold a public post. Russians are an intensely personal people who have never succeeded in translating their warm human feelings into the impersonal relations required for the effective functioning of social and political institutions. Hence they require a "strong hand" to regulate their public lives: vertical controls to substitute for the missing horizontal bonds, so well developed in Western societies. I dislike this feature of Russian life and I dislike the people who implement it. I further have no sympathy for Russian nationalism and the anti-Westernism which provide a convenient bond between authority and the uneducated masses. (Incidentally, my attitude toward the United States is neatly reversed: I have the highest respect for its public life but much less for its culture.) All of this has nothing to do with Russophobia. I would hardly have devoted my life to studying a people I disliked.

Expanding Intellectual Horizons: Isaiah Berlin

Harvard is the oldest American university and the most prestigious. Ever since Charles Eliot took charge as president in 1869 and, adopting European institutions as a model, transformed it from a provincial seminary into a blend of the English college and the German research university, Harvard has been the foremost center of higher learning in the United States. It achieved this status by drawing on the support, moral and financial, of the Boston elite who had greater cultural ambitions than those of any other American city. Judging by the opinion of the academic profession, Harvard retains this status to this day. It reached the pinnacle of its excellence and fame in the two decades that followed World War II. During this period Harvard was perceived and perceived itself as without peer not only in North America but in the world at large. Suffice it to say that after I had received tenure in the Department of History, one of its senior members told me in all seriousness: "You have no idea how close it was: on knife's edge—on the one side Harvard, on the other utter darkness."

Harvard enjoyed its unique status by virtue of several factors. There was, of course, its faculty, which included a number of refugees from Nazi-occupied Europe and, for the first time outside of New York City, some Jewish scholars previously all but barred from America's leading universities. It was the richest institution of higher learning in the world, which meant that its facilities, especially its remarkable library, were without peer. Last but not least, it had a lofty sense of its own worth that easily passed into arrogance—it used to be joked that "you can always tell a Harvard man, but you can't tell him much." If it did not become disagreeably conceited, it was because Harvard deemed its superiority so obvious, so predestined, so universally acknowledged that it felt no need to flaunt it.

Into this splendid vessel, virtually emptied during the war, poured in 1946 and 1947 thousands of recently demobilized students. Most had been on active service for several years; they were starved for knowledge as probably no generation before or since. They thronged to classes; they devoured books. I do not recall any discussions among graduate students during these years of jobs, a subject of increasing concern to those who would follow them.

When I read my diaries from the years 1938–46, I sense a disturbing undertone of frustration and self-pity at being prevented by the war from realizing any of my aspirations and having no one with whom to share thoughts and interests. All this vanished the instant I arrived in Cambridge. I found no end of young people who shared the same preoccupations and were as well if not better informed than me. The air was permeated with respect for intellectual achievement. I had never experienced anything like it. And it is symptomatic that soon after enrolling at Harvard, I stopped keeping a regular diary.

Harvard at the time was still in the grip of Anglophilia. Oxford, and to a lesser extent Cambridge, provided the model of both academic and social life. Much of the instruction was conducted through tutorials rather than lecture courses.* The Harvard house system modeled itself on the Oxbridge colleges and copied their "high tables." Many English scholars and writers visited Harvard in the 1940s and 1950s, reinforcing the English influence. Pedantry was frowned upon. One did not discuss one's work, and salary talk was taboo: the pretense among the faculty was that they were gentlemen of independent means who happened to have chosen scholarship as a vocation. It was a bit silly but it could be interpreted as homage paid to learning.

Harvard was greater than the sum of its parts. Much of the faculty consisted of tired professors, bored with their subjects and their students, some of them appointed because of their social connections. But the tone was set by the stars who enjoyed an international reputation. In history, there was the colonial specialist Samuel Eliot Morison; in European diplomatic history, William Langer (for a while on leave in Washington to set up the research division of what became the Central Intelligence Agency); Crane Brinton; Gaetano Salvemini, a political refugee from Mussolini's Italy; the Schlesingers, father and son. History was probably the most popular university department at the time, with the largest number of undergraduate "concentrators," and its morale was correspondingly high. The atmosphere was clubbish in that virtually all the permanent members of the department had Harvard Ph.D.'s and had been each other's teachers and/or pupils.

In the first year I took the required number of lecture courses and two

---

*In time, the tutorial system shrunk and increasingly knowledge was imparted by lecture courses. The Harvard catalogue of the Faculty of Arts and Sciences for the last prewar year (1938–39) numbered 183 pages; its successor for 2002–3, 910.

seminars, the first with Karpovich, the second with Brinton. Karpovich's seminar, which was devoted to the reign of Alexander I, enrolled some of the future leaders in the field: Marc Raeff, who would hold the Russian history chair at Columbia; Leopold Haimson, who would teach at Chicago and Columbia; Nicholas Riasanovsky, later of the University of California at Berkeley; Donald Treadgold of the University of Washington. My paper dealt with "Russian Thinkers and Europe, 1820–1840." In Brinton's seminar I wrote on the Russian military colonies under Alexander I: it would be my first scholarly publication when it appeared in the *Journal of Modern History* in 1950.

Irene wanted a business, and so my father gave us $400 to buy a small dry-cleaning establishment located near our apartment house. We ran it for a few months, Irene ironing and me delivering. But when the midterm grades arrived and proved to be not too brilliant, we sold the shop. The next term my grades were solid As.

Because of widespread fear of an imminent war with the Soviet Union, I decided to take my master's degree so as to have at least some concrete result of my studies in case I was unable to complete the doctoral program. This merely required me to make a degree application. At commencement in June 1947 the speaker was General George Marshall. I paid close attention to his address and was disappointed to find in it nothing but commonplaces. So apparently did everyone else, including the heads of European governments, until the Department of State alerted them to the programmatic passages that invited the Europeans to present the United States with a coordinated plan of postwar economic reconstruction. These remarks gave birth to the Marshall Plan, and thus the 1947 commencement address may be classed as one of the most important public speeches of the century. It certainly did not appear so at the time of delivery.

No war broke out and my second year was devoted to "reading courses," essentially independent study under nominal professorial supervision for the four "fields" to be presented at the General Examination, which we were expected to take at the year's end. I chose to be examined in the medieval history of Poland and Bohemia, the Renaissance and Reformation, modern England, and modern Russia. I passed the two-hour ordeal at the end of May reasonably well and began, in summer 1948, to cast about for a dissertation subject.

But before I plunged into my dissertation we took a trip to Europe. We thought that given the tension between the United States and the Soviet Union this could well be our last glimpse of the old continent before it was reduced to rubble. We crossed the Atlantic in a miserable converted Dutch troop ship, the *Kota Inten*, manned by Indonesians. The food was poor; we slept in separate dormitories; the ship permanently listed to one side. But after a ten-day voyage we arrived safely in Rotterdam. From there we proceeded to Paris where I met my uncle Max, a survivor of the Holocaust, the very same who had accompanied us to the train in Warsaw on that memorable October morning in 1939. He owed his survival to his Polish common-law wife who risked her own life to hide him in her apartment. I also met with Olek, who was his old self, at least outwardly. We traveled on a shoestring but the dollar was all powerful—in Paris, a room with kitchen and bath near the Gare St. Lazare cost us one dollar per day. Our wants were modest and we had a marvelous time. From there were traveled to Switzerland and Italy. In Brussels, on the return trip, I briefly met with Wanda who was married to a Belgian baker she had met in a German labor camp.

When we returned in September 1948 we settled in New York City, largely because Irene wanted to be close to her parents. A few days later we drove up to Cambridge so I could register in graduate school for the coming year. It turned out, however, that I had confused the registration dates and arrived late. The dean chided me for this and told me to wait until the end of the registration period to file my papers. During those two or three days of idleness, which I spent largely in Widener, the main university library, I ran into Charles Taylor, the department's principal medievalist. It was one of those fortuitous events that change the course of one's life. Taylor offered me an appointment as a teaching fellow in History 1, a survey of Western civilization, obligatory for concentrators but also attended by many other undergraduates. Lectures for History 1, one of Harvard's giant course offerings, were given twice a week in the New Lecture Hall on Kirkland Street, in the fall term by Taylor, in the spring by Karpovich. On Fridays, the students were broken up into sections of some twenty each under the supervision of a graduate student who answered questions and administered tests on the week's work.

It was my first teaching experience, and I enjoyed it greatly, even though it required feverish preparation and occasional improvisation. I recall a student once asking me out of the blue why the medieval French king Philip II was given "Augustus" as his middle name. Today I would say that I did not know, but being too young then to admit ignorance, I took a stab and responded that it was because he had been born in August. As soon as the class was over I rushed to the library to find the answer and was much relieved to learn that Philip II, indeed, saw the light of day on August 21, 1165.

I chose as my dissertation topic Bolshevik nationality theory. This was the time when Russian chauvinism, actively promoted by Stalin, was at its apogee: Russia was depicted as having been throughout her history the leading country in the world, always the victim of aggression, never the aggressor, as well as the source of humankind's greatest intellectual and scientific achievements. One Soviet publication of the time conceded to the Americans only two inventions: the waffle iron and the electric chair.* It struck me as puzzling that a regime officially committed to Marxism, an ideology that condemned nationalism as a bourgeois ploy to deflect workers from the class struggle, would espouse rabid nationalism. I wanted to find out why this had happened. To this end I began to study the theories of nationalism espoused by the founders of social democracy and their disciples, especially in Austria-Hungary and Russia. I worked very intensely because I wanted to finish my doctoral requirements in two years. This was difficult since I had to combine work on the dissertation with teaching. My load was lightened the next, and final, year in graduate school when the newly founded Russian Research Center offered me a one-semester fellowship that freed me from teaching. My thesis was ready at the beginning of 1950. I had worked so hard on it that after handing in the bound manuscript to the departmental secretary, I was rushed to the hospital with excruciatingly painful colic.

Half a year earlier Irene had given birth to our first child, Daniel. The experience, even if vicarious, of bringing a living being into this world was unlike any I had ever known: while she was in labor I felt as if I were being reborn. In honor of this event, on that day I stopped smoking and have not touched a cigarette since.

While I was working on my dissertation in February or March 1949, I made the acquaintance of Isaiah Berlin who was considerably to influence my intellectual development. Marc Raeff invited me to his Bow Street apartment to meet with Berlin who, as a visiting professor from Oxford, was teaching a course on Russian intellectual history. I had no idea who Berlin was but agreed to come. Assembled were six or eight graduate students. Berlin arrived, dressed, as was his custom, in a three-piece black suit. He sat himself in a chair across from us and in his deep voice asked: "Very well, what shall we talk about?" Paralyzed, we sat in silence. He quickly sized up the situation and posed the question, "What

---

*A wit, mocking this line of argument, claimed that Ivan Pososhkov, a minor Russian publicist in the reign of Peter I, was a greater economist than Adam Smith who lived half a century later. "Why? you may ask. Because of the use he made of the theory of marginal utility." "But neither economist knew anything about marginal utility?!" "True, but Pososhkov didn't know about it earlier."

was the difference between the generation of Russian intellectuals of the 1840s and that of the 1860s?" Since we continued to sit mum, he answered his own query: "The earlier generation loved art and music, the latter despised both." And then he launched into a monologue which, delivered in a rapid, partly British, partly Russian accent, was not always easy to follow.

Thus began a friendship that lasted for nearly half a century, until his death in 1997. I met with Berlin many times in New York, Rome, and London; I stayed at his Oxford home. He was always available. He was an extraordinarily versatile intellectual with wide knowledge of philosophy, art, music and the ability to converse with people of all ages and all walks of life. I always thought one could drop him into any era and country of the modern age—Moscow of the 1840s, Paris of the 1860s, London of the 1890s or 1920s—and he would find himself perfectly at home.

Years later, he called me at home one evening to say he was passing through Cambridge. It happened that we were giving a party, and so I invited him to come over. I soon saw a taxi cab pull up in front of our house. But time passed and there was no sign of Berlin. Thinking that perhaps he had forgotten his wallet, I went out to meet him. It turned out that he was deep in conversation with the taxi driver. "What a man!" the driver exclaimed.

He was a wonderful conversationalist because he instantly grasped what one was saying and responded in a way that kept the conversation going and expanding. He had that rare quality which Trollope attributed to one of his characters, that of taking up the other persons' subject, whatever it was, and making it his own. He was thus an excellent listener; but when the conversation lagged, he took over. He was always witty and in good humor, at least in company. If, as Max Beerbohm wrote in his essay on Ibsen, "great men may be divided into two classes: the loveable and the unlovable," Isaiah emphatically belonged to the category of loveable.

He was very witty. Two examples of his wit must suffice. While we were spending the year in London on leave in the early 1970s he called to invite us to a performance of *Faust*. I told him that, unfortunately, we could not come because we had accepted an invitation that evening from a man who happened to enjoy the reputation of being a leading host in England. "Ah, yes, café society," Berlin mumbled, and then corrected himself "No, Nescafé society." On another occasion the name of a well-known literary historian and critic came up. "A common type on the Continent," he remarked, "rather rare in England." Adding, after a pause: "A genuine charlatan."

It is hard to find any major ideas that he contributed: for the contrast between "hedgehogs" and "foxes" he borrowed from a minor Greek writer, and the distinction between two kinds of liberty strikes me as muddled. People were his passion rather than ideas: his greatest gift was biography. He could portray individuals with remarkable deftness. He went about it like a sculptor working in clay, adding a trait here, modifying one there, rounding it out until the personality stood out in all its complexity. And this he could do not only with people he knew personally but also those known to him secondhand, from reading, as he demonstrated in what is probably his single most outstanding book, *Russian Thinkers*, in which he drew splendid portraits of the intelligentsia in the 1830s and 1840s.

Yet, for all my admiration and friendship, in the end Berlin somewhat disappointed me. He seemed emotionally detached from events of our time, so full of tragedy. I used to think that this was because he did not want to alienate liberals and socialists who dominated his milieu, but years later I was surprised to learn from his biography that he had displayed the same detachment in the early 1930s toward nascent Nazism. Although he said more than once that our century was the worst in human history, he was loath to commit himself politically. I know that he despised the Soviet regime, yet he avoided criticizing it in public, perhaps because anticommunism was considered vulgar in the circles he frequented: this despite the fact that communism bore a great, perhaps principal blame for the miseries inflicted on the twentieth century. In 1971, when the Democratic Party nominated George McGovern for the presidency, I found myself in a quandary because I was a registered Democrat and had always voted Democratic, yet I felt I could not in good conscience cast a ballot for a man so unsuited for the post of chief executive. Even so, I hesitated to support Richard Nixon, his Republican opponent. "What would you do in my position, Isaiah?" I asked. He thought for a moment and responded, "I would vote for Nixon but tell no one." He adopted the incorrect view that Italian Fascism was a conservative doctrine, ignoring its radical roots, because that, too, was the fashion. He never commented on my histories of the Russian Revolution, either in public or in private, although he had encouraged me to write them, I suppose because they were too uncompromisingly hostile to the intellectual left in Russia and Western Europe. And yet he had no illusions on the subject.

I was struck to read in his recollections of Boris Pasternak that at their meeting in the mid-1940s the Russian poet criticized him to his face for lack of empathy for Russians and their misery. As Berlin recalls it—and it is greatly to his credit that he would do so publicly:

> Pasternak reproached me . . . not, indeed, for seeking to impose my political or any other opinions on him—but for something that to him seemed almost as bad. Here we both were, in Russia, and wherever one looked, everything was disgusting, appalling, an abominable pigsty, yet I seemed positively exhilarated by it: "You wander about," he said, "and look at everything with bemused eyes"—I was no better (he declared) than other foreign visitors who saw nothing, and suffered from absurd delusions, maddening to the poor miserable natives.[1]

I felt the same moral detachment in him, and it ultimately somewhat estranged me from this man whom in all other respects I liked and looked up to. His biographer says that one reason Berlin so admired Alexander Herzen was that Herzen presented him with a "moral challenge": "someone who showed the courage and political commitment that Isaiah himself knew he lacked."[2] I always thought him a very happy man, yet from his biography I learned that he was tormented by self-doubts of various kinds: as a Jew in a Gentile and often anti-Semitic English society, as an intellectual unable to produce a major book, as a man who had difficulty dealing with women. Although in the last years of his long life we were no longer as close as before, I owe him a great debt in that he extended my intellectual horizons, encouraging me to study subjects and to express opinions on subjects outside my academic specialty. This conformed to my natural inclination, but it was not in tune with the American academic culture.

In his old age, and even more so posthumously, he had the misfortune of becoming a media "celebrity," that is, a person known not for what he has accomplished but simply for being known. There were numerous anecdotes about him and his bon mots: his nighttime encounter with Anna Akhmatova in Leningrad in 1945 became the subject of articles and even a book which touted their meeting as the greatest literary event of the twentieth century! I am quite certain he would not have welcomed such superficial fame. The encomia lavished on him after his death as the foremost thinker of our time were grossly exaggerated, for as he himself realized he was not a thinker of the caliber of a Frederick Hayek, or a Karl Popper, or a number of others who come to mind. His was not so much a creative talent as a reflective one.

Early Scholarship and Teaching

Prior to completing my doctorate, I had never given any thought to jobs. But in June 1950 I had to face the fact that I was an unemployed doctor of philosophy. There were virtually no openings at universities because their administrators had decided that after the wave of war veterans had passed through, enrollments would shrink substantially, and hence there was no need to increase faculties. (College enrollments in 1950, compared to 1940, had more than doubled thanks in large measure to the G.I. Bill.) Many fledgling historians found themselves in the same situation as me. The best our department could do was to recommend us for instructorships at MIT to help give budding engineers some patina of a liberal education. I did not find this offer attractive and turned it down. Two years later an offer of an assistant professorship came from Indiana University, and I turned that down as well.

Fortunately, I obtained an instructorship with the History and Literature Committee—an interdepartmental body made up of members of various departments in the humanities—that offered no lecture courses but taught entirely by means of tutorial. I would spend the next six years tutoring bright undergraduates specializing in Russian culture, but occasionally also those of other countries. It was an all-honors field of concentration, restricted in enrollment, and something of an elite field. The morale among the small tutorial staff—there were a dozen of us—and the students (eighty-five admitted annually) was superb. We met with sophomores and juniors, either in small groups or individually, and also directed the writing of honors theses. In addition, we supervised general discussions on such subjects as the Bible, the ancient Greek historians, and Shakespeare. The years I spent doing this provided me with a further education because I had to offer instruction in some subjects in which I was no better informed than my tutees and hence I had to do rapid preparation. I also received financial help from the Russian Research Center to transform my dissertation into a book.

In June 1950 we packed our car and departed for California so I could spend the summer doing research at the Hoover Institution. I had served since 1948 as a second lieutenant in the Army Reserves, with a specialty in military intelligence and interrogation of prisoners of war. This commission entailed attending weekly evening sessions at a Boston army base to hear and give lectures on sundry subjects: I was once asked to speak on the construction of open-air latrines. Most of the junior officers were, like myself, students, and we were treated with disdain by the professional non-coms who staffed the base. Before leaving for California, as required, I gave the military my summer address but requested that my dossier not be forwarded because I expected to return to Cambridge in the fall.

As we were passing Cleveland we heard on the radio news of the North Korean invasion of South Korea. When we reached Stanford, I fully expected to be recalled to active duty, but weeks passed and no such call came. When we returned to the East in September, I learned that my unit had been activated and shipped to Korea. I was not included because, as it turned out, contrary to my instructions, my papers had been forwarded to the West Coast. This bureaucratic fluke spared me at least two years of military service in the Far East.

While working on my dissertation I made a stunning discovery: I discovered that Russia had been, both before the revolution, and since, a multinational empire. This fact may seems so obvious today as to require no comment: by now a whole academic industry has grown up devoted to the study of the nationalities of what had been the Soviet Union. This was not the case in the early 1950s. Both Russians and Americans tended to think of the USSR as a vast melting pot, much like the United States, made up of numerous ethnic groups that voluntarily discarded their ethnic identity in favor of a new, "Soviet" nationality. The few native-born Americans who could claim expertise on the Soviet Union had been trained by Russians and identified completely with Russia and her culture. Suffice it to say that George Kennan, a well-informed and clear-headed expert, wrote at the time that the Ukraine was economically as fully integrated into the Soviet Union as Pennsylvania was integrated into the United States: "The future should see a minimum disruption of these economic ties, and that in itself would normally warrant a close political connection," he wrote in 1951.[3] This kind of economic determinism unconsciously echoed Lenin's writings on the subject before 1917, where he argued that economic interests overrode nationalism and would prevent the disintegration of the tsarist empire. In its updated version, this premise held that the Soviet empire was certain to survive even though all other empires had either dissolved or were in the process of dissolution.

It did not take me long to realize how faulty were such analogies between the United States and the Soviet Union. With the exception of native Indians and African slaves, the United States was inhabited exclusively by immigrants who had of their own free will severed links with their homelands and come to America to acquire a new national identity, that of Americans. Scattered across the continent, they lacked historical roots in the regions where they settled. In Russia the situation was entirely different. Russia was not a multinational state but an empire. That empire was built by conquests made possible by Russia's superior political and military organization. The great majority of the conquered nations continued to live on their historic lands and to speak their native languages. Although the non-Russian elites had to master Russian for purposes of self-advancement, they did not, for that reason, become Russians, any more than the people of India, communicating in English, turned into Englishmen. Even the Soviet government came to acknowledge this reality by granting the minorities, which constituted one-half of the country's population, nominal statehood and limited cultural autonomy.

My plan, suggested by Karpovich, was to expand my thesis by tracing first the disintegration of the tsarist empire in 1917–18 and then the construction, on its ruins, of a new, Soviet empire. The scope of the book and even its title were fixed in my mind as early as 1950, although judging by the notes I made at the time, I had quite unrealistically expected to complete it in one year. In fact, it took three years. The subject presented considerable difficulties because each region and each ethnic group had its own peculiar history conditioned by a past that in most cases reached back centuries. My general sense was that conflicts which in the regions inhabited predominantly by Russians acquired during the revolution and civil war a social character, in the borderlands of the empire found expression in ethnic strife. The Bolsheviks succeeded in reconquering the separated borderlands partly by virtue of greater military might and partly through the support of the Russian minorities there.

The reconquest of the empire was bought at a heavy price, however. Lenin, in his pre-1917 writings, stressed the desirability of the minorities assimilating so that ethnic differences would not interfere with the construction of socialism: those that did not wish to become Russian were free to separate and create their own sovereign states. There was to be no third alternative. But his calculation proved wrong: Lenin had thought that economic ties to Russia would inhibit separatism, but the desire to escape the Communist regime and the civil war which followed its establishment transcended economic self-interest, prompting nearly all the minorities to seek independence. Thus Moscow found itself compelled to grant them the kind of political and cultural concessions that had been anathema to Lenin. These gave nationalism a certain legitimacy. After completing my studies of the subject, I was left with no doubt that should central authority in Russia weaken again, as had happened in 1917, the empire would fall apart. This prediction was vigorously contested by nearly all Russian specialists.

At the end of May 1951, with financial assistance from the Center of International Affairs at MIT, Irene and I left Daniel with our parents and went on a four-month trip to Europe and the Middle East. My purpose was to interview the surviving members of national governments of what had been the Russian empire during the period 1917–21. I located quite a few of them in London, Paris, Munich, and Istanbul, and they helped me appreciably to understand the complex situations of that era. In Paris I established contact with the Georgian émigré community. Two years later, I spent another summer in Europe, this time in Munich, interviewing refugees from Soviet Central Asia, nearly all of them ex-German prisoners of war. The information they furnished on life in their regions in the 1930s reinforced my conviction that nationalism was well and alive in the borderlands of the USSR and that no mass assimilation was taking place.

The results of my researches came out in 1954—the year that saw the birth of our second son, Steven—in a book called *The Formation of the Soviet Union: Nationalism and Communism, 1917–1924,* under the imprint of Harvard University Press. It was the first survey of the subject. I was especially pleased by the comments of Karpovich who, having read the manuscript and made some minor criticism, closed it saying, "Well, you have done it." For though a kind man, he was not lavish with praise. The reviews were uniformly favorable. I received a personal letter from Kennan in which he wrote that he was "full of gratitude and admiration," singling out for praise the chapter on the Ukraine as "the first really coherent and dispassionate treatment of the subject." I also received a complimentary letter from E. H. Carr, although his (unsigned) review in the *Times Literary Supplement* complained of "over-simplification." It was the only book of mine that found grudging favor in the eyes of the Soviet authorities—presumably because, unlike my later works, it did not assail their central concern, Lenin and the legitimacy of the regime he had founded. In 1964, following the publication of some archival materials on Stalin and his disagreements with Lenin, I brought out a revised version of the book. It has been in print ever since, and in 1997 Harvard published a new paperback edition.

The book had a welcome side effect in that it gave me an opportunity to offer my first lecture course. This was arranged by a newcomer to

Harvard's History Department, Robert ("Bobby") Lee Wolff. A Byzantinist, Wolff had come to Harvard from the University of Wisconsin. He took great interest in Russian history and in me personally. He was a remarkable man in many ways, a person with extraordinary knowledge in a wide range of subjects, including the Victorian novel on which he later published a standard bibliography. Appointed director of the Soviet Union Program, an area studies program leading to the master's degree, he invited me to give in the spring term of 1953–54, under the auspices of the program, a course on the Soviet nationalities. (In 1955–56 the course was shifted to the History Department.)

I well recall the first day I came to Boylston Hall to offer the opening lecture in what was to be my *own* course. I quickly surveyed the classroom: there were seven students present. I was dismayed when after I had introduced myself and announced the subject of the course, two of them got up and walked out, apparently having come to the wrong classroom. I offered the course until 1960 to much larger audiences.

In March 1951, I wrote Wolff a letter suggesting that I be given an opportunity to offer a course on the Russian Revolution, but he never responded. When I ran into him some time later he told me it was an "ill-advised" letter, though he never explained why. My proposal evidently was interpreted as a direct challenge to Martin Malia, an instructor in the department, who was scheduled to offer a course on the history of the Soviet Union the following year.

Many laymen regard historical research with certain condescension, believing that everything about the past is already known and that historians merely retell the same story from various idiosyncratic viewpoints. Thus, writing history is a dull and uncreative occupation, though if vividly done, it is of some value as entertainment. That is, unless new source materials come to light. When people learned in the 1980s that I was working on a history of the Russian Revolution, they typically would ask whether I had located some fresh sources. In reality, "fresh sources" add less to knowledge than is generally believed. The art of the historian consists of selecting, according to his own criteria, some evidence from the boundless store of available facts and then weaving them in a convincing and, if possible, aesthetically satisfying narrative. Beyond this, he seeks to arrive at some synthetic judgments about the story he tells. The task is difficult but for that reason, if well done, immensely satisfying. It is hard to convey the thrill that comes upon the historian when he feels he has succeeded in making the inchoate clear and the meaningless meaningful. For me, it has always been an experience akin to the artistic.

Having finished *The Formation*, I faced the question of what to do next. I first considered continuing my study of the Soviet nationalities, carrying the narrative into the late 1920s or early 1930s. But I was held back by the realization that do this properly I had to learn a number of difficult and, for me, not very useful foreign languages, beginning with those belonging to the Turkic group. I began halfheartedly to study Ottoman Turkish with the help of a Linguaphone set of records given me by a young woman who found no use for them after she had broken off with her Turkish fiancé. All went well until I ran into vowel harmony, a peculiarity of the Uralo-Altaic group of languages, which requires that the vowels of each word belong to the same group, which makes it difficult to locate them in the dictionary. I gave up. I continued to write, from time to time, in newspapers and magazines on the "nationality question" in the USSR, as well as to advise the government on the subject, but with the one exception mentioned below, I did no more research on it.

Instead, I turned to a topic more central to Russian history, namely, its political culture. Struck by the many similarities between pre- and post-revolutionary Russia, I wished to look beyond the radical slogans of Soviet propaganda to ascertain the elements of continuity in the country's political life. It seemed clear that for all its revolutionary posturing, the Soviet Union was "revolutionary" only as far as foreign countries were concerned; in its domestic politics, it was a rigidly conservative regime that had more in common with the absolutism of a Nicholas I than with the utopian fantasies of nineteenth-century radicals. Why should this be the case? Why would a government that had seized power in the name of the most radical ideals ever conceived turn so quickly into a bastion of reaction, exploiting radical slogans exclusively for purposes of external expansion? As I jotted down in a notebook in 1956–57:

> The conservative movement in Russia is much more indigenous, national, than either liberalism or socialism. While both liberalism and socialism had native roots, their intellectual content was largely imported from the West whereas conservatism was local both in inception and development. What it lacked in intellectual originality it made up in intimate contact with Russian life. It throws, therefore, a better light on the driving forces of Russian history than any other political movement of the prerevolutionary era.

This perception ran contrary to the consensus which saw Russia as a radical country and the Soviet regime as the embodiment of Marx's socialism.

In line with this premise, I resolved to write a history of Russian conservative thought. I began with a monograph on an outstanding conservative, Nicholas Karamzin, Russia's earliest professional historian, whose *History of the Russian State,* published in 1816–29, was the first account of that country's past to attract a wide readership. On the eve of the Napoleonic invasion, he had written an essay, "A Memoir on Ancient and Modern Russia," meant exclusively for the eyes of Alexander I and his sister, in which he courageously challenged the tsar's domestic and foreign policies, especially his vague plans to dilute the country's autocratic form of government. In this essay Karamzin argued on the basis of historical evidence that absolutism was Russia's "Palladium" or protective shield: its momentary disappearance or even dilution invariably brought ruin.

Karamzin attracted me for several reasons: he was highly educated; he wrote excellent, although somewhat antiquated Russian; and he was a liberal-conservative rather than a dyed-in-the-wool reactionary. His "Memoir," a work of some one-hundred pages, had never been translated or even issued in a scholarly edition in Russian.

In 1955, I published two articles. One, based on the interviews with Central Asian refugees conducted two years earlier in Germany, offered evidence that religious and ethnic loyalties remained very strong in Soviet Muslim regions. The other dealt with Max Weber's views of Russia. This essay originated in the informal discussions we had in the Russian Research Center about the proper methodology to use in studying alien cultures. The dominant methodology at the center was sociological. The center's founder, the anthropologist Clyde Kluckhohn, a student of Navajo Indians, laid no claim to being a Russian expert. He established the center in order to replicate the accomplishment of a fellow anthropologist, Ruth Benedict, who during World War II had provided astute insights into the Japanese psyche. The whole purpose of the center was to get away from politics as well as history and to approach the Soviet Union as a "system"—a system which, regardless of one's feelings about it, had proven its viability by surviving forty years of social turmoil and war. Assisting Kluckhohn were such sociologists as Alex Inkeles and Barrington Moore, who knew Russian. But they, too, shied away from history. In general, historians were not welcome at the center in these early years, and I received a fellowship there only because of Karpovich's support.

I was very skeptical of an abstract sociological approach to a country with the history of five or six centuries of statehood, and moreover a history very different from the Western. It seemed to me that to understand why it was behaving as it did one had to delve deeply into its past, especially its social and political institutions. To prove my point, I analyzed Max Weber's two monographs on Russia, both brought out in the wake of the 1905 revolution, along with his occasional subsequent pieces. I shared the widespread admiration for the German sociologist, but in reading his essays on contemporary Russia it became apparent to me that the man had been hopelessly blinded about the meaning and implications of developments there by his theory that under modern conditions professional bureaucracies were so entrenched in power that revolutions had become impossible. He interpreted the February 1917 events in Russia not as a genuine revolution but as the overthrow of an incompetent monarch. The Bolshevik coup appeared to him as a "pure military dictatorship" of corporals, a "swindle" without a future. My article, which appeared in the April 1955 issue of *World Politics* under the title "Max Weber and Russia," greatly annoyed the Harvard sociologist Talcott Parsons, the leading Weberian in the United States. He later told me he had intended to write a rebuttal, but he never did so; nor did he tell me what he found objectionable in my article. I suspect it was lèse majesté.

Now I must say something about the Harvard system of appointing professors in general, and the situation in the History Department in the 1950s in particular. During the depression, Harvard's President James Conant introduced a system of appointments based on what was popularly known as the "up-or-out" principle. In order to prevent the permanent faculty from being surrounded (and serviced) by hordes of underpaid and overworked junior faculty who had no future at Harvard, he instituted a rigid system of promotion. At the lowest rung of "the ladder" was the assistant professor who received a five-year contract and was presumed to be qualified for tenure provided he proved himself and there was a vacancy in his field. By December of his fourth year, he came up for review in the department, which either recommended promotion to associate professor, a rank carrying tenure, or else declined to do so, in which case the candidate had a year and a half to look for a position elsewhere. Because departments occasionally required "off-the-ladder" teachers, the titles of instructor and lecturer were instituted: these were strictly term appointments.

After I had received my doctorate in 1950, I was appointed an instructor, a position renewable annually for up to three years. I tutored undergraduates enrolled in History and Literature until 1954 as an instructor. That year I was made lecturer for one year. My prospects for gaining tenure at Harvard, therefore, were very slim, since as a rule tenure was granted to assistant professors who were "on the ladder." The future appeared even bleaker for me inasmuch as in 1954 the department conferred the assistant professorship in Russian history on Martin Malia, a Yale graduate and also a pupil of Karpovich's, who had served the preceding three years as instructor and was allowed, exceptionally for a person of this rank, to offer a graduate seminar. During the next four years, Malia taught every course offered on Russian history, alternating with Karpovich and Wolff; he also taught the history of the Soviet Union. Strange as it may seem, this situation did not trouble me in the least: I was so confident of myself that I paid no attention to departmental politics. I was too busy doing research, writing, and teaching to bother with such practical matters. I felt certain that something would turn up—if not at Harvard then elsewhere—that would enable me to carry on my scholarly work.

Relations between senior and junior faculty at Harvard in those years were cold and distant. Professors, in whose power it lay to bestow the supreme gift of a tenured professorship, wanted to avoid any taint of favoritism and for this reason refrained from social contacts with us. With one exception, I do not recall ever being invited to the home of a senior member of my department: the exception was Oscar Handlin, who with his wife, Mary, used to invite young scholars to their house on Agassiz Street. Generally, we were observed from a distance, closely and attentively but impersonally, like fish in an aquarium.

In September 1954, I received a call from Wolff. He told me that Malia, who had been scheduled to give the course on imperial Russia in the spring term, was unable to do so because he had decided to spend the time in Paris. Would I take his place? I accepted the offer with enthusiasm. In a frenzy of excitement I prepared during the next couple of months about half of the lectures covering the history of Russia from 1801 to 1917. I was bursting with facts and ideas accumulated over the past decade. On the first day of classes, Thursday, February 3, 1955, at 11 A.M., I entered Harvard Hall 201. The room, which has 140 seats, was packed. My head swam. To my surprise and delight, the first lecture and the subsequent ones met with a spirited response from an audience ranging from freshman to graduate students. I realized quickly that the attention span of undergraduates did not exceed ten to twelve minutes and hence interrupted the lecture at such intervals with stories and anecdotes that had some, even remote, bearing on the subject. Students then were very ready to laugh and they responded. I taught various lecture courses during the following forty years, but I never quite recaptured the exhilaration of this first experience.

During that term, while visiting Karpovich, I met Alexander Kerensky, the war minister and prime minister of Russia's Provisional Government in 1917. I invited him to give a lecture in my course on the Russian prerevolutionary parliament, in which he had served as deputy. My students were stunned to see him in the flesh. Kerensky began slowly and clearly, then worked himself into a frenzy which made him almost incomprehensible. I subsequently met him many times and found him invariably cordial. Discussing the revolutionary era with him, however, was quite useless because he had published three autobiographies and never deviated from them. During the Khrushchev era he displayed a sympathetic interest in the reforms, for he was, first and foremost, a Russian patriot and carried no grudge against the nation that had rejected him. He once told me his recipe for longevity: no freshly baked bread, three martinis before dinner, followed by a long walk afterwards, and a fourth component, possibly the most important, which I have unfortunately forgotten.

In 1955 more good news arrived, namely, an invitation from the University of California at Berkeley to come for one term as visiting assistant professor. Berkeley at this time was driven by an ambition to become the Harvard of the West, an ambition that would be frustrated by the radical delirium of the 1960s which had its beginning there. Its Russian historian, Robert Kerner, Czech by origin, wrote mostly on Bohemia and Central Europe: his principal contribution to Russian history, *The Urge to the Sea* (1942), gave a unilinear explanation of the course of Russia's history in terms of her (alleged) quest for warm sea ports. This interpretation was not widely shared, and the younger faculty looked eagerly to his imminent retirement. As his potential successors, Berkeley chose three of Karpovich's pupils: Malia, Nicholas Riasanovsky (then teaching at Iowa), and myself.

The summer of 1955 I spent with my wife in Rome attending the Tenth International Congress of the Historical Sciences. I delivered a paper on nineteenth-century Russian apologists of absolutism, the early fruit of my studies of Russian conservative thought. Here we met, for the first time, a Soviet delegation which had been sent to reestablish contact with the West. They trooped into the room where I was to lecture like soldiers, all dressed in ill-fitting suits, apparently made for the purpose, the sleeves of which were a good six inches too long. I had conversations with some of them, notably the economic historian A. L. Sidorov, head of the Institute of History of the Soviet Academy of Sciences. He and the others were most eager to rejoin the international scholarly community, which they had been forced to cut all relations with in the 1930s.

At the end of January 1956 we arrived in Berkeley. I was warmly welcomed by the Harvardians on the history faculty who seemed to form a party. I paid a courtesy visit to Kerner, who told me in all seriousness that as Archibald Cary Coolidge, the principal professor of modern history at Harvard, lay dying in 1928, he was asked whom he would like to see as his successor. "Kerner" he whispered with his last breath, but those around him thought they heard him say "Langer," and so it happened that Langer and not he became the Coolidge Professor of History at Harvard. I did my best to convey to Kerner that I believed this story.

Berkeley was most agreeable, although being a state university, it granted its faculty less freedom than Harvard: thus the number of weekly lectures in each course was prescribed, and I was expected to keep the door to my office open at all times. Still, I was happy to be there and, though homesick for Cambridge, would have gladly accepted an appointment at Berkeley had Harvard not come through.

When I returned to Cambridge for the summer to teach a course in nineteenth-century Russian history in the summer school and to assist Denis Brogan in his course on modern Britain, the fate of the Russian chairs at Harvard and Berkeley was still up in the air.

To get away from the heated competitive atmosphere I decided to spend a year in Europe. I had applied for and received a Guggenheim grant and on September 13, 1956, sailed with my family for Paris on the French liner *Flandre*. Karpovich advised me against going abroad for he thought I should be in place and available when the appointments were made, but I took the chance. I carried the distinct impression that Karpovich wanted me to get the Berkeley post rather than his own chair. The reason was not personal or even academic but political. Karpovich made it his mission in life to fight the notion, then widespread in the United States, that communism was native to Russia, that it reflected that country's culture, and that Russians were altogether "different"—he had nothing but scorn for the notion of a Russian "soul." Coming from Poland, a country which had bordered Russia for a thousand years and lived under its occupation for over a century, I unconsciously shared Polish attitudes toward Russia. I must have absorbed them from the air because, as I have said earlier, while in Poland I had had no interest in our eastern neighbor. My scholarly research confirmed me in some of these attitudes, and in my principal survey of Russia's political institutions and culture, *Russia under the Old Regime,* published in 1974, I stressed their distinctiveness and continuities.

Karpovich never tried to sway me, but I believe he found more congenial Malia's approach, which held that Russia was a European country, all of whose "peculiarities" could be found replicated in the West. As Malia wrote many years later in *Russia under Western Eyes* (1999), the notion that Russia was fundamentally different from Europe reflected Europe's own problems rather than Russian reality. The idiosyncracy of the Communist regime, in Malia's view, was due solely to the influence of Marxist ideology, a Western import—although why Marxism should have found so congenial a home in Russia whereas in Western Europe it was always a marginal phenomenon he never, as far as I know, explained. For the subject of his doctoral dissertation, Malia had chosen Alexander Herzen, a fervent Westerner (though with some lapses). It was published in 1961.

The view that Russia was a European country could be reasonably argued only by concentrating on her "high" culture—literature, art, science—which indeed was European, and ignoring political and social institutions along with "low" culture, which were not. This is the reason why Russians like Karpovich and those students of his who shared his viewpoint focused on intellectual history, moreover intellectual history of socialist and liberal currents, paying little heed to conservative movements which far more accurately reflected Russian reality.

Shortly after we had landed in France, two important international events took place: the anticommunist uprising in Hungary and the Middle East war during which England, France, and Israel attempted to seize control of the Suez Canal. Paris was very agitated. But what I recall best is that due to gas rationing introduced immediately after the opening of hostilities against Egypt, French highways, normally so busy, were eerily deserted. As foreigners with access to special coupons, we had the roads almost to ourselves.

To be in one's thirties, to have enough money for moderate comforts and pleasures, and to be in Paris—what bliss! We found an apartment in Auteuil, the southern half of the Sixteenth Arrondisement. I spent my days in libraries working on Karamzin; Daniel went to a nearby school; and Irene and three-year-old Steven simply enjoyed what the city had to offer. Most of our acquaintances were Americans, but I did strike up friendships with two Europeans. The first was Boris Souvarine, one of the founders of the French Communist Party and the author of a brilliant Stalin biography, published in 1935, which the left-leaning French intelligentsia dismissed as unworthy of attention. A small, wispy man of exemplary intellectual integrity, Souvarine had broken with the communists in the late 1920s and since then turned into one of their most implacable foes. He was virtually isolated in a Paris where the intelligentsia was either communist or procommunist. I greatly valued his judgment: his friendship and approval also meant much to me.

On the recommendation of Irakly Tsereteli, the Georgian Menshevik who in 1917 had chaired the All-Russian Soviet in Petrograd and now lived in New York City, I contacted Noe Tsintsadze, one of the leaders of the Georgian exile community, through whom I became acquainted with other Georgians. This relationship was to bear fruit many years later.

Our stay in Paris was marred by the fact that my academic future remained clouded. Neither Berkeley nor Harvard were as yet ready to make their Russian history appointments. Friends on the Berkeley faculty advised me that the department was leaning toward Malia. I was left in limbo to the last moment.

Face to Face with Russia

The great event for me of our year in Paris was a trip to the Soviet Union. It is difficult today to conceive to what extent the Soviet Union was, at the time, a closed world for foreigners. We could more readily picture life in medieval Europe than in contemporary Russia, all information about which emanated from official channels whose overseers released nothing but positive news. Foreign diplomats and journalists were subjected to round-the-clock surveillance and restricted to a few major cities. Any one of them who failed to cooperate, was declared persona non grata and expelled. Curiosity about the Soviet Union, therefore, was immense. My hostility to communism immunized me against fantasies about the USSR: I thought it self-evident that a country that went to such lengths to shield its citizens from contacts with foreigners and prevented them from leaving could not be a happy land. However, I had no concrete image of what it was like and approached it in some measure with an open mind.

After 1956, when Khrushchev delivered his attack on Stalin for crimes against fellow communists, the Soviet government made vigorous attempts to extricate itself from the isolation into which the dead dictator had driven it. One of them was to revive tourism which had been well developed in the interwar years. This was not the free-wheeling tourism familiar to Westerners, but controlled travel managed by Intourist, an organization closely affiliated with the KGB. Itineraries had to be approved by Intourist and throughout their stay in the USSR foreign travelers were under constant KGB surveillance, which in the case of Russian-speakers was particularly intense. One could walk freely in the cities listed on one's itinerary and, in theory, converse with the natives, but the latter were so well trained that they avoided all contacts with foreigners; if one managed to have a meaningful conversation with a Russian, one immediately suspected him of being on the police payroll.

Early in 1957 I learned that an American organization based at Indiana University, the Inter-University Committee on Travel Grants, offered scholars financial assistance to visit the USSR. Such help was essential because, in order to pay for the police escorts, one had to travel "de luxe" which cost, in addition to air travel, $30 a day, a sum equivalent to $300 today and well beyond my means. I worked out with a Paris travel agency a thirty-day itinerary that would take me from Russia to the Ukraine and Georgia, followed by Central Asia. The Congress for Cultural Freedom invited me to visit India at the end of my trip, to deliver lectures on my Soviet journey.*

I flew to Helsinki on March 31 and from there proceeded by train to Leningrad. The train made a lengthy stop at Viborg, once Finnish, now Soviet. I took a walk through the town and was appalled by what I saw. The war had been over for twelve years and most European cities which had suffered destruction had been rebuilt. Viborg, as far as I could tell, the scene of fighting in the Soviet-Finnish wars, had not been destroyed, but it was in a state of advanced decay: the buildings were crumbling, the sidewalks and roads full of potholes, there was not a single object to please the eye. Even worse was the appearance of the people who looked as if they had emerged from caves: some carried pails with water.

I arrived in Leningrad late in the evening. Two black limousines awaited me. I was driven to the Astoria, the city's premier hotel built before the revolution and located next to St. Isaac's Cathedral. As we were crossing the square, I heard a woman screaming in the darkness. When we drove up the well-lit hotel entrance, doormen rushed to my cars to remove the luggage. At that moment a woman emerged into the light: "My purse has been stolen!" she cried. "Beat it," one of the doormen hissed, "Don't you see there is a foreigner in the car?" It was a foretaste of things to come.

---

*When it learned that the purpose of my visit was to speak at local branches of the congress, the Indian Embassy in Paris refused me an entry visa, apparently because it was aware—as I was not—that the congress was financed by the CIA. The Indian Embassy in Moscow, however, issued me a visa without difficulty.

The next morning I was asked to report to the Intourist office in the hotel. I was advised that I would be escorted on my journeys during the next thirty days by one of their female employees. I immediately objected, saying that I spoke Russian and needed no escort. Such were the rules, I was told, but I stood my ground, with redoubled determination after being introduced to the proposed chaperon, a heavily made-up woman in her thirties with the repulsive expression of a professional KGB agent, made still uglier by a feeble attempt at an ingratiating smile. I finally won the argument and for the rest of the trip was escorted by local police personnel, some of them quite pleasant young men and women.

Leningrad was depressing. The crowds looked just as poor and morose as in Viborg, but here the backdrop of what had been a splendid imperial capital heightened the appearance of shabbiness. I spent two days walking the streets, some of the time with tears in my eyes. As I wrote Karpovich soon after my return to Paris: "Everything made the impression of waiting for something, as if it had known life and would know it again, but did not know it now." I did not quite realize what depressed me so much until I read, years later, the recollections of Princess Zinaida Shakhovskaia, who had visited Russia at the same time. She wrote that looking closely at the crowds on Moscow streets "it was hopeless trying to find one single face which clearly belonged to a born city dweller. It was an immense *kolkhoz*."[4] Worse than that: the Soviet regime had "liquidated," i.e., murdered in one way or another, the most intelligent and enterprising peasants, so that what one saw were culturally and even physically the most backward elements of Russia's rural population who had been evicted or fled from their villages. They looked like barbarian invaders who had conquered and taken over what had once been a flourishing center of civilization.

I knew that around the corner from my hotel, on Gogol Street (previously and now again Malaia Morskaia), lived my mother's brother Henry and his family. On the second evening, having reconnoitered the area, I slipped out of the hotel and made my way there. No one seemed to be following. The concierge told me the apartment number: I walked up to the top floor. From my travel diary:

> I rang the bell and the loud barking of a dog answered. The door opened and a woman whom I instantly recognized as my aunt (from the photographs I had seen), holding on to a large barking German shepherd asked me whom I wanted. I said the name and she asked me in. I walked into the living room. At a table sat a man in his shirtsleeves eating from a dish of soup. I stood silently for a minute while they tried to hush the dog. I then asked them once more for their name and when they confirmed it, I told

them my name. My aunt gasped and threw herself into my arms; my uncle, as if some great and unexpected force had struck him, rose dazed from the table. We embraced, and kissed, and cried.

After a while we calmed down. I was received with a mixture of joy and trepidation. I assured them that no one was following me. Soon the front doorbell rang. It was a friend of my cousin Nora. "What is going on?" she asked, "The stairwell is crawling with people running up and down." So much for my skill in eluding the police. We saw a great deal of each other during the few days I spent in Leningrad, always aware that wherever we went police agents followed us. Victor, Nora's brother, once pointed them out to me in the streetcar: an elderly *babushka* with a shopping bag seemingly absorbed in her own thoughts, or a well-dressed young man who looked like a student. I was very depressed by this surveillance. But as we were taking leave of each other one evening, Victor said with a smile: "Don't worry. You take care of your problems, and we will take care of this." Unfortunately, he did not live to see this wish fulfilled, dying of cancer before communism's collapse.

Next came Moscow where I was put up at the most prestigious hotel as well, the National, across from the Red Square. Moscow seemed less depressing whether because I was getting accustomed to the sights of the Soviet Russia or because, being the capital, it was maintained in better shape. I was contacted by Sidorov, whom I had met two years earlier in Rome, and through him made the acquaintance of several historians. I gave a lecture at the Institute of History on American scholarship on Russia. My mentor at the institute was one M. M. Shtrange, a specialist on French history: I later learned that during World War II he had been a high-level Soviet agent in Nazi-occupied Paris. He was very friendly: not from any personal or intellectual sympathy but because he apparently was charged with recruiting me for the "organs."

I spent much time in secondhand bookstores buying for pennies pre-1917 historical monographs that were entirely unavailable in the West. It was forbidden to export pre-1917 books, but Shtrange secured for me a permit to mail them. These books formed the nucleus of my library on Russian history.

From Moscow I proceeded to Kiev. That city had been thoroughly destroyed during the war and offered little of interest. Odessa, my next stop, was even less interesting: it was a low point in my trip when on a rainy day my young, unshaven cicerone showed me a deserted beach on the Black Sea. I spent most of my stay there holed up in the hotel room, reading.

I next traveled by train to Sochi and from there to Tbilisi. The ambience in the capital of Georgia was quite different from anything I had encountered on the Soviet trip: Mediterranean rather than Slavic, happy-go-lucky. In the center of the city I could see holes in buildings, testimony of the shooting during riots that had erupted a year before my arrival when Georgians had taken to the streets to protest Khrushchev's attack on Stalin. I gave a talk to some members of the local Institute of History and could not but help admire how much freer in their thinking they were than their Moscow counterparts. Thus began my infatuation with Georgia that was to lead, forty years later, to my being granted honorary citizenship.

From Tbilisi I returned to Moscow from where I was scheduled to fly to Central Asia. Another meeting was arranged at the Institute of History. When I concluded my remarks, Shtrange, with an unctuous smile, invited me to share my impressions of the Soviet Union. I sensed a trap and responded, noncommittally, that I had had too many unsorted impressions from my voyage to form an opinion. "But you must have some impressions," he insisted. I still refused to comment. This exchange marked the end of the KGB's efforts to enlist me. On my next trip, neither Sidorov, nor Shtrange, nor any other member of the institute found the time to see me: I had become an enemy: Henceforth, the "organs" concentrated on compromising me.

During my brief second stay in Moscow, I attended a reception at the American Embassy. The ambassador, Charles ("Chip") Bohlen, asked me where I was going next. I told him that I was scheduled to fly the following morning to Tashkent, the capital of Uzbekistan. "Are you sure?" he asked: it seemed that all flights to Tashkent had been canceled. Upon my return to the hotel, the Intourist office informed me that this, indeed, was the case. The reason, of course, unknown to us at the time, was that secret preparations were being made north of the Caspian, on the flight route Moscow-Tashkent, for the launching of the Sputnik: in fact, it was subsequently revealed that the original plans had called for it to be sent aloft at the beginning of May, the very time I was to fly over the region, but the launch had failed.[5]

I insisted that I had to go to Central Asia because of my speaking engagements in India. The authorities relented and offered me a special flight by small plane that took a circuitous route to Tashkent by way of Sverdlovsk (today, once again, Ekaterinburg). The plane had only one other passenger, a young radical chic art dealer from Paris. He gushed over the wonders of the Soviet Union and the marvelous people he had met. I finally could stand his rhapsodies no longer and assured him that all his personal encounters were either with police informants or individuals required to report to the police, and that he was constantly under surveillance. This thought had never occurred to him. He seemed troubled. Finally, during dinner which we ate at the Sverdlovsk airport, his face lit up: "I know why you are so sure I was being followed. It was you who followed me!"

Tashkent was not terribly interesting—unfortunately both Bukhara and Samarkand were closed to foreigners. I was struck how the Muslim quarters of the old city were separated from the modern Russian ones. I went to a performance by a traveling troupe of Jewish actors. The whole show was so anti-Semitic in spirit that I left in disgust during the intermission. I meant to go back to the hotel but got lost in the maze of the Muslim quarter. I felt no anxiety, confident that my invisible KGB chaperon would help me out. However, there was no KGB chaperon: it seems the police assumed that once a visitor procured tickets to the theater, he would remain there to the end. This impression was confirmed to me subsequently.

In Alma-Ata, the capital of Kazakhstan, my last stop, I witnessed a May 1 parade, complete with portraits of Stalin carried by expressionless Kazakhs. The Tian-shan Mountains surrounding the city were most impressive. My young escort—I believe he had been a Leningrad student exiled to Central Asia for dissidence—pointed out proudly Russian achievements in the region. I asked: "What would happen if the Kazakhs would say to you, as the Algerians did to the French—'Thank you very much, and now please leave'?" "*Pust' pobrobuiut*" (Just let them try), he replied.

From Alma-Ata I flew to Kabul in a nonpressurized Soviet plane, full of Russian "experts" en route to Afghanistan to provide friendly help. Once there, I was surprised by the extent to which the Afghans allowed the Soviet Union to intervene in their internal affairs, permitting them to construct a highway from Termez in Uzbekistan to Kabul, a road which could serve only one purpose, namely, to transport Soviet troops into the heart of Afghanistan. The head of the American mission, whom I met at the airport and who offered me the hospitality of his residence, said that our principal aid project was constructing a bakery.

After a brief stay in India, which dazzled me with its colors and enervated me with its heat, I returned to Paris. Word got around of my return, and I received many invitations to talk about the trip and to show the slides and films which I had brought back. One person who took a keen interest in my impressions of the USSR was Walter Stoessel, then a

staff member of NATO, later U.S. ambassador to Moscow. He arranged
for me to meet several high level NATO officials. I described to them the
dismal impression the Soviet Union had made on me and expressed
doubts that a country so poor and so backward presented a serious
threat to us. They eyed me with ill-concealed skepticism.

What most troubled me about visits to the Soviet Union, then and
later, was not the poverty and drabness but the pervasive lying. I do not
mean the brazen lies pouring out of the official propaganda machine: no
one I met paid much attention to them. Rather, it was that all human
relations there, except in the intimate circle of friends and family, rested
on make-believe: everyone was lying, everyone knew you knew they were
lying, and yet one had to pretend otherwise. Nothing had changed since
the 1930s when André Gide paid his famous visit to the USSR: "truth,"
he wrote on his return, was "spoken with hatred and falsehood with
love."[6] This created the suffocating ambience that made it such joy to
leave the country.

A memorable incident illustrating this feature of Soviet life occurred
on one of my subsequent trips. I entered a streetcar in Leningrad and to
buy a ticket took out the loose change from my pocket: mixed with Soviet
coins was a Kennedy half dollar. The woman selling tickets, sitting by the
entrance, spotted it instantly and asked, "Are you an American?" When I
confirmed, she insisted on yielding me her seat. As the streetcar lum-
bered on its way she pointed out to me various landmarks and, loudly
extolling the beauties of her city, urged me, as a Russian-speaker, to
resettle there with my family. The streetcar stopped: passengers poured
in and out. Taking advantage of the temporary commotion, the woman,
her facial expression suddenly transformed from falsely amiable to gen-
uinely anxious, bent down and asked me in an urgent whisper: "We live
like dogs, don't we? Tell me, please." It was a shattering experience, a
momentary falling off the mask that Soviet citizens habitually wore.

Yet when I returned to Cambridge and told of this oppressive sensation, one of the senior professors, echoing Pontius Pilate, responded:
"Dick, how do we know what is a lie and what the truth?" This deliberate
eschewal of the human and the moral in dealing with the Soviet Union
characterized the entire profession of "Sovietology" and accounted in
good measure for its dismal failure to foresee that country's fate.

The more I learned about communism, whether from personal experience or reading, the more I came to despise it. My mounting hatred of
it can best be explained in words which Chekhov used in a letter to a
friend when he wrote: "I detest lies and coercion in all their forms. . . .

My holiest of holies is the human body, health, intelligence, talent, inspiration, love and the most absolute freedom, freedom from coercion and lies, no matter how expressed."[7] I suppose not everyone has the same low level of tolerance for coercion and lies which lay at the heart of communist regimes: those who did not were prone to view my hostility as an obsession.

The summer of 1957 we spent in the Engadine Valley in Switzerland, at Sils-Maria, a stone's throw from the house where Nietzsche had spent much time in his declining years. Signs posted all over the village announced "Nietzsche House for Sale." I used the summer to write up my trip to Soviet Russia. I never finished it.

Professorship

We returned to Boston in September 1957 without my having any commitment from the university: my appointment as lecturer in History and Literature and research fellow of the Russian Research Center for one academic year came through only in October. Nevertheless, matters in the department were coming to a head. Karpovich was but one year away from his seventieth birthday, an age at which, by rules of the time, he had to retire. (He would die of cancer in November 1959.) Moreover, Malia was in the fourth year of his assistant professorship, at a point when he either had to be given tenure or let go. I was not privy to the departmental discussions in the fall of 1957. But on December 3, I was called in to the office of the chairman, Myron Gilmore, and told that the department, "after long and careful scrutiny," had voted the previous evening to recommend me for an associate professorship in Russian history, a rank which carried tenure. According to my diary of that time, "The news nearly lifted me out of my seat."

The offer was formally extended to me in April 1958 by the dean of the Faculty of Arts and Sciences, McGeorge Bundy, who was barely three years my senior in age. I accepted it without hesitation: I asked no questions and posed no conditions. My salary for the year 1958–59 was to be $8,000.

In *Anna Karenina*, Tolstoy describes the restlessness of Vronsky after he had won Anna and taken her away from her husband. He attributes it to Vronsky having committed the "eternal error of those who imagine happiness to lie in the satisfaction of a desire."[8] This may be true in some general way, but it certainly did not apply to me: I had imagined happiness to be the opportunity for the rest of my life to engage, undisturbed, in scholarship. When it was granted to me, I gained lasting happiness.

The rewards of a full professorship at a major university are not widely known. They are unique. First there is tenure which assures the holder of a secure job until compulsory retirement, then set at seventy; today, compulsory retirement has been abolished on the grounds that it constitutes "age discrimination" and a professor can teach for as long as he wishes, even into senility. Second, the working load—at any rate, at major research institutions—is light. At Harvard we were expected to teach two courses per term, but this was never spelled out formally, and many professors taught less. Third, the academic year is short: at Harvard we had two terms of twelve weeks each, which meant a twenty-four-week calendar year with some five hours of lecturing a week. Fourth, we were entitled to take a year's leave without pay every fourth year and a semester with full pay every seventh year. For someone like myself who took full advantage of this provision, the result was that I gave formal course offerings for some 120 hours annually over every three-year period and then went on leave. Finally, our teaching burden was eased by the provision that for lecture courses that enrolled more than thirty undergraduates, as most of mine did, the department engaged teaching fellows to grade the examination papers.

Of course, our responsibilities were not limited to lecturing: we taught graduate students and we sat on university and departmental committees. Still, all in all, the combination of security and frequent vacations along with leaves of absence gave one an enviable opportunity to carry on research and engage in such other activities as one found of interest. A tenured professor was entrusted with his field on the assumption that he knew best how to take care of it: he taught, therefore, what he wanted when he wanted.

Scholarship is lonely work in which one communes mainly with oneself: Montaigne must have been thinking of intellectuals like himself when he wrote "*Nous avons une âme contournable en soi même; elle se peut faire compagnie*" (We have a soul that winds around itself; it can keep itself company). It does not suit every temperament, and I learned in time to discourage graduate students who gave signs of chafing under its regimen from pursuing an academic career.

Academic life is not all sweetness and light. Scholars are psychologically less secure than most people: by and large, once they pass the threshold of middle age they strike me as becoming restless. A businessman knows he is successful when he makes money; a politician, when he wins elections; an athlete, when he is first in sporting contests; a popular writer, when he produces best-sellers. But a scholar has no such fixed criteria by which to judge success, and as a consequence he lives in a state of permanent uncertainty which grows more oppressive with age as ambitious younger scholars elbow themselves to the fore and dismiss his work as outdated. His principal criterion of success is approval of peers. This means that he must cultivate them, which makes for conformity and "group think." Scholars are expected to cite one another approvingly, attend conferences, edit and contribute to collective symposia. Professional associations are designed to promote these objectives. Those who do not play by the rules or significantly depart from the consensus risk ostracism. A classic example of such ostracism is the treatment meted out to one of the outstanding economists and social theorists of the past century, Frederick von Hayek, whose uncompromising condemnation of economic planning and socialism caused him to be banished from the profession. He lived long enough to see his views prevail and his reputation vindicated by a Nobel Prize, but not everyone in this situation is as fortunate. Such behavior, observed also in animal communities, strengthens group cohesion and enhances the sense of security of its individual members, but it inhibits creativity.

What particularly disenchanted me about many academics was [the way they treated] a professorship not as a sacred trust but as a sinecure, much like the run-of-the-mill Protestant ministers in eighteenth- or nineteenth-century England who did not even pretend to believe. The typical academic, having completed and published his doctoral dissertation, will establish himself as an authority on the subject of his dissertation and for the remainder of his life write and teach on the same or closely related topics. The profession welcomes this kind of "expertise" and resents anyone who attempts to take a broader view of the field because by so doing, he encroaches on its members' turf. Nonmonographic, general histories are dismissed as "popular" and allegedly riddled with errors—doubly so if they do not give adequate credit to the hordes who labor in the fields. In "A Boring Story," Chekhov diagnosed this kind of sterility as due to the absence of the "main element of creativity: the sense of personal freedom . . . without the freedom, the courage to write as one pleases . . . there is no creativity."*

*The protagonist of Chekhov's story, an elderly professor of medicine, observes his assistant and reflects: "During his whole life he will fill several hundred prescriptions of extraordinary

Such are the dark sides of the scholarly profession, but they need not trouble those who choose to strike their own path.

My appointment was greeted with warm congratulations from well-wishers and howls of envy from the others (the latter sounds reached me secondhand). Those who had aspired to the chair but failed to get it, never forgave me. As I was to learn at the time, envy is in some ways the worst of the seven deadly sins: whereas the other six harm the sinner, this one harms its object, who can fend it off only at his own expense. Balzac has well characterized envy as that "ignoble accumulation of disappointed hopes, frustrated talents, failures and wounded pretensions."

During the next thirty-eight years, interrupted only by periodic leaves of absence and two years' service in Washington, I taught at Harvard a variety of Russian history courses: medieval Russia, imperial Russia, Russian intellectual history, history of Russian institutions, core courses on the Russian civilization and the Russian Revolution, graduate seminars, and freshmen seminars. With my colleagues Walter (Jack) Bate and David Perkins, I once participated in a course on Coleridge in the English Department. Enrollments in my Russian history courses fluctuated with the political situation: when the press devoted much space to the Soviet Union they rose, when domestic problems came to predominate, they declined. (I was told that enrollments in courses of the Japanese language tracked the Nikkei Index of the Tokyo Stock Exchange.)

Undergraduate students admitted to Harvard were generally very bright in the sense that they were quick learners. Their knowledge, however, was appallingly slight. When in 1985 I offered my first freshman seminar on Russian intellectual history, I had 127 applicants for 12 places, and so I administered quick personal tests. I did not expect that the students would know anything about Russia, but I did think that a someone interested in intellectual history would be familiar with the classics of world literature. I was sadly disappointed: apart from *Crime and Punishment* which, I believe, they read as a thriller and *Madame Bovary* (for those who studied advanced high school French), they knew nothing: Dickens, Tolstoy, George Eliot, Chekhov, Cervantes were to them names, if that. I was dismayed how culturally *deraciné* America's young were, how they lacked any cultural background to fall back on when they faced life's inevitable problems. The situation was so bad that

---

purity, he will write many dry, very decent papers, make a dozen conscientious translations, but he will not invent gunpowder. Gunpowder requires fantasy, inventiveness, the ability to imagine, and Peter Ignatevich had none of this. In short, he was not a master in science but a toiler."

when a prospective student revealed familiarity with any major writer or thinker of the past, I admitted him or her on the spot.

I also supervised the work of many graduate students: by the time I retired I had turned out more than seventy Ph.D.'s. Some, possibly most, of my graduate students espoused political views that were to the left of mine, but I never pressured them to conform. I also gave them a great deal of latitude in the choice of dissertation subjects. My personal relations with them varied: some, after receiving their doctorates and assuming their own professorships, dropped out of sight entirely; others maintained desultory contacts, usually when requiring letters of recommendation; a few became lifelong friends. By and large, it is my impression that American graduate students treat their professors not as intellectual and spiritual mentors but as individuals who, at a certain stage in their life, happen to assist in the advancement of their careers—essentially not differently from the way they regard their high school teachers. Russians to whom I described this attitude found it incomprehensible.

I sat on various departmental and university committees, but I was not good at this sort of thing. In 1968 I began a five-year term as director of the Russian Research Center: in this capacity, too, I did not distinguish myself, though I did raise some funds from the Ford Foundation.

In 1964, when I had more than a dozen graduate students, I discussed with them how to put their talents to some general use, a use benefitting them and the profession at large. The idea occurred to me to found a periodical devoted to reviews of books on Russian history published in the Soviet Union which were usually ignored in Western publications. The students liked the suggestion and thus came into being *Kritika*, a journal published three times a year, edited and written entirely by graduate students under my overall supervision. We had more than five hundred subscribers and became self-supporting. The journal came out until 1984, when it had to be discontinued because by then the graduate student body in Russian history at Harvard had dwindled to a mere two or three. I believe that *Kritika* was a unique publication in the country, one that enabled predoctoral candidates to do professional work and acquire a bibliography.

One of teaching's great rewards is contact with the young, which helps one stay young. It also improves one's scholarship. Whenever I was writing a book on a broad subject, such as *The Russian Revolution*, I first offered it as a lecture course. Confronting an uninformed but bright and eager audience, I was forced sharply to focus my presentation: there was an instant reaction to any vagueness or confusion. On two occasions critical comments by students made me aware of major flaws in my argument and persuaded me to reorganize a book in progress.

Struve

After completing Karamzin's *Memoir on Ancient and Modern Russia* in November 1957, I cast about for another major Russian conservative thinker. In the summer of 1958, having read Simeon Frank's recollections of him, I chose Peter Struve, one of the most outstanding as well as controversial figures in Russian intellectual and political life between the 1890s and the 1930s.

Struve was born in 1870 into a family of assimilated Germans. His grandfather Wilhelm had fled to Russia to escape the Napoleonic draft: he became a leading astronomer of his age, the founder of the Pulkovo Observatory near St. Petersburg, and among his offspring were three generations of prominent astronomers. Peter's father, a high official in the Russian civil service, having gotten into trouble with his superiors, moved his family to Stuttgart for several years: as a result, the precocious youth was as much at home in Germany as in his native Russia. Throughout his life, Struve espoused ideas that in Russia did not readily mix: he was a socialist in his youth who accorded liberty precedence over equality, then a liberal who thought freedom would be brought to Russia not by the bourgeoisie but the working class. An ardent Russian patriot, he saw his country's greatness inextricably bound up with Western culture. In the 1890s, first as a university student and then as a publicist, he popularized in Russia the doctrines of Marx. When in 1898 Russian Marxists attempted to form a Social Democratic Party, they entrusted him with the drafting of the party's founding manifesto. He was a celebrity before attaining the age of thirty.

Then troubles began. In the late 1890s, Struve, whom Maxim Gorky called "the St. John the Baptist of all our Renaissances," fell under the influence of the German Revisionists who found flawed Marx's predictions of the inevitable and progressive impoverishment of the working class. In brilliant essays Struve pointed out the inconsistencies of Marx's social theory, concluding that socialism could come about only as the result of evolution, not revolution, that is, the gradual improvement in the condition of workers and the gains in political power that would result from it. The Revisionist argument, in retrospect, appears utterly persuasive, and it certainly has been borne out by events. But in the heated atmosphere of Russian radical intellectual life, such ideas were heresy: the revolutionary faction, more interested in gaining power through revolution than in improving the condition of the working class, closed ranks and expelled Struve from the party, something that did not happen to Eduard Bernstein, his Western counterpart.

Struve next joined the nascent liberal movement, assuming the editorship of its principal organ, *Liberation* (*Osvobozhdenie*), which he published abroad. After the revolution of 1905, disenchanted with the unwillingness of Russian intellectuals to work within the new constitutional order and their continued commitment to revolution, he abandoned politics altogether and devoted himself to economics and journalism. In 1917 he was elected to the Academy of Sciences. He was one of the few liberals who did not welcome the February revolution, fearing it would unleash primeval anarchy. He emigrated to the West in 1919 and died in 1944 in Nazi-occupied Paris.

I was attracted to Struve not only by his prophetic analyses of Marxism and communism, so sound despite the resistance they encountered. In the 1920s, for instance, when the introduction of the New Economic Policy persuaded many Russians and foreigners that Soviet Russia had entered the Thermidorean phase of her revolution, he predicted that communism could tolerate no political or economic freedom and hence that the system was unreformable: any reform would lead to collapse—a prediction fulfilled seventy years later. I found even more appealing his uncompromising intellectual integrity and civil courage: the readiness to follow his thoughts to their logical conclusion no matter how unpopular they might prove to be. In my biography I wrote that he possessed to an unusual degree the quality of virtue the ancient Greeks called *arête* and defined as complete self-fulfillment. This quality, combined with immense erudition and remarkably sound judgment, turned me into an ardent admirer.

When I first conceived the idea of writing Struve's biography, I thought it would take me two years. But I had no inkling of how vast and scattered was the body of his writings or how difficult it would be to assemble. As it turned out, I spent, on and off, ten years—extended over a period twice that duration—on what turned out to be a two-volume biography. The first volume appeared on the centenary of Struve's birth in 1970, the second in 1980. To the extent that I expected this effort to result in a general reappraisal of Struve's achievement and place in Russian history, I was disappointed. The Russians, of course, ignored my book: to them, he was, in Lenin's words, nothing better than a "renegade."* Western scholars of Russian history, by this time in the grip of their own kind of "revisionism," which in all essentials followed the Soviet interpretation and was committed to the view that all that mattered was "history from below," i.e., the class struggle, paid virtually no attention to the biography of a "failure." Even so, I never regretted the many years I spent on this extraordinary man, partly because of the privilege of familiarizing myself with such a noble personality, and partly because of what I have learned from him about communism and Communist Russia. He influenced me profoundly in many ways. Later, when I turned my attention to the issue of private property and its bearing on political liberty, whether this happened consciously or not I cannot tell, I found my ideas on the subject surprisingly close to his.

In the academic year 1961–62 I took leave, and we set off once again for Paris. Our second stay there was even more pleasant than the first because we knew more people and felt more at home. De Gaulle was president and he spared nothing to beautify the capital city, having its buildings cleansed of decades of grime. Apart from occasional terrorist acts by the OAS, the illegal organization of disgruntled French nationalists opposed to granting independence to Algeria, the country was calm and prosperous. I worked on Struve in the Bibliothèque Nationale and the École des Langues Orientales Vivantes. We traveled extensively, to Switzerland, the Loire Valley, Spain. The first half of the summer of 1962 we spent at St. Maxime, on the Riviera, on an estate extending over many acres covered with parasol pines and a vineyard.

As a result of a trip several of us had taken to Leningrad in January 1959, Harvard and Leningrad universities signed an accord calling for academic exchanges. In 1962, I was proposed as such a visitor and after overcoming delays in obtaining a Soviet entry visa, departed in mid-March for Moscow. From Moscow, where I spent several days, I took the night train to Leningrad. Before going to sleep, I had a sip of Martell's Cordon Bleu cognac which I had brought from France to console me during the bouts of depression that frequently afflicted me in Russia. It had come in a handsome gold-and-blue carton featuring Louis XIV, which the hotel chambermaid in Moscow could not resist appropriating.

---

*At any rate, until 2001 when the Moscow School of Political Studies published a Russian translation. In March 2003, the Moscow School organized a conference in Perm, Struve's birthplace, dedicated to his memory. During this conference I delivered a lecture at the local university and was pleasantly surprised to learn how many professors and students had read my biography. It meant something to them whereas in the West it was a mere curiosity.

At my request, she repackaged it in ordinary wrapping paper but in a such a way that the neck stuck out prominently. I asked the sleeping car attendant to wake me half an hour before we reached our destination.

He apparently forgot my request, for the first thing I heard in the morning was him opening the door and shouting "Leningrad!" I had barely time to dress when the train came to a halt and two porters barged into the compartment to take my luggage. I grabbed my briefcase and the bottle of cognac. As I stepped out, I saw the entire history department of Leningrad University lined up to welcome me: all eyes focused on the miserable bottle. I was mortified. Fortunately an American graduate student present relieved me of the embarrassing object.

Before leaving Paris, I had written out, in Russian, the text of four lectures on Russian conservatism in the nineteenth century. My purpose was frankly political: I wanted to show, without directly criticizing the Soviet regime, how tsarist-era conservatives foresaw the miseries of a socialist/communist society, such as the one they were living in. The interest in my appearance was enormous: several hundred students and not a few professors turned up for my lectures. I was told at first that each of my four talks would be followed by a discussion, but subsequently the department thought better of it: afraid of "provocative" questions, the chairman adjourned the meeting as soon as I finished. After the third lecture, however, the students, apparently on a prearranged signal, rushed forward, surrounded me, and asked all sorts of questions, most of them, indeed, "provocative."

The faculty treated me with utmost cordiality. When I fell ill with the flu, they postponed my lectures until I recovered. They also obtained for me penicillin, which was available only on the black market. Such friendliness, however, as I was to discover, was conditional on my following the rules of the game, which required that I neither say nor write anything that would get them in trouble with the authorities. The difficulty with this condition was that it was likely to clash with the truth: and when truth confronted expediency, I unhesitatingly opted for the former, following the dictum, attributed to Aristotle, that while "Plato is dear to me, truth is still dearer." The unfortunate corollary of this principle is that it tends to turn friends into enemies.

While working on Struve's biography, I learned of his early encounters with Lenin. Pursuing the leads, I studied in detail Lenin's first contacts with St. Petersburg labor—the only time before 1917 that he had direct relations with workers. Some of this research I carried out during my stay in Leningrad. I learned to my surprise that the minuscule group of trade-union-oriented workers in the capital kept aloof from the radical intelligentsia, Lenin included, because it was more concerned with economic and educational self-improvement than politics. From this experience, Lenin concluded that the proletariat was not really committed to revolution, and hence the revolutionary spirit had to be instilled in it from the outside by cadres of full-time professional revolutionaries, who, of necessity, had to be intellectuals. This un-Marxist inference led Lenin to formulate in *What Is to Be Done?* the Blanquist doctrine of revolution from above which became the essence of Bolshevik theory and practice.

The slender volume, *Social Democracy and the St. Petersburg Labor Movement, 1885–1897* (1963), in which I expounded these views, provoked an extraordinary stir in Soviet historical circles because it challenged head-on, on the basis of detailed historical evidence, the mandatory doctrine that the Bolshevik Party had always represented Russia's laboring masses. The history faculty at Leningrad got into trouble for having hosted someone as deviant as myself and for assisting me in gaining archival access for such wicked purposes. (In fact, I found few if any relevant archival materials on this trip.) Hence, they were forced to disown me. On orders from above, two poor Russian women historians, one of whom I had consulted, wrote a book called *Mister Paips falsifitsiruet istoriiu (Mr. Pipes falsifies history)* (Leningrad, 1966). It was so full of errors, misrepresentations, and outright lies that I never finished reading it. The very cover of this scurrilous booklet—black with yellow lettering—was repulsive because it conveyed an anti-Semitic message.

The incident had a curious epilogue. As I learned from American exchange students in Moscow, the person who most aggressively assailed me for writing such a seditious book was "Academician" I. I. Mints, a Stalinist flunkey charged with supervising all historical work on the Soviet period. (As I later learned, in early 1953, he—himself a Jew— had played a prominent role in pressuring Jewish intellectuals to beseech Stalin to deport all Jews to Siberia.) When Mints turned up in the United States a few years later and asked to see me, I refused. He somehow managed, however, to make his way to my Widener study. Before he had a chance to take off his overcoat, he exclaimed: "Congratulations! You have written a brilliant book." "You really think so?" "Oh, yes." When we sat down to talk, he told me I had made one mistake, namely, criticizing Lenin in the introduction, before presenting the evidence, which gave the impression that I had prejudged him.

Edmund Wilson and George Kennan

Our life back home followed an agreeable pattern: fall and spring in Cambridge teaching, summers in a cottage we had purchased in 1960 in Chesham, New Hampshire, high above Silver Lake, less than two hours' drive from Cambridge. Ever since, I have done most of my writing there. Surprisingly, I became thoroughly Americanized only after spending several summers in the countryside. Only after I had familiarized myself with the wild flowers and trees, with the rabbits and chipmunks, did I sink roots in the soil, as I had not been able to do on city pavements. Gardening, which I took up in the 1980s, reinforced this sense of belonging.

In the early 1960s I made the acquaintance of two distinguished men who were to influence me, though in different ways: Edmund Wilson and George Kennan.

Wilson, America's premier literary critic of his generation as well as a prominent literary historian and novelist, enjoyed the reputation of a gruff, self-centered person, very difficult to get along with: referring to him, the *Britannica* drops its customary reserve and refers to his "crotchety character." To some extent this reputation was justified. He hated crowds, felt uncomfortable when treated as a celebrity, and suffered agonies when required to speak in public.* His instinct, on such occasions, was to bolt. He could be rude to people who bothered him. Once, when he had gone through the torment of accepting the Mac-Dowell medal in Peterborough, New Hampshire, a lady approached him in my presence and asked what he thought of Mary McCarthy's recently published novel, *The Group*. "I never read books by my ex-wives," he brusquely answered. A Polish émigré poet, well known at home but not in the United States, related to him a complicated personal story of someone giving him a hard time. "You see, he did not know who I was," he added by way of explanation. Wilson responded with mock innocence: "And who were you?"

---

*He told me once of an event in New York at which he was the guest of honor and which he attended only because it involved a prize of $30,000. When he arrived, the company was well in its cups. They passed to each other, under the table, copies of *Who's Who in America* to find out whom they were honoring. One swaying lady approached him and said: "I know who you are." "And who am I?" he asked. "You wrote 'Finlandia.'"

In judging his manners one has to bear in mind that he was constantly importuned by writers eager to solicit his endorsement of their work: a favorable review by him could make an author's reputation. To protect himself from such assaults so as to be free to pursue his own work, he adopted the shell of inapproachability. He even had printed cards which listed every conceivable request that could be made of him: "Edmund Wilson regrets that it is impossible for him to: read manuscripts; write articles or books on order . . . give interviews . . . deliver lectures . . . autograph books for strangers . . . supply photographs of himself," and so on, so that he merely had to check off the appropriate box and mail it.

Because I never wanted anything from him and because we had many interests in common we got along famously. We first met in February 1960 at a "champagne picnic" supper in the home of Marcus and Mitzi Cunliffe who had come to Harvard for a year from Sussex University. Wilson at the time was working on *Patriotic Gore*. He at once impressed me with his insatiable curiosity, his unwillingness to rest on his reputation, and his readiness to serve as an apprentice in ever new fields of knowledge. One day it was French Symbolism, the next Lenin and the Russian Revolution, followed by the Dead Sea Scrolls and Hungarian language and literature. I have never met another person of his age and reputation who displayed such youthful inquisitiveness. We had many conversations, sometimes in Cambridge when he would drop in (I suspect that he occasionally suffered from bouts of depression and needed cheering up), sometimes in his house at Wellfleet. Our conversations ranged widely: he spoke with some effort and even a slight stutter but he listened attentively. He was an incurable romantic to the end: a common friend said that every time Wilson went to a party he expected some dramatic experience.

In politics he was a child. I refer not only to his infatuation with communism in the 1930s, about which he once told me, "We have been had." I mean that he understood nothing of what government did, why it collected taxes, why it needed armies. All matters that did not bear on literature and culture broadly defined were to him useless distractions.

He had a stroke in 1970. When he came to visit us shortly after his recovery, Irene, opening the door, took one look at him and said, "Edmund, you look fine." He winced but did not respond. When leaving, however, he said: "You know, Irene, there are three ages of man: youth, middle age, and old age. You have just put me in the fourth: when one 'looks fine.'"

The last time we saw him he had apparently come into money and had rented a suite at the Boston Ritz, where, spread out like royalty, downing one martini after another, he received visitors. He was in a wonderful mood. We chatted but then started to take our leave because we had to go to a party. "Stay," he urged but we declined. I have always regretted preferring a run-of-the-mill cocktail party to another hour with Edmund.

His widow, Elena, told us that he had given a great deal of thought to the last words he would utter on his deathbed. In any event, he died in Talcottville, New York, his parental home, where he spent every summer in the company of a nurse. That morning the nurse asked him what he would like to do first, take a bath or eat breakfast. "I will have breakfast first," he answered and collapsed.

I was very gratified to read in his posthumously published diaries of the 1960s that he was really fond of us because he could be most acerbic about people.

George Kennan was in many respects Wilson's opposite. Where one was short and pudgy, the other stood tall and elegant. Speaking in public was torment for the one, to the other it came with a natural grace. Kennan's most admirable quality to my mind was an uncommon ability to grasp the essential features of communism without any of the illusions of American liberals, as well as the complex relationship between communism, the Russian people, and Russian history. His "long cable" of 1946 and the "Mr. X" article in *Foreign Affairs* are too well known to require elaboration. In them he articulated the "containment policy" which posited that vigorous action to halt Soviet expansion would cause the communist system to implode. In spring 1960 he delivered at Harvard's Sanders Theater a series of historical lectures—they were published the following year as *Russia and the West under Lenin and Stalin*— that held the audience of hundreds spellbound. Without any concessions to the crowd, without any attempt to make the complex more palatable by oversimplifying or sensationalizing, by the mere force of his intellect and eloquence, Kennan delivered one of the most impressive rhetorical performances I have ever witnessed.

But he had faults, which over time affected his judgment and ultimately brought him deep disappointment. His principal character flaw was inordinate vanity—the greatest enemy of the intellectual because it places gratification of the ego above truth. Although he came from a midwestern family of modest means, he fancied himself an eighteenth-century aristocrat: I heard him say that his notion of an ambassador was of a diplomat who sat down once a week to write by hand a report to his minister, the way it was done two centuries ago. Indeed, he believed that the eighteenth century was the apex of Western civilization, a civilization that collapsed under the onslaught of the Industrial Revolution.[9] He founded in Washington, D.C., a scholarly center devoted to the study of Russia and the Soviet Union and named it the "Kennan Institute," ostensibly in memory of his great-uncle and namesake, a minor late-nineteenth-century figure who had written on the Siberian exile system, but in fact to honor himself. Later he founded a chair in his name at the Princeton Institute for Advanced Studies.

Another of his shortcomings was bizarre political ideas which he could entertain alongside very realistic ones without any awareness of contradiction. He was convinced, for instance, that all great powers were entitled to their sphere of influence. When I met him in New York in December 1960, he told me, apropos nothing in particular, that Soviet Russia had a "right" to Iran, something Moscow did not even demand. For balance, he felt, we ought to invade Cuba and get rid of a Soviet base so near our shores. When we testified jointly before the Senate Armed Service's Committee in 1980, he insisted that Russia's recent invasion of Afghanistan was a "defensive" move.

I imagine that he thought himself destined to be secretary of state, but his views disqualified him from holding significant public office. He never came close to realizing his political ambitions. Moscow declared him persona non grata as ambassador after he had made some undiplomatic remarks comparing the Soviet Union to Nazi Germany. Eisenhower's secretary of state, John Foster Dulles, unceremoniously dismissed him from the department. Under Kennedy, he went as envoy to Belgrade, but he did not perform very well and soon retired permanently to Princeton.

Career setbacks left him embittered and disillusioned about the country that in his eyes had treated him so shabbily. He felt disgusted with the United States as it was and resented the influence on it of immigrants. He never tired of complaining about sex shops a few blocks from the White House. Personal failures affected his view of the Soviet Union. He increasingly apologized for Soviet actions and in effect repudiated his own containment policy: at one point he said that on rereading his famous "Mr. X" article he found it hard to believe he had written it. On another occasion he denied that in recommending containment he had in mind military action, although there is a great deal of evidence to the contrary. In his "Mr. X" article he had stated unequivocally, "It is entirely possible for the United States to influence by its actions the internal developments" in Russia and the international communist movement.[10] Yet thirty-five years later, in objecting to Reagan's policy of pushing the USSR toward reform, he just as unequivocally denied that we could in any way influence developments inside the Soviet Union. In the 1980s he continued to warn that Reagan's hard-line policy vis-à-vis Moscow would inevitably lead to World War III. When the Soviet Union collapsed suddenly in 1991, he found himself in the embarrassing situation of receiving congratulations for the triumph of a strategy that he had long repudiated. There were really two Kennans living side by side. Bertram Wolfe, author of *Three Who Made a Revolution,* said of Kennan that his unpredictable political vacillations brought to mind Hamlet's "I am but mad north-north-west: when the wind is southerly I know a hawk from a handsaw."*

It so happened that in spring 1960, Wilson and Kennan as well as Isaiah Berlin were visiting Cambridge. I thought this coincidence presented a unique opportunity to invite three world-class intellects to our home for dinner, there to sit back and delight in their conversation. For good measure I included Arthur Schlesinger Jr. I looked forward to a sublime conversational quartet: but, alas, as it turned out, these were four soloists, unused to playing in tandem. The conversation during and after the meal was fitful and trivial. All I recall of that evening was Wilson and Berlin discussing the various ways of saying "necktie" in Russian, and Schlesinger picking up the whole cutlet with his fork, bringing it his mouth, and biting off pieces.

Western Civilization

William Langer was one of the luminaries of our department. Before the war he had published several standard works on the diplomatic history of pre–World War I Europe in which he drew on an amazing array of sources in various languages. He also edited *The Encyclopedia of World History,* which remains to this day an indispensable reference work. He was notoriously demanding of himself and his students. A story made the rounds that he had once returned a seminar paper to a graduate student, explaining that he had given it an A-minus rather than a straight A which it otherwise deserved because the student had not drawn on Italian sources. "But Professor Langer," the student remon-

---

*Hamlet, II, ii. "Handsaw" here refers to a heron.

strated, "I don't read Italian." "How do you know?" Langer is said to have replied. "Have you tried?" His nickname was "Butch." When I asked him why, he answered in his peculiar nasal twang, "Butch for butcher." But by the time I came in closer contact with him, he had considerably mellowed.

In July 1963—I had just turned forty—I received a letter from him inviting me to contribute to a two-volume freshman textbook on the history of Western civilization which he had undertaken to edit. The book was to be richly illustrated by American Heritage which copublished it with Harper and Row. There were to be four authors; my responsibility was Europe since 1800. The proposal attracted me for several reasons. I did not mind putting aside the Struve biography on which I had been working for five years to write something that called for a broad brush. I further saw an opportunity to weave the history of Russia and Eastern Europe into that of mainstream Western civilization in which it usually played a marginal role. And, finally, the financial rewards promised to be substantial, which appealed to me since at the time I had no assets other than my salary. So I agreed.

I labored on the textbook very hard for three and a half years, absorbing a large quantity of secondary literature on every aspect of European history during a 160-year period of extraordinary vitality. I paid special attention to cultural and intellectual developments as well as to Russia and Eastern Europe. These were the strengths of my contribution. The political and economic chapters were more conventional. My chapters received high praise when the two-volume history, sumptuously illustrated, came out in March 1968.

The initial reception by the profession was as good as could be expected: there were nearly 200 college adoptions, and first year sales for volume 2 came to 33,000. Yet sales soon dwindled: the next year, they fell to 21,000, and then to 9,000. For one, the contributors to volume 1 ("Paleolithic Man to the Emergence of European Powers") wrote turgid prose that freshmen found hard to follow. Teachers dropped it, and along with it, volume 2. Then, too, the timing of the publication proved most unfortunate. The late 1960s was a period of turbulence at the colleges, of revolt against all traditions and authorities, including textbooks and the very concept of "Western civilization."

In 1970, the publishers repackaged my section as *Europe since 1815* and the next year, volume 2, the first half of which was written by J. H. Hexter, as *Europe since 1500*, but, of course, the potential readership for these books was much smaller than for a textbook on Western civilization as a whole. In 1975 a second, abbreviated version of the original book came out as a paperback under the imprint of the same publisher, minus the sumptuous color illustrations, but by that time the book had lost its novelty. "Western civilization" now yielded to "world history," a subject that lacks cohesion since the various regions of the world run on different historical clocks. Furthermore, inspired by a worthy but nebulous feeling of human equality, it neglected to teach the young about the sources of their own culture.

The year 1967 marked the fiftieth anniversary of the Russian Revolution, and at the suggestion of the American Council of Learned Societies in April I organized at Harvard a conference on the subject. I came under considerable pressure from some scholars and the foundations to which I had applied for funding to invite Soviet historians. I refused to do so on the grounds that unlike scientific topics or histories of remote countries and eras, in the Soviet Union the Russian Revolution was a subject not of scholarship but of politics, strictly controlled by the authorities who considered it vital to their legitimacy. At least one scholar refused to come under these conditions, and one or more foundations declined financial support.

But the conference met anyway and it was a notable affair. The list of participants was stellar. Among them were Hannah Arendt, Isaiah Berlin, E. H. Carr, Merle Fainsod, George Kennan, Leonard Schapiro, Hugh Seton-Watson, and Bertram Wolfe. No attempt was made to arrive at a consensus. The record of the conference was published in 1968 as *Revolutionary Russia*.

In June 1968 I spent time in Helsinki working on Struve materials at the University Library. Before 1917 it had been one of Russia's depository libraries, and it held publications, notably daily newspapers, unavailable elsewhere in the West. I lived in a small hotel room, spent most of the day in the library, and then roamed for hours the city streets. I felt very happy and wondered whether I was not really meant to be a monk. When finished, for a couple of days I explored the pristine Lake Saimaa on a small steamer.

On June 21 I arrived in Prague where my wife joined me. The city was in the throes of a quiet revolution led by Alexander Dubček. I was surprised how quickly all the emblems of communist power—hammer and sickle, red flags, portraits of Lenin—had vanished. One shop displayed in its window nothing but a photograph of Thomas Masaryk, the founder in 1918 of the Czech Republic: it attracted a crowd which stared at it, because Masaryk's likeness had been outlawed for over twenty years.

But underneath the relaxed air of normalcy one could detect signs of acute nervousness that the Russians would not tolerate these developments. Uniformed Soviet officers roamed Prague's streets, looking aloof and disapproving. In one beer hall I watched with dismay a group of Czechs trying to persuade some Russians, who sat in glum silence, that they in no way threatened their country or its regime. It occurred to me they would have been more effective had they emphasized what bloody resistance the Warsaw Pact would encounter if it invaded.

The invasion came two months later and it was bloodless.

Historical "Revisionism"

The 1960s were a period of much change at the university. At Harvard, the first signs of this change appeared in 1961 following the election of John F. Kennedy. Like the rest of the Kennedy clan, President Kennedy was a product of Harvard. The clan's reputation here was not the best. On the eve of the 1960 election, Dr. Ronald Ferry, the master of Winthrop House, of which all the Kennedys had been members and which I had joined as tutor, invited me to lunch in a vain attempt to dissuade me from voting for JFK. He told me of the blatant pressure that old Joseph Kennedy had applied on the university after Teddy Kennedy had been caught cheating. But like the rest of Harvard, I was dazzled by the handsome Democrat, who, in contrast to Eisenhower, seemed so eloquent, so well read, and so respectful of intellectuals. After several Harvardians, headed by our dean, McGeorge Bundy, had left to join the Kennedy administration, we began to think of the White House as an annex to the Harvard Yard. The university now became more politicized and more partisan. Suffice it to say that when I joined the Reagan administration twenty years later, one senior member of the faculty referred to me in private conversation as a "traitor." The insult was passed on to me, but he never seemed to realize why I would refuse to shake hands with him.

In the classroom, too, changes became apparent. Students of the 1960s were less eager to learn and less disposed to laugh. I noticed a glassy look in the eyes of some, the effect of drugs. The air was suffused with an unfocused atmosphere of resentment, induced in part by the Vietnam War, which threatened students with military conscription, but running deeper since it also affected students in Western European countries which did not participate in the war.

In the mid-1960s, violent disturbances broke out at several major

American universities, notably Berkeley and Columbia, but Harvard seemed immune. This proved an illusion. In 1969, the student "revolution" struck Harvard. The disturbances were meticulously organized by a group which called itself Students for a Democratic Society (SDS) but seemed to be run by older radicals quite contemptuous of democracy; many of the younger members came from Stalinist families.

At noontime on April 9 as I emerged from my lecture, I saw a crowd of several hundred students gathered in the rear of University Hall, the administrative seat of the Faculty of Arts and Sciences and the office of its dean. Standing on the steps, some young people harangued the throng. At one point, a student, dressed in a freshly pressed railroad engineer's suit, emerged from the crowd and advanced toward the building bearing the Stars and Stripes: this baby-faced youth apparently was meant to represent the American "proletariat." From the steps of Widener, a camera crew filmed the proceedings. The crowd appeared more amused than agitated.

At a certain point, the principal haranguer shouted through the bull-horn, "All right, shall we go in?" The crowd responded with a roar: "NO!" He yelled back: "They didn't ask us whether to go into Vietnam, so in we go." And in they went to manhandle the staff and rifle through confidential files. Unfortunately, the administration, though forewarned, had not taken preventive measures, such as surrounding the building with police, which might have defused the crisis. The Yard now was sealed off while University Hall was "occupied." Later that night, the police were brought in to eject the trespassers forcibly.

This was exactly what the organizers of the event had hoped for. The police violence instantly radicalized the rest of the student body, which ignored the cause and focused on the effect. The next day the university was in chaos. I was asked to have lunch at Winthrop House to help calm the undergraduates: one of them sat at the table with a bandaged head, rambling incoherently.

The unrest had no clear objective: that is, although endless "programs" were drafted, it was an emotional explosion which affected both students and faculty. All sorts of frustrations and resentments, previously held repressed, floated to the surface. Graduate student assistants wanted higher pay; Orthodox Jewish students wanted kosher food served in the houses. Lectures were disrupted by radical students: here and there a bolder professor expelled them, sometimes with the assistance of the class, but most were helpless. Strangely, for all my conservative reputation, I never experienced such disruptions: the main victims were liberal professors afflicted by a guilty conscience. Anyone who has observed such events at close range becomes aware that mass hysteria communicates from person to person like a virus, for no apparent reason and with no clear purpose. It is next to impossible to resist. I recall during those days drafting various "memoranda" and "appeals" which never left my desk because they had no specific addressee. They simply helped me find bearings in the midst of collective madness.

The faculty split on the issue of the administration's response. One part backed President Nathan Pusey's decision to call in the police; another turned against him. The former organized into a "conservative" caucus, while the latter formed a "liberal" one. Each comprised some thirty professors. The remaining 90 percent of the faculty pretended that nothing had happened and pursued their normal routine. The conservative caucus, which I joined, met informally in the homes of its members to draft policy statements for faculty meetings, which at that time convened every few days. The liberals did likewise but their stress was on a "dialogue" with the rebellious students, which in practice meant finding ways of appeasing them. The faculty meetings, usually staid gatherings devoted to the discussion of trivia, turned into raucous affairs. Because attendance was much greater than normal, the meetings were transferred from University Hall to the Loeb Theater on Brattle Street. The proceedings were broadcast to crowds assembled outside. I listened to the discussions with a sensation akin to nausea. I had a hard time believing how many of the frightened faculty were prepared to give up all that made our university great in order to pacify the mob and how dishonestly they rationalized their fears. It was in this mood that the faculty voted to establish a black studies program and to allow black students to participate in faculty appointments to it, although hardly anyone believed that this program made for a legitimate field of concentration. The faculty acted under the impression of a newspaper photograph which showed a group of black students, armed with guns, leaving Willard Straight Hall at Cornell, where similar events had taken place and where the administration collapsed completely.

I never quite regained the esteem I had for my colleagues: their self-interest and cowardice lurked all too clearly beneath the facade of academic concerns. Nor did the students' behavior raise them in my eyes. The majority were intimidated and lacked all initiative. The instigators of the disturbances acted at no risk to themselves: liberal opinion, even as it condemned their excesses, assumed that their violence was inspired by genuine grievances and sympathized with them. A neighbor of ours, when told of an explosion set off by a radical at the Harvard Accelerator, killing one scientist, wondered aloud what the killer wanted to "tell us." When, half a year earlier, a small band of young Russians had demonstrated in Red Square to protest the invasion of Czechoslovakia, they were instantly seized and sent to prison, as they expected to be. This was heroism; the actions of our university dissidents were antics.

Harvard changed profoundly after the 1960s. It began to view itself as an agent of social change and increasingly devoted itself to solving society's problems: instead of acquiring knowledge, no matter how esoteric, and teaching it to its students it emphasized "outreach." Rather than select its faculty and students solely by criteria of talent and creativity, it pursued sexual and racial diversity. Elitism, even when it involved exclusively intellectual excellence, was frowned upon. Much of what Harvard now did reminded me of the early Soviet educational experiments which aimed at breaking down the isolation of institutions of higher learning and harnessing them in the cause of social reform. Altogether, the drift was of a Soviet kind, with every institution, universities very much included, being expected to contribute to the solution of social problems.

Shortly after these events I left for California to spend the academic year 1969–70 on leave at the Stanford's Center for Advanced Study in the Behavioral Sciences. My parents joined us there. It was not a happy time for them because father soon suffered a minor stroke and then began to show symptoms of confusion which doctors diagnosed as Alzheimer's—a disease I had never heard of previously.

Father's postwar years were altogether sad. Business turned sour. By 1948 he had realized that with the lifting of sugar rationing, he could not compete with chain candy stores like Fanny Farmer and closed his outlets. For a while he dealt in wholesale toys. He could make no sense of the world around him in the turbulent sixties: returning from Harvard Square on visits to us he would shake his head in bewilderment wondering why everybody and everything was so "ugly." He was acutely depressed. In May 1971, mother decided to move to Boston to be near us. She took care of father as long as she could and then placed him in a nursing home. In the last months of his life—he died in April 1973 at the age of eighty—he could no longer recognize either of us. One of the last times I saw him was sitting in a chair in the nursing home, holding hands with an elderly woman patient, a total stranger, and staring uncomprehending at the flickering television screen. At his funeral I read the wonderful thirty-eighth chapter of the Book of Job, where God, having listened patiently as Job and his three friends attempt to discover the reason for Job's misfortunes, speaks up from the whirlwind and tells them His purposes are beyond their comprehension: "Where wast thou when I laid the foundations of the earth? Declare, if thou hast the understanding. Who determined the measures thereof, if thou knowest? Or who stretched the line upon it?" I read the same passage at mother's funeral twenty years later.

During my year at Stanford, I completed the first volume of the Struve biography. When I returned to Harvard in the fall of 1970, the atmosphere had changed dramatically for the better. The main reason was President Nixon's repeal of the draft: the calming effect of this measure suggested that behind the *Weltschmerz* of the rebellious students lay no little self-interest. But though peace was restored and university life returned to normal, Harvard was never quite the same. For one, it had lost its uniqueness: when the country was swept by a wave of university disturbances, Harvard found itself as susceptible to mass hysteria as other institutions of higher learning. Second, in response to egalitarian pressures, Harvard abandoned many of its "elitist" practices. Thus, the college houses gave up "high tables" and professors were encouraged to mix with the undergraduates who seemed, to me at least, to prefer each other's company. Students, who previously had stood a good chance of ending up in a house of their choice, were now assigned at random. History and Literature had to abolish its limited admissions policy and throw itself opn to all qualified applicants. Soon affirmative action made itself felt as the university yielded to Washington—the source of a good part of its budget—in the matter of hiring, enrolling, and promoting minorities, a concept which included women. Students were encouraged to "rate" their professors. Whereas previously, many and perhaps most of the administrators had a Harvard background and felt strong loyalty to the institution, many of their successors were professional managers for whom Harvard was just another job, which they readily abandoned when a better paying one turned up. By the 1970s Harvard came to resemble more a midwestern state university than its old self. The word "campus," previously taboo, now entered the vocabulary. This process was facilitated by the decay of the Boston Brahmin community and the decline of the British and German universities which had served Harvard as models.

In summer 1970, I attended another International Historical Congress, this time in Moscow. The political atmosphere in the Soviet Union had relaxed considerably during the preceding decade, and I no longer felt under constant surveillance. Even so, as I later found out, Soviet citizens were permitted to attend my session only by special permission. I submitted a paper on Russian conservatism in the second half of the nineteenth century: once again, as in my 1962 Leningrad lectures, I meant to point out the contemporary relevance of conservative thought. In my spoken remarks I emphasized that only liberalism, which decentralized decision-making, was capable of coping with the complexities of modern life. When I finished, the designated opponents mounted the podium to raise the conventional objections. But, surprisingly, one Russian speaker defended me: she was Valentina Tvardovskaia, daughter of the celebrated editor of *Novyi Mir,* the most liberal of Soviet thick journals. The fact that she dared to do so in public indicated that something was changing.

In 1970, concurrent with the publication of volume 1 of *Struve,* I brought out an edition of Struve's collected works (minus newspaper articles) in fifteen folio volumes. In preparing these materials for publication, I took advantage of xerography. Struve's publications were first xeroxed and placed in chronological order, then microfilmed, and from the microfilms reproduced in bound volumes. I financed the undertaking out of my own pocket, taking a chance that I would sell enough copies at $950 to cover my costs. I did better than that: thirty-five libraries purchased the set, yielding me a modest profit. I believe this edition may have been the first in which the collected corpus of any writer's work was made public not by typographical but by xerographic means.

In spring 1972, I was invited to the University of Jerusalem. I was asked neither to give public lectures nor to address classes: my talks were delivered exclusively to faculty seminars. I did not attach any significance to these facts. But nearly thirty years later I was startled to receive a letter from an ex-student of Jerusalem University who wrote: "We were not allowed to attend [Pipes's] guest lectures which were confined to the academic staff only. Off the record I was told that because of his right-wing views our professors did not wish his ideas to have contacts with our minds (his lectures were not advertised on the campus and it was only by word of mouth among the professors that his talks became known)."

From Jerusalem my wife and I traveled by way of Jordan, Syria, and Lebanon to London, where we spent the summer.

Russia under the Old Regime

Sometime in 1956–57, when I was spending my first leave in Paris, an idea occurred to me that was in good measure to dominate my writings on Russia. It had to do with the relationship between political power and property. I never felt any attraction to the Marxist notion that political power was nothing but a "function" of property relationships, and the state but an instrument of the propertied classes, since it seemed evident that the abstraction called "the state" was staffed by individuals whose own interests often clashed with those of property owners. It struck me that sovereignty and ownership were really alternate ways of controlling people and assets: it was a zero-sum game in that what the one gained, the other lost. The most dependable means of thwarting government from expanding its power and encroaching on citizens' liberties, therefore, was to make certain that the bulk of the wealth rested in the hands of citizens in the form of inalienable property. I did not learn until many years later that this thesis had been anticipated three centuries earlier by the Englishman James Harrington. In March 1958, I read to an informal group of younger Harvard historians a paper on "Property and Political Power" in which I outlined this thesis and stressed how in Russia, the late and incomplete development of private property made possible the monstrous growth of state power. Despite the prompting of some colleagues, I did not publish it. I did, however, introduce the idea into the course on Russian medieval history which I gave for the first and last time in the spring term of 1960–61. There I applied to Muscovite Russia the term "patrimonial regime," which I had adopted from Max Weber, meaning a regime under which the ruler is both sovereign and owner of the realm.

An opportunity to develop this thesis presented itself ten years later. After finishing in 1969–70 the first volume of the Struve biography, I decided, before completing that undertaking, to honor a contract I had signed ten years earlier with the English publisher Weidenfeld and Nicolson to contribute a volume on Russia to their new "History of Civilization" series. I received complete freedom as to contents and scope.

I completed this book in London where we spent a year's leave in 1973–74. Having lived in London several summers as well as a full year, we had fallen in love with the city and felt that if fate had given us the choice of where to be born and where to live our lives, we would have picked this city. London's social life was much more open than that of Paris. It also had an advantage over Cambridge, Massachusetts, where one's social contacts were confined to academics with a sprinkling of retired politicians and an occasional businessman or professional. In London all groups intermingled: intellectuals (not only of the academic kind), members of parliament, business people, and even actors and movie directors. It made for an exceptionally spirited social life. I also liked the bluntness of the English of a certain class, who have no inhibitions telling you in your face, even publicly, when they think you are wrong. Once during the question and answer period following a lecture I had delivered at the University of London in which I criticized the political and social record of the Russian Orthodox Church, a Russo-English theologian rose to his feet to dismiss my remarks as "sheer nonsense." On the other hand, when not long afterward I lectured at the London School of Economics on the Russian gentry and a friend told me that everyone felt it was a "brilliant" performance, I took it as a genuine compliment. In the United States you never quite know what people think of you because they are afraid to hurt your feelings.

The book which came out in 1974 as *Russia under the Old Regime* was an essay on the evolution of Russian statehood from the earliest times to the late nineteenth century, with stress on the patrimonial nature of tsarist power. I depicted this power as very different from Western absolutism because the latter had always been constrained by the instituton of private property. In the conclusion I hinted that the Communist regime in Russia, under which the ruling party enjoyed unrestrained control over both politics and economic resources, owed a great deal to this patrimonial tradition.

The book was well received, adopted in many colleges, and translated into several foreign languages. Its most severe critics were Russian nationalists headed by Alexander Solzhenitsyn. Solzhenitsyn had recently arrived in Switzerland, and in November 1975 I sent him a copy of the English edition with a letter and personal dedication, adding that I thought he would "find several coincidences in our views." Solzhenitsyn did not respond and it occurred me that this was probably because he was ignorant of English. At the time, next to nothing was known of his politics except that he was fiercely anticommunist. For this I admired him greatly and in the summer of 1974 even canceled a trip to the Soviet Union to protest his expulsion. It came, therefore, as something of a shock when, in late 1976, in the course of an address at the Hoover Institution of California, Solzhenitsyn delivered a blistering attack on me and my book. What aroused his ire was my linking tsarism and communism, phenomena which in his mind were polar opposites. Quite innocent of historical knowledge, he had a naively romantic view of prerevolutionary Russia and blamed Russia's current miseries entirely on the influence of Marxism and other noxious ideologies imported from the West. When I met him in June 1978, at a dinner that preceded the Harvard commencement where he received an honorary doctorate, I asked him how he thought it possible that the same people, with the same history, speaking the same language, living on the same territory, could, in the course of one night—October 25–26, 1917—turn into something entirely different because a group of radical intellectuals had seized power in their country. "Even biology does not know such sudden and extreme mutations," I argued. But though personally amiable, he would not yield an inch and in the years that followed blasted me on every occasion that presented itself, to the extent of protesting to the BBC when that network broadcast in Russian excerpts from my book to the Soviet Union. I never responded to his attacks because they were personal and emotional, lacking in serious content.

The failure of the "Holy Russia" of his imagination to reemerge the instant Russia's government gave up Marxism must have sorely disappointed him. His hate-driven intellectual intolerance along with his fanaticism disqualified him, in my eyes, from claiming greatness: he was a false prophet even if he did display remarkable courage in standing up to the equally hate-filled and equally fanatical Communist regime. He was, in fact, its mirror image; and when that regime fell, he found himself as irrelevant as any member of the old Communist *nomenklatura*.

But even for Russians who did not share Solzhenitsyn's utopianism, my thesis was difficult to accept. Communists disliked the notion that they owed anything to tsarism; anticommunists resented my linking tsarism with communism; and both, because of their sensitivity to being regarded an oriental people, took exception to the notion—implicit rather than explicit in my book—that Russia's political culture bore many similarities to oriental despotism. The book, however, was published in Russia in 1993 and attracted considerable attention.*

After finishing that book, I returned to Struve to complete the second volume. While tracing his activities in 1917–21, I became increasingly interested in the Russian Revolution as an event that determined in large measure the history of the twentieth century.

But before I had the chance to immerse myself deeply in the revolution, I became involved in politics, which were to occupy me for much of the 1970s and 1980s and all of 1981 and 1982.

China

My reputation as an uncompromising hard-liner toward the Soviet Union reached Beijing, and in winter 1977–78 I received an invitation from the Chinese Institute of International Affairs.

---

*I published privately the original Russian version, which I had commissioned, in the United States in 1980.

I arrived in Beijing on April 3, 1978. The city made, on the whole, a melancholy impression, being ugly in a Soviet sort of way. From my hotel window, which looked out on the main boulevard, I saw hordes of bicycle-riding people—they resembled a swarm of blue and green ants—and heard the incessant hooting of automobile horns. My opinion of the capital improved considerably the next day when I visited the Forbidden City, which impressed me with its remarkable use of space and the subdued use of color. I met a number of professors at Beijing University, some of them old intellectuals who had somehow managed to survive the Cultural Revolution, others semiliterate party hacks. The former told me of the many changes in the curriculum that were under consideration, while the latter sat silent and ill at ease.

I gave a seminar at the institute, attended by some thirty attentive listeners. The questions concerned mostly the reasons for U.S. "flabbiness" in dealing with Moscow. It was a foretaste of things to come because throughout my visit I would be hectored on the need for a firmer U.S. policy toward Russia.

I was driven east of Beijing to inspect the 196th Division which had fought in the civil war and in Korea. The division (I was told) was in large measure self-supporting, growing its own vegetables, raising its own meat, and even manufacturing alarm clocks. I observed exercises staged especially for me. They resembled acrobatics: hand-to-hand combat and climbing buildings. Sitting at a table and watching the proceeding through binoculars provided by my hosts, I thought of myself as General von Moltke the Elder inspecting the Imperial German Army. When the show was over my commissar asked me what I thought: "Very impressive," I replied. "Good for nothing," he countered, "that is for previous wars, not for modern warfare." At lunch, toasts were raised "Down with the common enemy—the Polar Bear!"

A meeting was arranged with the director of the Institute of International Affairs, the seventy-three-year-old Mr. Hao Teh-Ching. Most of the time he talked while I listened and took notes. The thrust of his remarks was that the United States and China were traveling the same road—meaning, containment of the Soviet Union—but separately. We had to contain them militarily, while the Chinese foiled them in the Third World. He believed another world war unavoidable; the best we could do was delay it. The war he envisaged would be conventional, not nuclear. He did not think China was in danger of a Soviet invasion because that would require a minimum of three million troops, far more than the Russians had deployed in the east. The thrust of his remarks was "have no fear." To my question whether there was not a risk that, since they shared the same ideology and system, China and the USSR would not once again unite against the West, he replied that there was no chance of this happening because Russia was not a communist state but a "bureaucratic monopoly." He categorically denied the possibility of the USSR reforming after Brezhnev: such matters, he said, were resolved not by individuals but by the "social system," a prognosis which time proved very, very wrong.

I received a similar briefing from the deputy director of the Foreign Affairs Bureau. He told me that throughout China, tunnels were being dug to protect the population from nuclear fallout. In Beijing on the day of my departure I was taken to a small, out-of-the-way shop. A trapdoor on the floor behind the counter led down steep stairs to a vast subterranean city built on three levels that stretched for miles in all directions. Equipped with all sorts of amenities, it was a city-sized underground shelter. The massive structure—whatever its utility—was awesome.

I observed one profound difference between the way I was treated by the Russians and by the Chinese. The former were trying to pick my brains; the latter, to influence my thinking. Altogether, I found the Chinese lacking in curiosity. Whenever I mentioned life in the West, the subject elicited no notice, in sharp contrast to Russia. Their mind was made up on most issues, and they had no interest in learning my reactions. In contrast to Russia, where everyone was reading, in China I saw no one with a book in hand (apart from students in the university library). In my travel diary I wrote: "One has the feeling that this ancient civilization of so many hundreds of millions can withstand it all—whereas Russia with its 125 million might not. Hence their serene confidence as compared to Russian strutting, bullying, neurosis, apprehensions."

The Chinese did not brazenly lie, as the Russians were wont to do. When asked a question they did not wish to answer, they would be evasive but not downright dishonest. Russian *vranyo* is a peculiar form of lying because it need not serve any ulterior purpose: it is a feat of imagination, an escape from reality which is why Russians rarely feel embarrassed when found out. A character in Dostoyevsky's *Crime and Punishment* thus extols it:

> I like it when people lie! *Vranyo* is man's only advantage over all other organisms. Lie and you will find the truth. I am human because I lie. They haven't found a single truth without having previously lied fourteen, and perhaps one hundred fourteen times. . . . To lie in one's own way—why,

this is almost better than finding the truth in someone else's way: in the former instance you are a human being, in the latter you are merely a parrot.[11]

Similarly, Turgenev's "superfluous man" declares lies to be as alive as truth, if not more so.[12]

China enchanted me. I realized, of course, that being an "honored guest" I was treated with special deference for political reasons, and I made every effort to avoid the trap which ensnared so many "honored" visitors to the Soviet Union. The sights that met my eyes proved to me once more that culture is more important than ideology: that ideas accommodate to the cultural soil on which they fall. Thus Marxism in Scandinavia, where traditions of property and law were relatively strong, evolved first into social democracy and then into the democratic welfare state. In Russia, where both traditions were weakly developed, it reinforced the autocratic, patrimonial heritage. In China, it produced something very different from Soviet communism although what distinguished it I did not know enough to say.

The quality that immediately and forcefully struck me was the outgoing, optimistic attitude of the Chinese people, an attitude that Americans call "can-do," that stood in such contrast to the gloom and fatalism prevalent in Russia. True, there were many signs of what had been euphemistically labeled the "cultural revolution" but what was, in reality, a barbarian counterrevolution: disfigured buildings, graffiti on monuments, closed museums. True, too, except for the children, people dressed uniformly and shabbily. Modern architecture had all the panache of its Soviet prototype. But there was a dynamism in the air that I had never seen in Russia, either before or after 1991. Adding to the charm of China was the countryside, which still lingered in the preindustrial stage so that one was spared the incessant din of motors that accompanies life in the West. The fields that I observed from the train were lovingly tended. There appeared to be plenty of food in the cities.

Shanghai, traditionally the most Westernized Chinese city, retained more of the flavor of old China than Beijing, the capital. There were many narrow streets with small shops selling everything imaginable: cutlery, buttons, dumplings, shoe soles. Foreigners must still have been rare here for unlike Beijing, I was stared at everywhere, and in some places crowds followed me and my official guides.

In Soochow I saw the charming gardens for which it is famous: large enclosed areas with ponds and rocks. In some of them, elderly and even young Chinese sat on benches in silent contemplation. I also visited a factory that manufactured fans. From my travel diary:

> Incredible sight—500 hundred women (a few men) doing by hand the most intricate labor to produce cheap fans (camphor wood and silk, mainly) for export. Work with great intensity. The most expensive fan, intricately carved out of ivory, sells for 800–1000 yuen ($500–600)—it takes "over half a year to produce" and the material is expensive. Wages? Apprentices who remain 3 years in this status get 20 yuen a month—the rest from 35 to 80, with 48 yuen ($30) average. . . . No vacations—get 6 or 7 days off a year, work 48 hours a week (6 days at 8 hours)—which means that average hourly wage is 14 U.S. cents an hour. Women retire at 50, men at 60 and then receive 70 percent of salary as pension. I buy for 50 yuen a nice fan with classical landscape, a whim on which a worker here slaves for 220 hours!!

The last city I visited was Nanking. Here the art museum was opened especially for me: I saw some remarkable watercolors and woodblock prints. Since I have been collecting Japanese prints (Hiroshige's "Great Tokaido") for some time, I had an interest in their Chinese prototypes. Quite unconsciously, whenever shown a print, I would ask for the date of origin because the information was not provided: it turned out that some preceded the Japanese by a century. My museum guide, though obliging, was puzzled why I paid so much attention to the date when a work had been created. I became aware then that our obsession with chronology is not shared by Oriental civilization. A person educated in the history of art can date a Western painting within a few decades. With Oriental paintings this is almost impossible to do because the artists strive not at originality—that is, surpassing their teachers—but at perfection, at the best possible representation of an object, which may have been attained a thousand years earlier. The same holds true of our music. This constant striving for originality is a source of Western creativeness, but in the end it has led to self-destruction. When twentieth-century painters and composers were no longer able to improve on their forerunners, they capitulated. A painting that is a pure white canvass or a composition consisting of several minutes of silence mark a rejection of art, since, by definition, a painting is a design and a musical composition, sound.

I may add that except for banquets, I had to take my meals at the hotels alone: even my assigned guides disappeared during meal times.

Throughout my stay, my hosts never allowed me to forget the perfidy of Russians: they pointed out to me time and again projects that had to be delayed or abandoned because Moscow had reneged on its promises. As I was being escorted to the airport on my last day, the parting message of my guide was: "Remember, Mr. Pipes, the Russians always lie."

The concluding remarks in my travel diary were as follows:

> Very impressive, especially the energy, vitality, work discipline of Chinese people—can only be compared to Japanese and obviously has nothing to do with the political system. Also their courtesy and manner which are much superior to Japanese.
>
> Badly impressed by lack of curiosity of outside world, little evidence of reading, bad taste. A certain "peasantization" of life much in evidence.
>
> But they could well be the people of the future: given technology and a certain intellectual relaxation, what is there to stop them? Certainly not Russia which looks sleazy by comparison. . . .
>
> No attempt was made to "buy me." There was a lot of spontaneous warmth. Unlike Russia which I could never leave fast enough, I left China with certain regret—and a wish to return.

I did return, this time with my wife, in June 1984. I once again gave talks and visited sights, but my impressions did not change. The picture that remains etched most sharply in my mind from this trip is a scene we witnessed in Shanghai. In the evening we took a stroll along the Bund, the section of the city which before 1949 had been home to Western financial and business firms. Along the river embankment I saw a re-markable sight: dozens of young Chinese couples sitting on benches, locked in an embrace and kissing but so completely motionless that at first I took them for statues. They acted in open defiance of communist prudery codes which forbade such displays of passion. As I observed the scene, I became convinced as never before that communism was doomed.

Amalrik and Shcharansky

In the early summer of 1975, my wife and I spent five weeks in Mos-cow while I did research on Struve. The archivists of the Central Archive of the October Revolution were most stingy with materials: I usually got one folder a day, and when done with it, which sometimes took no longer than a few minutes, I was told to return for more the next day. By contrast, one of my American colleagues known for his friendly attitude toward the regime, sitting at a nearby desk, all but drowned in documents.

On this trip I befriended Andrei Amalrik, the author of *Will the Soviet*

Union Survive until 1984? He was an unusual Russian dissident in that he was cheerful rather than gloomy and possessed of a keen sense of humor. There was a childish impudence about him: he did not hate communism, he just laughed at it and mercilessly twitted his police interrogators. We visited his tiny one-room apartment off Arbat, a good part of it occupied by a grand piano which neither he nor his wife, the painter Giuzel, knew how to play. One evening he donned for us the uniform he had worn during his imprisonment at Magadan. I asked him whether his familiarity with us would not cause him harm, and he replied that, on the contrary, the more foreigners he was seen with the less likely was he to be troubled by the police. I later helped him to visit the United States and to spend some time at Harvard. Unfortunately, he died in a car accident in Spain before he had a chance to see his prediction almost come true.

During the month we spent in Moscow, a curious incident occurred. On July 4, 1975, the U.S. Embassy hosted its annual Independence Day party. When it was over, my wife and I went to the apartment of Vitaly Rubin, a specialist on China and what was then called a "refusenik," i.e., a Jewish citizen refused an exit visa to emigrate to Israel. Rubin and his wife, Ina, kept a salon to which they invited anyone interested in Israel and Zionism: they were not dissidents since they regarded themselves as citizens of Israel. For this reason, they did not carefully screen their visitors: as Rubin told me, they had nothing to hide. (Even so, when discussing sensitive matters we communicated by writing in order to foil the KGB men who monitored their apartment from a car parked under their windows and were believed able to overhear conversations.)

That evening among their guests was Anatoly Shcharansky, a courageous Jewish dissident, and also an architect by the name of Vladimir Riabsky with his wife. Rubin had met Riabsky in front of the main synagogue and invited him over although he knew nothing about him. The talk that afternoon, as we sat around the dining room table, was of no particular significance. Shcharansky was silent most of the time. Before the meeting broke up, I told him that after leaving the Soviet Union I would visit Israel where I could contact his wife, if he wished, and tell her that I had found him in good spirits. He agreed and gave me her phone number. But because he forgot to supply the area code, I was unable to reach her. Subsequently, Riabsky invited me and my wife to his home but then, for some reason, canceled the invitation. Later that year, after I had returned to the United States, however, he sent me warm new year's greetings.

I forgot the entire encounter until I learned two years later that Shcharansky had been arrested for espionage. One of the main charges against him at the trial which opened in July 1978 was that he had met with me and allegedly received from me instructions on how to carry out anti-Soviet work. At his trial, a key prosecution witnesses was none other than Riabsky, who described me as "an agent of the American government" who had come to the USSR with "specific instructions to act as a Zionist emissary."[13]

To quote Shcharansky: "Riabsky . . . claimed that Pipes had specifically recommended that we use the Helsinki Final Act to unite the Zionists and the dissidents of the Helsinki Watch group."

During the questioning, Shcharansky addressed Riabsky:

"You say that Pipes appealed to us to unite with the dissidents, utilizing the Helsinki Final Act. Was he familiar with the text of this act?"

"Of course! It was lying right there on the table."

"According to your testimony, the meeting took place on July 4, 1975. Is this correct?"

"Yes, I remember it well. It was American Independence Day, and that was mentioned, too."

"Correct. I also remember that. But the Helsinki Final Act came in August 1975. A month before that it wasn't even clear whether the conference would take place. Yet Rubin already had the text and Pipes was suggesting that we utilize it. How do you explain that?"

I hadn't managed to finish my question when Riabsky's expression quickly began to lose its confidence. He frowned, hesitated, and finally muttered, "Yes, yes, well, yes, apparently I simply made a mistake. The meeting with Pipes took place not in 1975, but on July 4, 1976."

It was easy to prove him wrong. In July of 1976 not only was Pipes not in Moscow but Rubin was already living in Israel.[14]

Such scoundrels kept the Soviet regime going.

Despite the total vacuity of the accusation, in his summary the judge ruled that Shcharansky

had met "confidentially" with American government adviser Richard Pipes at Vitaly Rubin's apartment "and had declared again the need to exert pressure on the USSR, and in particular the expediency of blackmailing the USSR with the threat of curtailing the Soviet-American cultural and scientific relationship". The Judge also alleged that Shcharansky had received from Pipes "concrete recommendations" concerning the methods of "stirring up" anti-Soviet activity inside the Soviet Union, in particular "of rousing national hatred" which, according to the judges' version of what Pipes had said, "influential circles in the USA see as a powerful catalyst, furthering the erosion of Soviet society."*

On the basis of such trumped-up charges, Shcharansky was sentenced to thirteen years "deprivation of liberty," three in prison and the rest in a strict-regime labor camp.

The second half of our Soviet stay we spent in Leningrad, where for nine days I continued my researches on Struve with greater success than in Moscow.

Before proceeding to Leningrad, we took a detour to Warsaw at the invitation of the U.S. ambassador, Richard Davies. It was the first time I had set foot in Poland since October 1939. What a difference between my arrival now and my departure thirty-six years earlier! Then my parents and I had to slink out of the city; now I was welcomed at the airport by the American ambassador with a bouquet of flowers and driven into town in the embassy limousine displaying the Stars and Stripes. It was a powerful emotional experience: I had a sense of personal triumph. We were put up at the ambassador's residence and treated royally. Polish intellectuals, however, shunned us for fear of being compromised: the birthday party Ambassador Davies gave for me was very sparsely attended.

The sense of elation which I had felt on arrival in Warsaw soon gave way to dejection as I walked the familiar streets. Warsaw had never been a beautiful city, I suppose: at any rate, it lacked the elegance of Polish towns under Austrian rule. But it did possess considerable charm which made some people compare it to Paris. Now it was all gone. Following the Polish uprising in 1944, the Germans systematically dynamited and set fire to the entire city save for those parts where they resided. After the Germans had withdrawn, the Poles, under Russian orders, rebuilt Warsaw in the most tasteless manner possible. Apart from the medieval quarter, which they reconstructed faithfully to the smallest detail, they favored huge blocks of office and apartment buildings that resembled barracks. In the center of the city they erected a massive Palace of Culture that dominated the skyline, a copy of the five skyscrapers that Stalin had planted around Moscow: it was as ugly as it was dysfunctional. Its one attraction, according to local residents, lay in the fact that it was the only building in Warsaw from which it could not be seen.

*Gilbert, *Shcharansky*, 268–69. I suppose that the reason I was declared an "American agent" had to do with the fact that in late 1976 I had chaired Team B for the CIA (see below, chapter 3).

Suffice it to say that in one opinion survey conducted in the 1990s Warsaw was voted the "least romantic city" in the world—presumably after Ulan Bator, Tirana, and even Magadan.[15]

My dejection was due primarily to the fact that the city which once been home to 300,000 Jews was now *Judenrein.* I had known this fact, of course, but abstractly: the reality of it was brought home to me as I searched in vain for Jewish faces on the streets. Communist Warsaw was much less oppressive than Communist Moscow, yet in Moscow one saw many Jews, which made its gloom more bearable to me. The Jewish section of Warsaw was totally gone, levelled to the ground, although here and there apartment buildings were beginning to rise on its ruins. My grandmother's house had disappeared, as had the house where Wanda lived. On the vast square in what had been the ghetto stood a socialist-realist statue of a Jewish resistance hero. Buses filled with tourists would pull up from time to time in front of it: people stepped out, snapped a picture or two, and hastily departed. The euphemistically named *Umschlagplatz* or "Transfer Square," where hundreds of thousands of Jews, including my own family and friends, were herded into cattle trains for the voyage to gas chambers of Treblinka, stood abandoned and neglected. It was all unspeakably depressing. Observing these scenes, I had the eerie feeling that I was the last Jew on earth.

What especially bothered me then and on my subsequent visits to Poland is that the presence of Jews in the territory of Poland simply vanished from the consciousness of the Polish people. True, an occasional book recalled Jewish life in Poland, but it left hardly any trace in the nation's collective memory. And this despite the fact that Jews had lived in Poland for seven centuries during which they made significant contributions to the country's economy and, in more recent times, its culture. It was as if they had never existed.

The site of the house where we had lived in 1939 was now occupied by the Palace of Culture. But four of our previous residences survived intact, presumably because they had been requisitioned by the Germans. I visited each one and experienced the peculiar sensation of having been there and yet being a stranger. I have revisited Poland a number of times since. I was very well treated by the government and the intellectuals of postcommunist Poland and even honored with a high Polish decoration, yet I have never been able to rid myself of the feeling that I and my people have been rejected by our homeland.

Irene, 1946.

Our wedding: Hotel Delmonico. New York City, September 1, 1946.

Our parents, Watertown, 1949. Irene's parents, second and third from left, her sister, Hanna, second from right.

Working on the *Formation of the Soviet Union,* my first book. Watertown, Massachusetts, 1951.

Irene in Celerina, Switzerland, 1957.

With the head of Central Asia's Muslims. Tashkent, April 1957.

With Alexander Kerensky in Stanford, California, summer 1959.

Freshly baked professor in his Widener study, c. 1960. Lyman W. Fisher/Copyright, *The Christian Science Monitor*.

Our sons, Steven (eight) and Daniel (thirteen) at an improvised Passover.
Paris, 1962.

Parents: last picture together. Chesham, New Hampshire, 1971.

With my graduate students Dan Orlovsky (now teaching at Southern
Methodist University) and Nina Tumarkin (now at Wellesley College),
1971.

Skating at the
Evening with
Champions at
Harvard, 1972.

With the Polish philosopher Leszek Kołakowski, the Italian historian
Franco Venturi (bearded), and Isaiah Berlin (with his back to the camera).
Oxford, February 1974.

Isaiah Berlin, aged eighty-four. London, 1993.

Edmund Wilson when we knew him. Photograph courtesy James A. Sugar.

With Andrei Amalrik. Outside Moscow, July 1975.

China: with the 176th Division, spring 1978.

My portrait by *People* magazine, 1977. Photograph courtesy of Arthur Grace.

THREE

Washington

Détente

I have always had an interest in politics but it was never a consuming
passion. I was quite prepared to express my opinions on the Soviet
Union and give advice to politicians interested in them, but I had no
ambition to hold office. Such vanity as I possess was and remains that of
an intellectual who wants to influence the way people think and feel
rather than one who enjoys power over them or craves the status of a
celebrity. My modest political career was unsought and came unasked.

The 1960s and 1970s was a period of "détente." The massive buildup
of nuclear arsenals in both the United States and the Soviet Union had
persuaded many in the West that the only alternative to nuclear war and
the extinction of life on earth was some kind of accommodation between
the two "superpowers." This belief led politicians and political scientists
("Sovietologists" as they came to be known) to devise a foreign policy
model which called for cooperation with the Russians where possible
and resistance to them where necessary. But when was it necessary to
resist? If the only alternative to nuclear holocaust was cooperation, then
resistance was in effect eliminated since nothing was worth annihilation. The slogan "Better Red than Dead" honestly expressed the premise
of those who thought in those terms. To buttress their position and the
policy recommendations that flowed from it, the proponents of détente
argued that a process of "convergence" between democracy and communism was already under way: hence those who harped on the differences
between the two systems and called for an aggressive anticommunist
stance—labeled "cold warriors"—were dangerous lunatics capable of ig-
niting World War III.

To understand the attitudes—and failures—of the Sovietological community in the United States one must bear in mind the conditions under which the study of the Soviet Union had gotten underway in this country. It first emerged at the start of the Cold War in the 1950s and took off, as it were, in 1957, after the Russians had launched the Sputnik, a potential weapon system which (for the first time in U.S. history) directly threatened its security and even survival. It is commonly believed that the circumstance of its origin infused Sovietology with irreconcilable hostility toward communism and the USSR, breeding a Cold War mentality. In fact, it had the very opposite effect. In Europe, where communist ideology had a history going back at least to the middle of the nineteenth century and communist parties had come into being in the early 1920s, scholars and publicists had analyzed communism on its own merits for a century before it attracted the attention of the United States. Some of them— notably the Poles—had predicted with astonishing accuracy the nature of a communist regime, anticipating its political despotism and economic failures.

In the United States, such analysis was impeded by the fact that the phenomenon of communism came to be inextricably linked with the dread of nuclear war. Largely ignorant of Marxist theory and the history of both Russia and the Soviet Union, Americans tended to see the problem exclusively in foreign policy terms: that is, how to avoid the conflict between the two camps leading to a nuclear holocaust. It made them conciliatory and this meant that they stressed positive developments in the Communist bloc and interpreted them in the best possible light. Quite unconsciously they minimized differences and emphasized similarities.

However well intentioned the sentiments behind this attitude, they misconstrued reality, as inevitably happens when truth is subordinated to politics. The Sovietological community was first and foremost committed to bringing the two adversaries together and in so doing ignored or downplayed whatever ran counter to this objective. As a result, it grossly misunderstood the nature of communist regimes and the forces that animated them.

This approach enjoyed popularity because it carried a comforting message. It appealed to those who had no sympathy for communism but were frightened of nuclear war and liked to think that patience and understanding would persuade the Russians to adopt a more friendly stance. Every evidence to the contrary was rationalized. Thus when it became apparent that the Soviet Union, having attained by 1970 nuclear parity with the United States, nevertheless proceeded to deploy additional missile systems, some of them MIRVed, this conduct was explained by (1) the alleged "paranoia" of Russians induced by frequent foreign invasions, or (2) the need to confront the Chinese with whom at the time they were at daggers drawn. Such rationalizations of what to any unprejudiced observer were aggressive buildups were the daily bread of opinion makers.

The misunderstanding of Russian motives and intentions had also deeper cultural causes. For most Americans the axiom that all people are equal leads, more or less inadvertently, to the belief that they are the same by which they mean that they are at heart like themselves so that, given a chance, they would behave like themselves. If a nation behaves aggressively toward the United States, it is because it is justly aggrieved: by extrapolation, the blame for aggression falls not on the aggressor but on his victim. The logic is quite flawed but psychologically understandable. Throughout the years of the Cold War, a high proportion of educated, affluent Americans felt guilty of provoking the Russians and pressed for concessions to them to make them feel more "secure."*

The Russians exploited such American perceptions with admirable skill. They projected the image of a country aspiring to become another United States—if not, perhaps, as affluent then, at any rate, socially more just. Americans fell for this cynical propaganda because they liked to believe both in fundamental human goodness and the desire of the world to emulate the American way of life. *The Soviet Union Today,* the slick propaganda magazine distributed in the United States, resembled remarkably the equally slick *Amerika,* which had great difficulty gaining distribution there. For the American elite, the Russians fielded teams of crafty propagandists, like the loathsome Georgii Arbatov, the head of the U.S.A. Institute, an organ of the KGB, who played to perfection the role of a pipe-puffing, jolly fellow which many businessmen and academics found irresistible. By pretending not to take communist ideology seriously and cracking an occasional joke about their regime, the Arbatovs made one wonder what the East-West confrontation was all about.

The theoretical foundation of this approach, whose true basis was fear coupled with greed, came from the Sovietological profession, recruited mainly from university departments of political science, economics, and sociology and enthusiastically endorsed by the scientific

---

*I must confess with shame that for a short time, in the years immediately following World War II, I, too, fell victim of this kind of reasoning. In November 1948, disgusted by what I considered Truman's provocatively aggressive policies toward the Soviet Union, I voted for Henry Wallace, a presidential candidate backed by the Communist Party.

community for which ideology and politics were not serious matters. Lavishly funded by the government and private foundations, its members held endless conferences in the United States, Europe and the USSR, published no end of symposia, and collaborated on many research projects. For the sake of harmony, scholars who held significantly different views were barred from these activities. In this manner, considerable unanimity was obtained and "group think" flourished. That is not to say that there was no room for controversy: there was room but it was strictly circumscribed. Thus, for example, it was permissible to maintain that the Soviet regime was more stable or less stable but not that it was unstable.

Insisting that moral judgments have no place in science (and they considered themselves scientists) the Sovietologists treated societies as if they were mechanisms. One of their basic premises held that all societies performed the same "functions," even if in different ways, on which grounds they interpreted in familiar terms all those features of the communist regime which to a mind untutored in social science appeared outlandish. One such "expert," for example, found no significant difference between the way New Haven was administered and any city of similar size in the Soviet Union.* The net result of this methodology was to depict communist societies as not fundamentally different from democratic ones: a conclusion that reinforced the policy recommendation that we could and should come to terms with them.

In this manner a consensus was forged. Nothing, not even travel to the Soviet Union or the appearance in the West of tens of thousands of Jewish refugees with their own tales to tell, could sway the Sovietological profession in its opinions because here science coincided with self-interest. None of these experts asked themselves—at any rate, aloud—such obvious questions as, for example, if things were indeed so normal and stable there, why did communist governments prevent their citizens from freely traveling abroad? or why did they insist on unanimity of public opinion? or why did they allow only one candidate and one party to run in "elections"? Such embarrassing questions were ignored, and when raised, went unanswered. To an unprejudiced mind such facts about the USSR suggested insecurity, and insecurity indicated fragility.

One had to see how American academics scraped and bowed before

---

*In the words of Jerry F. Hough: "If we could engage in a detailed case study of local government in the Soviet Union, it is highly probable that we would arrive at many of the same conclusions that Robert Dahl did in his study of New Haven": How the Soviet Union Is Governed (Cambridge, Mass., 1979), 512.

their Soviet "colleagues," most of whom carried out intelligence missions, at least part time, how ready they were to advise the KGB through its front organizations while indignantly refusing to cooperate with the CIA. Sometimes I would listen with disbelief when I heard them instruct visiting Soviet delegations on how to hoodwink the U.S. government. They would go to nearly any length to qualify for Soviet visas and sustain contact with their Soviet counterparts. Elena Bonner, Sakharov's wife, spoke to me with bitterness in March 1986 of her inability to persuade American scientists to come to the assistance of her imprisoned husband by declaring a boycott of Soviet conferences: they sympathized with her but thought it essential to "stay in touch."

Once in a while I publicly took issue with such positions as, for instance, in 1959 in a brief and angry essay in the *New Leader,* which the *Washington Post* reprinted under the title "Now It's the Babbitts Have Crush on Soviet," where I expressed disgust with the collective hysteria that had seized the United States following the launching of the Sputnik and the attendant admiration for the USSR for its demonstrated scientific competence. I made such interventions only sporadically: they sufficed, however, to earn me the reputation of a cold warrior that kept me out of Dartmouth, Pugwash, and similar conclaves devoted to the creation of an atmosphere of global good will, where like spoke to like and dissent would have injected a jarring note.

Those who called me a cold warrior apparently expected me to cringe. In fact, I accepted the title proudly. In dealing with the Soviet Union there were only two alternatives to the Cold War—appeasement, which promoted communist objectives, or war, which threatened general destruction. The Cold War steered a sensible middle road between these extremes: it was a policy that required sangfroid. Pursued by the United States from 1948 until 1991, with the interruption for détente, it achieved its purpose in speeding the downfall of the communist empire without recourse to arms.

An opportunity to launch a broad critique of détente and all that went with it presented itself in December 1969 when I was invited to deliver a paper at the annual gathering of the American Historical Association in Washington, D.C. The session was devoted to U.S.-Soviet relations: George Kennan and Louis Fischer were scheduled to be the commentators, with Harvard's William Langer chairing. Kennan withdrew for some reason, which meant that the only comment came from Fischer, a self-important journalist who in the 1930s contributed his bit to misinforming the American public about the USSR. My paper, which subsequently appeared in the London monthly *Encounter,* under the title "Russia's Mission, America's Destiny," drew an impassable line separating the two systems on both historical and ideological grounds. There was no "convergence" and there could be none: one or the other must give way. I concluded:

> There is little comfort in these reflections for anyone who believes that somehow, by a magic marriage of good will and enlightened self-interest, the foreign policies of the United States and Russia will come to coincide. The notion of what is "good" and what is "self-interest" is not the same for those who make policy in the two countries. The condition of international equilibrium existing since the mid-1950's, which so far has provided a precarious peace, does not result from the acceptance by the Communist leadership of the principle of an international community of interest. As seen from there, the cosmos consists not of majestic planets revolving according to the laws of nature, each in its allotted orbit, in the midst of which man has been placed to prove his worth. The vision there— when it is not completely drowned in cynicism—is one of chaos in which wondrous and terrible things happen, and God, in the guise of History, renders implacable Final Judgment.[1]

Fischer's contribution consisted of repeating, over and over and with mounting emphasis, "politics is power"—a statement about as meaningful as "business is money" or "medicine is healing."

Present in the audience at this session was Dorothy Fosdick, the daughter of the famous Protestant theologian and a close advisor of Henry Jackson, the Democratic senator from the state of Washington. Jackson, one of the most perceptive as well as incorruptible politicians I have ever met, took strong objection to détente and the whole drift of U.S. policy toward Russia. In this, he sought the support of specialists. After Ms. Fosdick had reported to him and his foreign policy advisor, Richard Perle, what I had said, Jackson invited me to testify at a March 1970 Senate hearing on the proposed SALT treaty. In my testimony I tried to get across that what mattered were not the capabilities of weapons but the psychology and political mentality of the people wielding them. Communists could not accept the notion of parity basic to American nuclear strategy because to do so would create a military equilibrium, and a military equilibrium meant that they could no longer count on victory in the global conflict which served as justification for both their dictatorship and the poverty in which they kept their subjects. Another professor testified along with me: when the session ended, he confided to me that he shared my views but preferred not to express them publicly for fear of being turned down for a Soviet visa. Jackson subsequently attached me as a consultant to his Committee on National Security and International Operations, which in 1972 published a paper I had delivered the previous year in Tel Aviv on "Some Operational Principles of Soviet Foreign Policy." My admiration for him never flagged, though I was disappointed by the haste with which he withdrew from the presidential race in 1976 after losing Pennsylvania. His death in 1983 loosened further my attachment to the Democratic Party, weakened a decade earlier by the nomination of George McGovern as its presidential candidate.

As a result of this political involvement, I was invited in 1973 to become senior consultant to the Stanford Research Institute (SRI), an organization based in Palo Alto, California, which maintained in Washington a Center for Strategic Studies under the direction of Richard B. Foster. The government regarded SRI as a right-wing, antidétente outfit and allocated to it meager research funds. My idea of systematically studying Soviet "grand strategy" elicited nothing but derision from State and Defense Department personnel. For the next several years I lectured, gave congressional testimony, and published widely on issues of national security, which established me as something of a leading proponent of the "hard line" vis-à-vis the USSR. (This is what it was invariably called: the contrary view was always referred to as "moderate," never "soft-line.")

In 1974, SRI organized in Moscow a joint conference with two Russian foreign policy institutes: it was the latter's effort to reach out to the conservative wing of American opinion. During one of the sessions I said some rather harsh things about Soviet policy in the Middle East, which at the time was directed against Israel and involved the deployment of Soviet military personnel. The American delegates congratulated me in private although publicly they remained silent. Following this session, one of the Soviet participants, Evgenii Primakov, a Middle East specialist, took me aside. He told me that I misunderstood Soviet policy in the Middle East and that the USSR could never, under any circumstances, allow the destruction of the State of Israel. "Why?" I asked. Just as he was about to reply, the door opened and Arbatov entered the room, asking us to rejoin the conference. I never found out the answer. But neither did I expect that Primakov, then a middle-level apparatchik with KGB connections, would in time become postcommunist Russia's prime minister and a candidate for the office of president. He impressed me as a shrewd bureaucrat, nonideological and lacking in a broader perspective.

Team B

In the summer of 1976, which I spent in London—a summer memorable for the drought that killed many trees in Hyde Park—I received a call from SRI's Dick Foster inquiring how soon I expected to return home. He would not tell me why he wanted to know except to say that there was an important assignment awaiting me. I planned to leave in a few days anyway.

On the bus to Heathrow a curious incident occurred. A young man, walking by me to the rear of the bus, deliberately kicked my foot, which stuck out a bit in the aisle; he repeated this act even more deliberately a few minutes later. I jumped to my feet and called him "deranged." "Go ahead, hit me!" he taunted. "A man your age should sit quietly in the corner," he added. I took this behavior to be a deliberate provocation though by whom and for what purpose I had no idea.

Then on the airplane, after I had taken the seat assigned to me, by the window alongside two passengers, the steward called out my name over the loudspeaker and asked me to move to another window, which had a vacant middle seat. This seat was soon occupied by a young woman who spoke some Russian and seemed to know who I was. We talked most of the way to Boston. This, too, had never happened to me before and made me wonder what lay behind it.

As soon as I returned to Boston (it was toward the end of July) I went to Washington to see Foster. The assignment he outlined to me was, indeed, most interesting and in some ways would change the course of my life. He had been approached by the CIA with a request for me to head a very secret project on its behalf. Its background was as follows: The intelligence community had been divided for some time over the meaning of the Soviet nuclear buildup of the 1970s as manifested in the deployment of new generations of both strategic and tactical missiles. According to the Mutual Assured Destruction or MAD doctrine, then accepted as axiomatic in academic as well as intelligence circles, nuclear weapons had no utility other than to serve as a deterrent against nuclear threats. A top secret CIA memorandum issued in April 1972 on "Soviet Defense Policy, 1962–1972" asserted that the Soviet leadership shared this view, although it offered no evidence for its claim: "The Soviets . . .

consider [their strategic] forces primarily as a deterrent. The major effort has been on programs which assure the ability of these forces to absorb a U.S. strike and still be able to return a devastating blow."[2] Hence, once an adequate level of deterrence had been attained—in the definition of Defense Secretary Robert MacNamara, one that assured the destruction of 25 percent of the aggressor's population and 50 percent of his industries—further deployments were not only useless but dangerously provocative. Rather than subject the MAD doctrine to reassessment, the CIA persisted in finding various explanations for the Soviet buildup consistent with it. It continued to do so although some competent observers, such as James Schlesinger and Albert Wohlstetter, expressed serious doubts about it. As is customary with bureaucratic bodies, the agency protected itself by conceding that the USSR was "influenced by a military doctrine which calls for war-winning capabilities" and rejecting "mutual assured destruction," but it dismissed such considerations as essentially theoretical, with MAD being "a reality which will be operative at least for the next decade."*

To prevent intellectual inbreeding and the congruous analyses likely to result from it, the government had established an overseer body called the President's Foreign Intelligence Advisory Board or PFIAB. In mid-1976 this group, consisting of sixteen persons, was chaired by an ebullient New York economist and head of the International Rescue Committee, Leo Cherne. It counted among its members Clare Boothe Luce; Edwin Land, the founder of Polaroid; George P. Shultz, the future secretary of state; Robert W. Galvin, the head of Motorola; the well-known Washington attorney Edward Bennett Williams; along with several retired generals and admirals. Troubled by the comforting assessments of Soviet nuclear deployments provided by the agency, PFIAB in August 1975 requested an independent audit of the evidence. William Colby, the head of the CIA then, would not hear of such an intrusion and in April 1976 proposed instead an in-house review. According to Lionel Olmer, PFIAB's executive secretary at the time: "The CIA produced a 'track record' study about 75 pages long. It was so astonishing that [George] Bush (Colby was gone by then) had absolutely no option but to accept the Team A–Team B proposal. The study was so condemnatory of the performance of the [intelligence] community over a period of ten

---

*National Intelligence Estimate 11-3/8-75, 16. The United States formally abandoned the MAD doctrine in 2002 under President George W. Bush by withdrawing from the ABM Treaty and declaring its readiness to construct antiballistic defenses and, under certain circumstances, to launch a preemptive strike.

years on those three issues [see below] that it left no room for argument that something ought to be done."[3]

After George Bush had taken over as director of Central Intelligence in early 1976, Cherne approached President Ford with a request for an external audit. Ford agreed and Bush fell in line. It was resolved to conduct an experiment in "competitive analysis" in the course of which six teams of experts, three from the CIA (Teams A) and three made up of outsiders (Teams B), would address independently of each other the same evidence in three areas—Soviet air defenses, missile accuracies, and strategic objectives, the most disturbing as well as controversial aspects of the Soviet military effort, all three of direct bearing on the premises underpinning our defense strategy.

I have described elsewhere in some detail what came to be known as the "Team A–Team B" experiment,[4] and thus here I will confine myself to a few generalities. By far the most important of the three experiments in competitive analysis concerned the Soviet strategic doctrine: for if the continuing deployments of Soviet ICBMs and other weapons' systems, both offensive and defensive, could be shown to signify Moscow's rejection of the MAD doctrine, then the entire U.S. nuclear strategy rested on a false premise with potentially catastrophic consequences. The agency first offered the chairmanship of the proposed team of outsiders on Soviet strategic objectives to Foy Kohler, the onetime ambassador to Moscow, then living in retirement in Florida, but he declined on grounds of ill health. Seymour Weiss, a retired Defense Department official, also felt that his health was not up to it. (Rumors had it, however, that his nomination was vetoed by the State Department on the grounds that as ambassador to the Bahamas he should not be distracted from his duties.) I was the third choice, appointed by George Bush at the recommendation of his staff of National Intelligence Officers.

I accepted the offer with some hesitation from fear that the assignment required knowledge of missile technology that I did not possess. But Foster persuaded me that there was no shortage of experts on such technology whom I could engage: what was needed was an understanding of the Soviet mindset, of the way the Soviet military looked on weapons. I queried both Robert Galvin, who was PFIAB's liaison with our Team B, and Henry Knoche, the deputy director of the CIA, about the scope of our undertaking but received vague answers and was told to make it as broad or narrow as we found it necessary. These responses refute the charge made later that Team B exceeded its "mandate."

The group that I assembled was outstanding. Two military officers, retired General John Vogt and Major General Jasper Welch, came from a list supplied by the agency. The others I selected. They were Paul Nitze, the onetime secretary of the navy and deputy secretary of defense; retired Lieutenant General Daniel Graham, the former head of the Defense Intelligence Agency; Paul Wolfowitz of the Arms Control and Disarmament Agency, subsequently deputy secretary of defense in the George W. Bush administration; Thomas Wolfe of the RAND Corporation; and Professor William Van Cleave of the University of Southern California. Kohler and Weiss served as consultants. We divided the work among ourselves and pored over the documentation which the agency placed at our disposal. We had to work rapidly because our report, as that of the CIA, was due in mid-December when the document, formally designated as NIE (National Intelligence Estimate) 11-3/8-75—the most important single product of the intelligence community and the basis of the annual defense budget presented to Congress—had to be made available.*

I did my share of the work while carrying a full teaching load: I taught my lecture courses and seminar the first half of the week and spent the second half in Washington. In all, between August 25 and November 23, Team B held ten meetings. I analyzed the texts of the CIA's past estimates in order to identify their unspoken assumptions, leaving the job of evaluating Soviet deployments to my more knowledgeable colleagues.

On November 5, the two teams, having previously exchanged drafts, met at CIA Headquarters at Langley in what turned out to be a tense confrontation. The agency fielded junior analysts for Team A whereas our team consisted of mature and experienced political and military figures: it was an engagement that pitted lieutenants against generals. The encounter, unfair by its very format, proved a disaster for the CIA as our people simply tore to shreds their criticism of our draft. On December 2, Team A and Team B presented their respective cases for PFIAB: the former's were conspicuously revised compared to what they had been one month earlier—whether as a result of Bush's pressure or the

*Liaison between Team B and the CIA was maintained by a CIA employee named John Paisley. Initially, our group was known as "the Paisley project"—the name Team B was coined later. Paisley retired from the agency in 1974, where he had served as deputy chief of the Office of Strategic Research that dealt with assessments of Soviet nuclear forces. In October 1978, two years after our work had been completed, he was found dead, a gunshot wound in his head, floating in Chesapeake Bay with thirty-eight pounds of diver's weights strapped to his body. He is reported to have had aboard his sailboat Team B materials as well as sophisticated radio equipment. It has never been determined whether he had committed suicide or was murdered, or even whether the decomposed body found and promptly cremated was his. See Tad Szulz in *New York Times Magazine,* January 7, 1979, pp. 13, 15, 60, 62.

force of our arguments I am unable to say. Team A's revised draft stressed the Soviet drive for a war-winning capability not, as before, as a theoretical possibility, but as a reality.[5] Even so, our case was much more stark, and Clare Boothe Luce told me afterwards that after we had left the room, the group sat in stunned silence for a while, so struck were they by the case I had made on behalf of our team—a case they had long suspected to be correct but which no one had previously made to them.

Our final report, submitted in December, consisted of three parts. In the first, which I drafted, previous strategic estimates by the CIA were subjected to methodological criticism. Part 2 consisted of analyses of ten Soviet weapons systems, written by individual members of the team, and the last part, drafted collectively, presented our conclusions and recommendations.

Our overall judgment was that CIA assessments had "substantially misperceived the motivations behind Soviet strategic programs" and as a consequence "tended consistently to underestimate their intensity, scope, and implicit threat:"*

> This misperception has been due in considerable measure to concentration on the so-called hard data, that is, data collected by technical means, and the resultant tendency to interpret these data in a manner reflecting basic U.S. concepts while slighting or misinterpreting the large body of "soft" data concerning Soviet strategic concepts. The failure to take into account or accurately to assess such soft data sources has resulted in the NIE's not addressing themselves systematically to the broader political purposes which underlie and explain Soviet strategic objectives. Since, however, the political context cannot be altogether avoided, the drafters of the NIEs have fallen into the habit of injecting into key judgments of the executive summaries impressionistic assessments based on "mirror-imaging," i.e., the attribution to Soviet decision-makers of such forms of behavior as might be expected from their U.S. counterparts under analogous circumstances.

The report went on to point out that the Soviet leaders did not think in stark dichotomies common to our culture (e.g., war vs. peace, confrontation vs. détente, etc.) but "dialectically," treating them as "complementary or mutually supporting concepts." One consequence of ignoring this fact was to assume that Moscow viewed the utility of nuclear weapons exclusively in terms of deterrence, treating "deterrence as an

---

*Officially published in a highly classified document called "Intelligence Community Experiment in Competitive Analysis. Soviet Strategic Objectives: An Alternative View," it was declassified and released, with some excisions, in September 1992.

alternative to a war-fighting capability rather than as complementary to it." Evidence, however, indicated that Soviet leaders

> are first and foremost offensively rather than defensively minded. They think not in terms of nuclear stability, mutual assured destruction, or strategic sufficiency, but of an effective war-fighting capability. They believe that the probability of a general nuclear war can be reduced by building up one's own strategic forces, but that it cannot be altogether eliminated, and that therefore one has to be prepared for such a war as if it were unavoidable and be prepared to strike first if it appears imminent.

In sum, the issue was one of understanding a different culture. The strategic balance was determined not just by the relative power of the two arsenals confronting each other but also and above all by the mentality and intentions of the people controlling them. (In 1940, for example, the Allies had deployed in France more men and more tanks than Germany, and yet they suffered a crushing defeat because their generals, conditioned by the experience of World War I, thought defensively and attributed a similar mindset to the enemy.)

These general conclusions were supported by detailed analyses of several specific Soviet nuclear programs: intercontinental ballistic missiles; civil defense; hardening of command and control facilities; mobile missiles; strategic bombers; and so on. We also attached, separately, a set of recommendations on ways of improving the NIE process, stressing the need to think in Soviet categories in order to avoid mirror-imaging, abstaining from offhand "net assessments," viewing the Soviet military effort in an integrated manner, resisting to the maximum extent possible political pressures on the estimating process, and providing diverse interpretations of the evidence.

On December 21 I presented our findings in a huge auditorium at Langley to the assembled CIA personnel. When the meeting was over, Bush, who was present, invited the three Team Bs to a private luncheon. It struck me that even though our team had the most distinguished personnel by far, Bush did not invite any of us to his table. He seemed deeply to fear the repercussions of the Team A–Team B experiment and probably regretted having authorized it. While our work was still in progress, word reached me that he had queried associates what effect it could have on his political future. Lack of political courage was his outstanding weakness: it would stamp his presidency with the brand of mediocrity. In my journal, under the date January 1, 1982, by which time I had gotten to know him better, I wrote of Bush, "I rather doubt he had much strength of character and self-confidence," which Ronald Reagan possessed in overabundance.

Although the entire undertaking was meant to be secret, word soon leaked. The first report, quite accurate, written by William Beecher, appeared in the *Boston Globe* on October 20, but it attracted little attention. The alarm bells began to ring only following a front-page story in the Sunday *New York Times* of December 26, 1976, filed by David Binder, who in the 1950s had been a tutee of mine in History and Literature. Binder telephoned me on December 20 requesting an interview. When I told him I could not grant him one, he informed me that the agency had already briefed him on this project. I contacted Richard Lehman, deputy to the director of central intelligence for national intelligence, requesting authorization, which he readily granted. I met with Binder at National Airport on December 21 for some thirty minutes. It was clear to me that he had interviewed high CIA officials and possibly Bush himself. Even so, after his article had appeared, I was suspected of being the "leaker." On December 30, someone asked the columnist Joseph Kraft to warn me against talking. Today, I would have asked him to leave; at that time I politely informed him that I considered leaking of state secrets to be a betrayal of trust. It rather surprised me, therefore, that in an appearance on CBS's "Face the Nation," on January 2, 1977, Bush hinted that Team B was the source of the leaks.

During the next several weeks things were in turmoil. The *New York Times,* in a typically pompous editorial, speaking from the journalistic Mt. Olympus where its editorial writers make their home, questioned the motives and intentions of Team B while ridiculing its effort to examine the motives and intentions of the Soviet military. It did so without having had access to the highly classified Team B report, although it undoubtedly got some biased leaks from the CIA directorate.[6] Kissinger dismissed the Team B report as "aimed at sabotaging a new treaty limiting arms" and called for a "rational debate on the issue of nuclear strategy"—"rational" presumably being defined as one that concurred with his own view that it was irrational to strive for nuclear superiority.[7]

The CIA immediately went on the counteroffensive to defend itself and impugn the motives of Team B. It did so through the medium of the Senate Select Committee on Intelligence chaired by Senator Daniel Inouye of Hawaii whose staff director, William Green Miller, I had known in the 1950s at Harvard as member of the staff of History and Literature. Miller had had to resign from the Foreign Service for displaying excessive zeal in seeking to topple the shah of Iran. Later, as an aide to Senator John Sherman Cooper, he helped draft the Cooper-Church Amendment that cut off aid to Vietnam. He arranged the hearings in such a way that not a single member of Team B was invited to testify: the prosecution had the field to itself. It was he also who selected Harold Ford to direct this study—an honorable man but one who, by virtue of his past career in the CIA, could hardly be expected to display impartiality.

Inoyoue appointed Senator Adlai Stevenson Jr. to head a subcommittee to determine whether the experiment in competitive analysis did not exert pressure on the CIA to "slant" its conclusions. I learned of its report, prepared in utmost secrecy, from Graham and requested Stevenson to grant permission to Graham, Nitze, and myself to read and respond to it. Permission was granted. What I read in August 1977 was appalling. The report charged that Team B had exceeded its mandate, that it made no reference to "raw data," that it "colluded" with PFIAB in the selection of personnel and the drawing up of conclusions, and even that it had reached its conclusions before beginning work.[8] (The latter charge came from Paisley's testimony.) It further hinted that Team B bore responsibility for leaking its findings to the press. The whole experiment was dismissed as having made no "constructive contribution" to improving NIEs. Yet at the same time, contradicting itself, the report agreed with many of our criticisms of the NIEs, including their stress on engineering at the expense of political science—that is, divorcing weapons from policy.

Senator Gary Hart, or more likely a staff member writing on his behalf, accused us of being in cahoots with the military-industrial complex and seeking with our estimate to force the incoming Carter administration to increase the defense budget: "The use of selected outside experts was little more than camouflage for a political effort to force the NIE to take a more grave view of the Soviet strategic threat" for purposes of increasing defense appropriations.

We were vigorously defended by Senators Daniel Patrick Moynihan and Malcolm Wallop. A year later, in a statement attached to the Senate Intelligence Committee's public release on the Team A–Team B experiment, Moynihan asserted that Team B's view that Russia was seeking superiority in strategic weapons "has gone from heresy to respectability, if not orthodoxy" in "what might be called official Washington."[9] Senator Wallop noted correctly that the revised Senate report was fundamentally flawed in that, in its own words, "it makes no attempt to judge which group's estimates concerning the USSR are correct," focusing instead on "procedural issues."

During the month that followed—it coincided with the installation of the Carter administration—I was bombarded with invitations from the major TV networks, all of which I turned down. I was also flooded with letters, all of which I tried to answer, from people across the country, some of whom praised me, while others condemned. I did, however, give a public speech on the Team B affair to a packed audience at the Lisner Auditorium of George Washington University on February 16.

Brezhnev felt impelled in January 1977 to deliver an address in Tula, directed at president-elect Carter, in which he indignantly denied that his country strove for military superiority or contemplated fighting and winning a nuclear war. The only effect of his speech was severely to tighten censorship of discussions of nuclear strategy in Soviet publications.

It is indicative of my inexperience in Washington's ways that reading the U.S. media on Team B I should have been surprised that everyone asked only one of two secondary questions: what were our motives and what were the implications of our findings? No one, the Senate Intelligence Committee included, seemed interested in finding out whether we perhaps were right. But this was nothing new. Montaigne four centuries earlier had remarked on this manner of thinking when he wrote, "I see ordinarily that men, when facts are put before them, are more ready to amuse themselves by inquiring into their reasons than by inquiring into their truth."

Team B had two important effects. For one, it deeply influenced Reagan and the thinking of the Reagan administration: this was so much the case, that some journalists initially referred to the Reagan administration as "Team B." Second, it contributed to improving the estimating process at the CIA. Although no outside teams were ever again employed, competitive analysis became part of the estimating process, in that estimates henceforth "routinely include[d] dissenting opinion."[10]

Its victim was PFIAB, which paid for its involvement in the Team B affair by being abolished by President Carter. As a result, the caliber of CIA reporting deteriorated so quickly for lack of oversight that in November 1978, President Carter formally reprimanded Admiral Stansfield Turner, its new director, for the low quality of political intelligence it was submitting to him.[11] One year later came the Soviet invasion of Afghanistan, for which the CIA was completely unprepared: once again it had mirror-imagined, convinced that after our fiasco in Vietnam, Moscow would not dare to engage its armed forces in a Third World country in the grip of a fanatical ideology.

While Team B was at work, Nitze and several other prominent public figures organized the Committee on the Present Danger (CPD) to alert public opinion to the growing disparity in the military balance between the United States and the Soviet Union. He, David Packard, the co-founder of Hewlett-Packard, and Eugene Rostow, the onetime dean of the Yale Law School, were the moving spirits behind this organization. Among the members of the executive committee were ex-Secretary of the Treasury Henry Fowler; ex-Chief of Naval Operations Admiral Elmo Zumwald; David Acheson, Dean Acheson's son; and Richard V. Allen, a Republican specialist on foreign affairs. Ronald Reagan served on its board of directors. As soon as Team B disbanded, I was invited to join the executive committee of the CPD. I drafted for it a number of programmatic statements, beginning with "What is the Soviet Union up to?" (April 1977), in which I stressed the need to understand Soviet behavior in terms of Russia's history and the communist concept of grand strategy.[12] The reputation of the committee's personnel and, I like to think, the persuasiveness of its argument assured it of a large and respectful audience. We spread the message far and wide through publications and lectures, and we certainly had an impact, counterbalancing the influence of the arms control lobby. Suffice it to say that our unhappy opponents, always quick with slogans and ad hominem appeals, declared that the real danger facing the United States was not the Soviet Union but the Committee on the Present Danger.

I was also amused to see how readily American liberals adopted the communist habit of attributing communist views to the critics of communism. Thus one Robert Scheer in the November 1982 issue of *Playboy* (!) claimed to describe "How the U.S. government has come under the control of men who believe that nuclear war can be waged and won."* I believe that we prevailed in the debate with the election of Reagan and the massive military buildup which followed because while we argued on the basis of facts our opponents either spoke in terms of vague generalities or else resorted to ridicule and abuse.

The greatest stir caused by anything I ever wrote was occasioned by

---

*This technique is stock in trade for liberals. In 1998, when Kenneth Starr reported in detail on the sexual escapades of President Clinton in order to prove that in denying them under oath he had committed perjury, he was labeled "sex obsessed." Similarly, in the 1930s, English appeasers called Winston Churchill a "war monger" for warning that Germany was arming to wage war.

the article "Why the Soviet Union Thinks It Could Fight and Win a Nuclear War" commissioned by Norman Podhoretz, the editor of *Commentary,* and published in its July 1977 issue. Here, carefully avoiding any reference to classified sources and having the text cleared by the CIA, I summarized the basic findings of Team B.

The vindication of Team B's work came two years after it had disbanded. On taking office, the Carter administration treated Team B's conclusions with great skepticism. Although Admiral Turner promptly agreed with them, expressing the view that Moscow was indeed seeking military superiority, incoming Secretary of Defense Harold Brown poohpoohed this thesis, as did Cyrus Vance, the new secretary of state. However, at the insistence of Zbigniew Brzezinski, Carter's national security advisor, a secret study was launched to determine the validity of Team B's conclusions. Less than a year after Team B had completed its work, Harold Brown conceded publicly that should "present trends continue" in Soviet nuclear deployments, in five years the situation could be "serious," adding that there was "a potential danger" the Soviets are "preparing to fight a nuclear war rather than simply deter one."[13] The secret conclusions of this inquiry were partly released in January-February 1979. According to the *New York Times:* "The study [Presidential Directive 59] concluded that Moscow did not accept the concept of 'assured destruction' and was acquiring forces that would enable it to fight a nuclear war. In particular, the study argued that by the early 1980's, Soviet forces would be able in theory to knock out a large number of United States Minutemen missiles housed in underground silos."[14] What an admission that Team B had been correct! In consequence of this analysis, the Carter administration abandoned the conventional view that to deter Moscow the United States needed only to threaten to inflict on Soviet citizens and industries "unacceptable damage." In its place it adopted a "countervailing" strategy directed at Soviet nuclear forces. In so doing, it embraced the Team B's point of view and drew from it the appropriate practical conclusions, albeit without giving it any credit.

Since I have been accused of holding all sorts of inane ideas on the subject—from scorning the danger of nuclear war to expecting the Russians any day to launch a nuclear attack on us out of the blue—I can do no better than summarize my actual views as I outlined them in a letter to the *New York Review of Books* a couple of years later. They rested on four premises:

1. The Soviet leadership does *not* desire war, hoping to attain its global objectives without a military confrontation with the United States;
2. This same leadership prudently assumes that a war with the United States *may*, nevertheless, occur;
3. In such a general war, it is their opinion that strategic nuclear weapons will play a decisive role;
4. Proceeding on this premise, they make preparations, both offensive and defensive, to emerge from the war with the least possible losses and their political system intact, i.e., victorious.[15]

This assessment received confirmation nine years later, under conditions of glasnost, from Vadim Zagladin, the deputy director of the Central Committee's International Department, who wrote in *Izvestiia* that the Soviet Union had pursued a double policy: "Rejecting nuclear war and struggling to prevent it, we, nevertheless, proceed from the possibility of winning victory in it."[16] After the collapse of the Soviet Union this view was bolstered with information obtained from the Soviet military. "Brezhnev allowed the military to develop the following formula," writes Lt. Gen. William Odom:

> Although nuclear war would be terrible and should be avoided if possible, one could not be sure that the imperialists would not unleash it, and if they did, the growing Soviet nuclear capabilities would ensure that the social[ist] camp would prevail and that imperialism would meet its demise. . . . In 1992, Colonel General Igor Rodionov, head of the general Staff Academy at the time and appointed minister of defense in July 1996, wrote that in the 1950's and 1960's the political leaders concluded "that a future war would be nuclear, with massed use of nuclear weapons. . . . And military science, striving to justify this thesis, proved that combat actions, using conventional weapons, had virtually become extinct, and that victory could be achieved in a world nuclear war."[17]

Recently released information about the war plans of the Polish army, a member of the Warsaw Pact, specified that its offensive operations against Denmark and Belgium were to be preceded by nuclear attacks on major Western cities (Hamburg, Bremen, Antwerp) as well as NATO concentrations (Esbjerg, Roskilde) to sow panic and devastation.[18]

It is baffling why such designs, evident in both Soviet military preparations and specialized literature, failed for so long to reach the American community of military theorists and why Team B, which had first articulated it, was the object of such abuse.

Joining the NSC

As a result of these activities, toward the end of the seventies I became involved in politics although I still had few political connections and spent most of my time on historical scholarship. In 1979, I completed the second and concluding volume of the Struve biography, *Struve: Liberal on the Right,* the subject of which was far removed from current affairs.

Richard V. Allen, a member of the executive committee of the Committee on the Present Danger, had close links with the Reagan camp and expected to receive a high post in it. He had served on the National Security Council under Nixon as deputy to Henry Kissinger. Kissinger, who took a strong dislike to him, forced Allen to resign after ten months' service and replaced him with Alexander Haig. The enmity between the two men had festered ever since. After the 1980 election, Allen, having been appointed Reagan's national security advisor, proceeded to assemble a team of experts untainted by the conventional wisdom on détente and arms control as centerpieces of U.S. foreign policy. He included me in this group.

Reagan and his advisors were determined to avoid the kind of tension between the NSC and State that had bedeviled the Carter administration by substantially reducing the role of the NSC in the formulation of foreign policy. Henceforth it was to serve exclusively as a conduit to the president of ideas emanating from State and the other branches of the executive. Unlike his predecessors, Allen was not to report directly to the president, but to Ed Meese, a member of the powerful White House troika which also included James Baker and Michael Deaver. Moreover, it was determined that the NSC would neither chair interagency committees nor clear State Department cables. The NSC professional staff, which under Kissinger and Brzezinski had numbered up to seventy-five members, was reduced to thirty-three. The new arrangement received symbolic expression in Allen's office being moved from the West Wing corner previously occupied by Kissinger and Brzezinski and now assigned to Meese, to the White House basement. This entire reorganization subsequently elicited a great deal of criticism as unworkable and causing chaos in the conduct of foreign policy.

Allen put on a good face on his reduced role, professing in public to be satisfied with it. In a press interview he gave upon being appointed, he said that the NSC would, indeed, be whittled down and that he, its director, instead of making policy, would serve as liaison between State,

Defense, and the White House.[19] In reality, I believe, he hoped through personal connections with Reagan to overcome the institutional obstacles placed in his way. On one occasion he told me he did not care who was appointed secretary of state because he would enjoy influence through "propinquity." This proved a miscalculation. It had worked in the case of Kissinger but not now, because Reagan chose as his secretary of state not a low-keyed bureaucrat but a feisty general, Alexander Haig, a politician trained in the Kissinger school and skilled at playing the Washington game. In lining up personnel to implement the Reagan foreign policy, Allen gravely underestimated the interests and powers of the incoming head of the State Department.

My relations with Allen during the ten months that he served as Reagan's advisor were a mixture of cordiality and discord, the latter caused mainly by his personal insecurity. Allen was bright and quick. He had a good sense of humor: sometimes he amused us during staff meetings with droll imitations of Nixon and Kissinger. Politically, he and I saw eye to eye. But he enjoyed neither solid connections with the Republican establishment nor a national reputation. Moreover, two powerful figures in the White House—Nancy Reagan and Michael Deaver—took a dim view of his conservative politics, since they were determined to tame Reagan's anticommunism and draw him closer to the mainstream. (Peggy Noonan, one of Reagan's speech writers, observed that Mrs. Reagan was always "suspicious [of people who] believed in things, which meant to her, that they were *ipso facto* disloyal. She didn't like people whose first loyalty was to abstractions and not to Ronnie.")[20] Allen came early under fire from the media for being "disorganized and lacking in detailed professional information."[21] As a result, he found himself in a precarious position and forever feared being eclipsed.

Although he liked me, admired my work, and whenever necessary sprung to my defense, I could not help but feel that he looked on me as a potential rival and hence kept me in the background. During his tenure, I was not allowed to brief the president even once; I was invited to attend only a single NSC meeting (October 16, 1981). On some occasions, when the NSC discussed subjects directly within my purview, he sent other staff members to attend. As I was to learn later from press reports, Allen never attributed to any member of the staff the memos which he submitted to the president, in effect taking personal credit for them.[22] Anything that could enhance my reputation was thwarted; any indication that I was well regarded by the outside world was resented.

I will cite examples to support these assertions later on and here confine myself to only one incident that sticks vividly in my memory. Sometime in 1981, Allen told the staff of the difficulty the administration was experiencing in coining a fresh acronym for arms control negotiations to replace SALT which stood for Strategic Arms *Limitation* Talks. For the new president wanted not only to limit the growth nuclear weapons but drastically to reduce existing stockpiles. Various alternatives were bandied about at the meeting but none seemed satisfactory until I came up with START (for Strategic Arms *Reduction* Talks). Allen immediately pounced on it, adding: "If anyone here says that Pipes coined it, his head will roll." He said it half jokingly, of course, but the fact that I never received credit for what will likely be my only contribution to the English lexicon suggests that he meant what he said and concealed my authorship.

Paradoxically, the determination to keep me in the shadows had the opposite effect of the one apparently intended, in that not a few journalists and Washington insiders, who, concluding that I was a sort of éminence grise quietly active behind the scenes, attributed to me much greater influence on the administration than I actually enjoyed.

In May 1980 Allen had invited me to join one of Reagan's advisory groups, in which capacity we drafted policy papers and occasionally contributed to the candidate's campaign speeches. On May 16 we met with the then candidate Reagan and delivered brief summaries of our recommendations. Having heard us out, Reagan recounted a story— whether true or not, I am unable to say—of how a certain Captain Ingraham of the U.S. Navy in the middle of the nineteenth century saved the Hungarian patriot Lajos Kossuth. Kossuth had been abducted from his ship by the Austrians, I believe in Trieste, and Ingraham warned his captors that if they did not promptly release him he would shell the city, whereupon Kossuth was set free. Since then, Reagan concluded, the U.S. Navy has always had a vessel named after Captain Ingraham. He spoke with utter conviction.

Shortly after Reagan won the presidential election, Allen assigned me to the Reagan transition team at the Department of State with responsibility for Europe, a term which included the Soviet Union: it was the largest and most important of State's regional branches with more than three thousand staff members. My compensation was $1.00. In this capacity I interviewed officials from the assistant secretary for Europe down about their functions and problems. Richard Perle, who also joined the transition team, advised me not to take my responsibilities too seriously since nothing would come of our work, and he was proven right. The one specific recommendation that I felt I should make concerning the European desk was to break it up: it seemed to me unrealistic to expect a single assistant secretary to deal on a day-to-day basis with our European allies and at the same time manage relations with our enemy, the Soviet Union and its dependencies. My interviews indicated that the assistant secretary for European affairs spent nine-tenths of his time on relations with our allies. I suggested, therefore, the establishment of a separate desk for the Communist bloc, at any rate, for as long as that bloc existed. In addition, I proposed the appointment of a special coordinator for Soviet affairs. These recommendations were promptly leaked to the press, I presume by personnel on the European desk alarmed at the prospect of having the scope of their authority diminished. Anonymous State Department spokesmen told the press that they opposed my proposal because they did not want to "institutionalize" the Cold War. The *Washington Post* carried a nasty article ridiculing my idea and attributing it to my desire to become the "tsar" of Reagan's Soviet policy.

I had met Haig, the new secretary of state once before, in Casteau, Belgium, in May 1979, where, at his invitation, I delivered an address to SHAPE.[23] At that time, he struck me as cordial and poised: someone who knew him then said he had "glacial self-control." But in the interval he had undergone open heart surgery which, I understand, can profoundly alter a patient's personality. When on the first day of his appointment, on the morning of December 22, 1980, we were assembled by Robert G. Neumann, the head of the transition team, to render an account of our work, Haig at once struck me as a different man. His eyes emitted a pugnacious light and on his lips played a sardonic smile. His whole sneering expression seemed to say, "I know what you are up to; don't try to pull anything over me." He retained this expression until his resignation a year and a half later.

Neumann, a political scientist and a refugee from Vienna, asked each member of the transition team to give a sixty-second (!) account of what he had learned. It so happened that three days earlier I had submitted a seventeen-page single-spaced report, prepared jointly with Angelo Codevilla, with our recommendations. After we had hastily delivered our summaries, Haig thanked us and Neumann brought the meeting to a close: it had lasted forty minutes. As we were walking out, someone said, "Well, we have just been dismissed." I could hardly believe my ears for traditionally transition teams worked until inauguration day. But it turned out to be true. The six weeks I had spent canvassing the Department of State were so much time wasted. According to the *Washington Post,* everyone in State was "absolutely delighted" with Haig's move.[24]

Haig demonstrated on this occasion, as he would time and again later on, that his principal concern was not with the substance of the country's foreign policy but with his personal control of it. Mindful of the way Kissinger had reduced the secretary of state to the status of a marionette, he fought, like a harried animal, for every inch of what he claimed to be his territory which embraced the totality of U.S. foreign policy. As became subsequently known, on the day of Reagan's inauguration he handed the new president a document in which he demanded that the entire conduct of foreign policy be turned over to him—a demand that not only violated the Constitution but completely misread Reagan's mind and laid the groundwork for Haig's future troubles. Reagan rejected it out of hand, but even so Haig never ceased to regard himself as the vicar of international relations. Every attempt by NSC to play a role in foreign policy Haig interpreted as encroachment on his authority, which led to endless petty squabbles.* His obsession with "turf" acquired manic dimensions, verging on paranoia.

I believe that Allen, greatly overrating his political clout, had me pegged to be assistant secretary of state for European affairs. This prospect fell through with Haig's appointment. Allen, therefore, invited me to join his National Security staff as head of the East European and Soviet desk, a position (grade 18) equivalent in rank to that of an assistant secretary or a three-star general at a salary of $57,500. (I later learned that his own salary was only $3,162 higher.) Initially he proposed that I take on this position half-time, commuting from Cambridge, but I rejected the proposal as unworkable, and so he offered me a full-time appointment. I took it on the understanding that I would serve for two years, the maximum period of time that Harvard allows its faculty to be on leave. We moved to Washington at the beginning of February 1981.

I cannot say that my appointment made headlines, at any rate not in

---

*In reflections on my first year in Washington, which I jotted down in my journal on January 1, 1982, I wrote of Haig as follows: "A tactician with very limited horizons. Smart on details. Personality disturbed in some way. His behavior at NSC meetings alternates between impassioned and often accusatory outbursts and sneering silence. I think he considers himself the only man in the room who understands the issues of foreign policy and regards the rest (president included) as nincompoops. He flatters the president but RR feels very uncomfortable with him, especially when caught in a crossfire between Haig ([sitting] on his right) and Weinberger (on his left). It is difficult to see how he can survive the whole presidential term. He has no support in the cabinet."

the United States. When my predecessor, Marshall Shulman, assumed an equivalent post four years earlier (albeit in State rather than the NSC), the *New York Times* reported the news on the front page, accompanying it with a photograph and an account of his views on relations with the USSR. It accorded the same treatment to my successor, Jack Matlock. But the "newspaper of record" apparently chose not to frighten its readers with the news that the chairman of Team B was advising the new president: it completely ignored my appointment. Only two years later, when I was about to leave Washington, did the *Times* carry a brief report on a back page, accompanied by a cartoon showing a man exchanging a top hat for an academic's mortarboard.

By contrast, Moscow noticed and paid a great deal of attention to me. Arbatov told a European diplomat that my appointment was a "tragedy" for I was "worse by far than Brzezinski." The Reagan administration he characterized as run by "troglodytes" and "Neanderthal men." Subsequently, the Soviet press regularly singled me out for criticism, usually sarcastic in tone, depicting me as a fanatic and ignoramus not only in politics but also in historical scholarship. Thus in February 1981, before I had even been able to do anything in my new position, *Pravda* carried an article headed "Attention: Pipes!" which described me as a "wretched anti-Sovietist" filled with "pathological hatred of the USSR and dense ignorance."[25] Later, after the Soviet Union had collapsed, Russians told me that in the anti-American propaganda of that period, I was singled out as a satanic figure, so that my name became very familiar. I felt nothing but pride at having aroused so much animosity—and, presumably, anxiety—among such vile people.

The National Security Council, founded by President Truman in 1947, is a body of officials of cabinet rank, composed of, in addition to the president and vice president, its chairman, the president's assistant for national security affairs, the secretaries of state and defense, the director of central intelligence, the chairman of the Joint Chiefs of Staff, and whoever else is considered relevant when a given policy issue comes up before it. It meets irregularly (under Reagan, usually once a week) to deal with current foreign policy issues. The president listens to its counsel but is not bound by it: in other words, the NSC is an advisory body. The council has a small professional staff, somewhere between twenty-five and seventy-five persons, which in Reagan's time was divided into six regional and five functional offices, each with a director and from one to several assistants.[26] My office, in charge of Eastern Europe and the Soviet Union, had, in addition to myself and a secretary, the services of one full-time staff member, Paula Dobriansky, who twenty years later would serve as an undersecretary of state, and the part-time assistance of a naval officer, Dennis Blair, who in the late 1990s would command the U.S. Pacific Fleet.

In theory, all recommendations or requests by Defense and State are to be routed through the appropriate desk of the NSC staff, which summarizes them for the president, and passes them on, with or without recommendations, to the national security advisor. In reality, any secretary is free to discuss his recommendations or requests with the president personally or by phone and in this manner bypass the NSC staff. This happened, for example, early in the Reagan administration, in April 1981, when the secretary of agriculture, John Block, secured from the president authority to lift the Soviet grain embargo imposed by Carter after the invasion of Afghanistan: neither Richard Burt, the new assistant secretary of state for European affairs, nor I had been consulted in the matter.

While the national security advisor officiates from the White House, his staff is installed nearby, in the gray Old Executive Office Building, built in the late nineteenth century to house the State, War, and Navy departments but now transformed into a nerve center of the executive branch. It is an elegant building with high ceilings and sumptuous ornamentation. One's floor space and location in it are matters of considerable importance. The most prestigious is a large office with a view of the White House and preferably a balcony, less so one that faces on Pennsylvania Avenue, least of all, one facing an inner courtyard: the last, I was told by an occupant, "could not be given away." I received a prime location (minus balcony), although its windows were so thickly coated with a white film of accumulated grime, the casualty of President Carter's parsimony, that I could not clearly see the presidential residence until they were finally washed months later.

No one briefed me on my rights, duties, and responsibilities, so that I had but the vaguest notion what we were expected to do. I asked Allen this question at the very first staff meeting which took place ten days after I had moved into my office: my innocent query immediately leaked and found its way to a newspaper column. I did not receive a clear answer. The next month, I got a job description that gave me wide authority but which, for various reasons, I found impossible to exercise. It transpired that what I did with my position depended largely on me.

This surmise was confirmed by Kissinger at a reception given toward the end of March 1981 by the departing correspondent of the *Neue*

Zürcher Zeitung. Kissinger, whom I had known vaguely at Harvard, had snubbed me for years, apparently holding me partly if not mainly responsible for the Jackson-Vanick Amendment which required countries that wished to qualify for most favored nation status and other commercial advantages to open their borders to unrestricted emigration. Directed at the USSR and its policy of refusing Jews the right to leave, it wrecked a major understanding which Kissinger had reached with Moscow and, in his eyes, dealt a fatal blow to the whole policy of détente. In reality, I had nothing to do with Jackson-Vanick: as I recall, when Richard Perle called me to solicit my opinion on this bill, sponsored by his boss, Senator Jackson, I expressed considerable skepticism about linking trade to emigration, although once it was enacted, I defended it. Be that as it may, in Kissinger's eyes I was compromised by my association with his bête noire, Jackson, the more so because in my writings I had criticized his foreign policy as misguided and opportunistic.

But his loathing of Allen was even stronger than his resentment of past injuries. As soon as he espied me in the crowd, he broke into a friendly smile and approached. For the next ten minutes, surrounded by other guests, he lectured me on how to unseat Allen (without, of course, mentioning his name) and take his place. Never mind, he assured me, what your present position is, if you play your cards right, you can rise to the top: what matters is not one's formal position but the uses one makes of it. I listened attentively not because I had the slightest intention of following his advice but because I was astounded by his effrontery.*

In the next two years I met Kissinger occasionally in Washington and abroad. One time, when I was breakfasting with the newspaper columnist Rowland Evans at the Metropolitan Club he walked up to me with his familiar smile, saying, "Pipes, I can destroy you." "How?" "By saying that I agree with you." It was a fine example of his self-deprecatory humor. A few years later I observed him at the Bohemian Grove in California making his way through a crowd of greater and lesser notables. His self-conscious smile seemed to say: "Yes, indeed, it is I, Henry Kissinger, in your midst; your eyes are not deceiving you, even as I myself am astonished by my existence."

But once he gave up hope of ever returning to office, a kind of sadness

---

*Before I left for Washington, a Harvard graduate student in the Government Department handed me a memorandum with hints how to take over Allen's job: I was to help Allen keep Kissinger at bay, feed the press anti-Allen stories while gaining his confidence, cultivate Nancy Reagan and her secretaries, and move against Allen "at the right moment" when he fell out with Baker and Haig.

settled over him: for although he was earning millions as head of a consulting firm, he craved the limelight. Watching him and others like him, I concluded that power and the celebrity that accompanies it are as habit-forming as a narcotic. I recalled Khrushchev saying that one can tire of everything—women, luxuries, food—but one never tires of power. As I will note later, however, this rule applies only to a certain kind of personality.

Still, I cannot deny the pleasure I derived in my early days on the NSC from the exercise of the power that came with my office. I received a desperate call from the director of Radio Free Europe/Radio Liberty, the headquarters of which were located in Munich, that due to the rapid rise of the German mark in relation to the U.S. dollar, the two stations might be forced to relocate to another, less expensive country. Could I please help? I contacted a person I knew in the Bureau of Management and Budget to ask whether additional funds could be allocated to these important stations. A few days passed and my acquaintance informed me that, indeed, several additional millions have been earmarked for this purpose. The stations stayed in Munich.

At about the same time I learned that Georgii Arbatov had requested a visa to attend in Virginia a congress of a spurious organization that called itself "Physicians for Prevention of Nuclear War." Though Arbatov could by no stretch of the imagination qualify as a physician, he received a short-term visa to attend this gathering. Having apparently become accustomed under the previous administration to disregard such restrictions as visa deadlines, Arbatov chose to ignore the dates on his visa and proceeded to make arrangements for television and other appearances weeks after it was due to expire. I thought he should be taught that the United States was not a Soviet satellite and asked the Department of State to make sure that his visa was not extended. Thus on the day when it lapsed, he was politely requested to leave the country. I was told he was quite enraged by such unaccustomed treatment.

My daily routine at the NSC was not strenuous, except in times of crisis. I would normally arrive at my office at 368 Old Executive Building around 9 A.M., read the National Intelligence Daily, and go over the "packages" placed on my desk for action. Three times a day my secretary would bring a pile of the raw intelligence data in the form of signal intercepts collected by the National Security Agency. "More *garbage*," she would sigh, pronouncing it as if it were a French word. I scrutinized this material carefully because it contained information that CIA analysts often missed. One official with much intelligence experience told me that I was the only person he knew of who regularly read these intercepts.

I was especially impressed by a report from an unnamed Soviet agent, apparently connected with the KGB, which I read in June 1982. Written after the appointment of Andropov to head the Soviet government, it painted a depressingly somber picture of the country, quite at variance with the consensus of the U.S. academic and intelligence communities. Its anonymous author stated at the outset that the Soviet Union was suffering from a malaise which could not be cured by changes of leadership but required the destruction of the entire system. He stressed the growing corruption and crime, aggravated by the militia's connivance with criminal elements. Although publicly the government fought alcoholism, in fact it encouraged it as a means of keeping the population docile. Workers frequently went on strike and farmers abandoned the *kolkhozy* because rural life was unbearable. The report stressed the important role of the creative intelligentsia, especially writers, who, according to its author, wanted less class antagonism and greater pride in Russian nationhood. It depicted the growing frustration of the KGB with the condition of Soviet society, especially the privileges and abuses of power by the Party and its inability to do anything about them. In conclusion, it expressed skepticism whether the system could weather systemic reform because such reform was likely to undermine the position of the Party. All of which proved remarkably prescient.

On the basis of my reading in open and classified sources, I drafted memoranda for the president, suggestions for his press conferences, and most of his letters to Brezhnev. Sometimes I contributed to his speeches. I met in my office or over lunch with journalists and foreign diplomats. And I battled the Department of State.

The Department of State and the Allies

The entire first year and a half of the new administration passed in an atmosphere of unremitting tension between the NSC and State. It brought to mind a remark attributed to General Curtis LeMay, the chief of staff of the air force, during a briefing by a junior officer: "Young man," LeMay interrupted him, "stop referring to the Soviets as 'the enemy.' They are our adversary. The enemy is the navy." So it was with us: the enemy was State.

State Department personnel views itself as a community of professionals in the field of foreign policy and tends to regard all politicians as amateurs who need to be coaxed or restrained (usually the latter) as the occasion requires. This holds especially true when the president and his staff are perceived as "ideologues," that is, people who want to direct foreign policy toward some specific objectives instead of accepting the world such as it is. Whenever I visited "Foggy Bottom" on business I had the feeling I was entering a gigantic law firm that abhorred confrontation with any foreign government and firmly believed that all international disagreements could be resolved by skillful and patient negotiation. Resorting to force is to its staff a mark of failure. They do not believe in irreconcilable differences nor attach importance to ideology. As good bureaucrats, they obey presidential directives: but they are quite capable of emasculating them by the various devices which bureaucrats have at their disposal. Thus, for example, they adamantly refused to share with the NSC transcripts ("memcons" or "memoranda of conversation") of talks Haig had with Soviet Foreign Minister Andrei Gromyko and Soviet Ambassador Anatoly Dobrynin, which made it difficult for me to make proper assessments of Soviet positions.

Although they attempted to create the impression of being disinterested professionals, State Department personnel did not neglect their private interests. On September 23, 1980, by which time polls indicated that Reagan would be the likely winner in the forthcoming elections, I was invited to address State Department personnel on the Soviet Union at the secretary's "Open Forum." The large room where I lectured was packed: the audience hung onto every word I said. When I finished, the first question was: "If designated secretary of state, would you appoint to ambassadorships professional diplomats or political figures?" It was the first time I heard that anyone considered me for the post of secretary of state, but apparently my name did appear on some list of candidates: it had to have been a very long list, indeed, since I had no connections with the Republican establishment. (Incidentally, according to some newspapers I was also on the short list of candidates for the post of director of central intelligence.)* I brushed the question aside. But that the matter of ambassadorial appointments should have been first and foremost on the staff's mind spoke volumes.

We had another problem with State personnel besides their presumed airs of "professionalism." As indicated above, their principal busi-

---

*With William Casey, David Abshire, Ray Cline, and Laurence Silberman: *Christian Science Monitor,* November 18, 1980. On June 7, 1979, p. A3, the *New York Times,* in an article called "New-Boy Network," William Safire mentioned me as a leading candidate for the position of national security advisor, along with Frank Carlucci, John Lehman, Edward Luttwak, and Richard Allen. The trouble with this prediction was that I did not belong to this or any other "network."

ness was with our European allies and in that capacity they assumed the
role of spokesmen for the NATO alliance. The difficulty with this was
that the alliance, forged after victory in World War II, was very much a
one-sided affair. Although in theory the North Atlantic Treaty called for
mutual assistance by its members to one another in case of aggression by
an outside power, in reality the United States committed itself to the
defense of Europe but the reverse was not the case. The Europeans
(with the possible exception of the British) acted on the premise that the
responsibility for countering communist aggression globally fell exclusively on America's shoulders. Whenever we felt the established order to
be threatened outside Europe's geographic confines and took action,
they either did nothing or gave us token support; on some occasions,
they publicly opposed us. The European allies simply refused to acknowledge that the Cold War, in which we acted as their ultimate pro-
tectors, was a global conflict. To make matters still worse, they accepted
the post–World War II order as permanent and viewed with alarm any
American attempts to tamper with it.

The heart of the problem was Germany, which had a vital interest in
reuniting with its eastern half, occupied by Soviet armed forces and
administered by a puppet communist government. To that end Bonn
was prepared to go far in accommodating the Soviet Union: it cooperated with Moscow by consigning all of Eastern Europe except East Germany to the Soviet "sphere of influence." Thus whenever we ventured to
help East Europeans resist the occupying regimes, the Germans openly
disassociated themselves from us. In the case of Poland, as I shall relate
below, Germany told us in no uncertain terms that it had no objection to
the imposition there of martial law in December 1981, denying us the
license to meddle in the "internal affairs" of countries controlled by
Moscow.

The problem ran deep. Leading public figures in Germany disavowed
the right to apply moral standards to countries that disposed of great
coercive powers. Thus C. F. von Weizsäcker, a prominent German scientist and brother of the country's president, in obvious reference to
Reagan, wrote:

> A policy which divides the world into good and evil and which perceives
> the greatest power, coexistence with which is our destiny, as the center
> of evil is not a policy of peace even if its moral judgments are correct.[27]

This mentality, of course, merely echoed what French or British appeasers before 1939 had said of Hitler's Germany. It reflected a spirit of
moral capitulation widespread in Germany which justified a policy of

appeasement—theoretically, at any rate, appeasement without limits. It had previously turned Germans into a nation of Nazis and Frenchmen into a nation of Nazi collaborators. In any event, it seems superfluous to exhort people to submit to superior power: this comes naturally. What is needed is the realization that moral resistance to superior power is a powerful weapon in itself. The trouble with appeasement is that sooner or later it does reach a limit beyond which the appeaser is unwilling to go, and then he is forced to act under less favorable conditions. This is what happened to England and France in the interwar period when instead of stopping Germany as soon as she began brazenly to violate the Versailles Treaty, they did nothing and then, in 1939, gave Poland security guarantees that they could honor only by going to war.

The French also frequently spited us. The reason was mainly their frustration that the United States, which they regarded as a half-civilized upstart nation, had become since World War II the leading Western power. They had no objections to being defended by it; but they acutely resented American hegemony and at every occasion opposed us and our policies.

All this anticipated the kind of problems we would experience later on, in the 1990s and early 2000s, after the Communist threat had vanished and the European governments began openly to resist our efforts to cope with the new global threat, Islamic terrorism.

The Department of State, anxious to maintain good relations with the allies, its principal client, did not openly identify itself with their point of view—this it obviously could not do—but it never wearied of reminding the White House that any hostile action against Moscow threatened to upset the alliance. Such empathy for the allied position readily turned into apologetics.

Allied hostility to our foreign policy became apparent to me in May 1981 when I attended the Bilderberg meeting at the Bürgenstock Hotel above Lake Lucerne. The Bilderberg meetings, held annually at different locations, are very prestigious events attended by some one hundred political, economic, and intellectual leaders, one-quarter of them Americans, to discuss the state of the world outside the glare of publicity.* Allen gave me grudging permission to attend, remarking irritably that he had never been invited. Jeane Kirkpatrick, then U.S. ambassador to the United Nations, was the administration's principal representative.

---

*Once, during the meeting, I repaired to the toilet, where a man told me he had met me in Portugal. "Are you Portuguese?" I asked. "Oh, yes," came the reply, "I am Portugal's prime minister."

In her talk, she criticized, in a sober academic manner, the "North-South" and "First World–Third World" dichotomies, then popular in Europe. As soon as she had finished, she came under vicious attack from the other participants: one German said that her remarks "sent chills down his spine." Jeane was shattered by the ferocity of the reaction and asked me to join her in a walk to explain what she had done to provoke it. She was convinced she had been singled out for assault because she was a woman. I disagreed: she was the target of opportunity as a representative of the Reagan administration which the allied establishment feared and despised. But I failed to persuade her. I suspect it is this sensitivity to personal attack that caused her ultimately to withdraw from politics.

Moscow had its own strategy for dealing with Reagan's truculence, and that was to convey the impression that unless checked, it could lead to war. Shortly after the Bilderberg conference, on June 30, 1981, I attended a meeting at the Carnegie Endowment in Washington to hear an address by the first minister of the Soviet Embassy, Alexander Bessmertnykh. During his talk, he casually remarked that the United States was "acting like Nazi Germany" and "readying for war against the Soviet Union." This incredibly provocative statement by a high Soviet diplomat went unchallenged by the audience. When, during the question period, I rose to ask whether I had heard him right, that the United States was planning to attack his country, Bessmertnykh backed off slightly, saying "it looked like it." It was the beginning of a campaign orchestrated by Moscow to force Reagan to soften his rhetoric lest it bring about a world conflagration—a campaign that was to bear fruit in early 1984, when, · alerted by intelligence of Soviet military deployments, Reagan extended an olive branch to Moscow. In a speech on January 16, 1984, he would say that "our working relation with the Soviet Union is not what it must be," that "we must and will engage the Soviets in a dialogue" to find "areas in which we could engage in constructive cooperation."[28]

A particular problem in our relations with the allies during the early period of the Reagan administration was that of energy imports. Reagan received advice from the CIA that the Soviet economy was faltering: it projected the rate of growth of the USSR's gross domestic product in the mid-1980s to decline to 1–2 percent a year. Such anemic growth was not sufficient to meet competing demands for investment, military needs, and improvements in living standards. The West, in the agency's view, could compound these difficulties by restricting credits to the USSR, tightening export controls, and imposing embargoes which could compel the Soviet Union to take the path of reform.[29]

This counsel, rather unusual for the agency, persuaded Reagan and underpinned his strenuous though ultimately unsuccessful efforts to limit Western subsidies to Russia's energy sector. Reagan wanted to decrease the Soviet Union's hard currency earnings in order to force a reorientation of its investment priorities from military buildup and expansion to domestic reform. (More about this later.)

The Germans, by contrast, beginning with Willy Brandt and his *Ostpolitik,* wanted to develop to the maximum Soviet energy exports, partly to create a putative bond based on shared economic interests, partly to provide Moscow with hard currency earnings with which to buy German goods. The two viewpoints proved irreconcilable.

The Soviet Union was a major supplier of oil and natural gas to Western Europe: the CIA estimated that 80 percent of the USSR's hard currency earnings derived from energy exports. There were further estimates indicating that by 1990, when the 3,500-mile pipeline from Yamal in Siberia to West Germany and from there to ten West European countries would be fully operational and paid for, Russian natural gas would account for 23 percent of Europe's consumption, earning the Soviet Union $10 billion a year.* Such earnings would not only enable the USSR to pay for technology imports with military applications as well as to subsidize client states, but also give it the ability, in the event of a major international crisis, to hold Europe ransom by shutting off gas supplies. (Five prospective recipients of Soviet gas were NATO members.) Despite our objections, the Europeans agreed with Moscow in September 1981 to proceed with the construction of the Yamal line, and to provide cheap credits with which to purchase equipment for it. This issue would come to a head before long when, to punish Moscow for forcing the Polish government to impose martial law, Washington enacted sanctions on the export of oil and gas technology—an action that would produce a major crisis in our relations with Europe.

Social life in Washington, especially for anyone holding a position of some importance, can be exhilarating. Unlike the university, where people do not like to discuss their work for fear that, in retaliation, they will have to listen to what others are doing, in Washington everyone is interested in everybody else's work because it may have direct bearing on

---

*By 1997, Russia, indeed, became the largest supplier of natural gas to Germany, accounting for nearly one-third of her gas imports. Russia's profits from these exports, however, fell considerably short of CIA's estimates, amounting, over twenty-five years (1972–97), to $31 billion: *Financial Times,* July 2, 1998, p. 3.

their own. One is courted by foreign diplomats and journalists eager to learn the "inside story." One frequents international conferences at the highest level. One also receives invitations to embassy receptions and dinners. Traveling abroad, one is an object of curiosity and attention. My wife enjoyed these perquisites even more than I did because at Harvard she could neither participate in my work nor take part in most university social functions. During my two years in Washington, I was—for the first and probably last time in my life—accorded respect and attention not for what I did, said, or wrote, but for what I was—or, at any rate, was perceived to be. It was a strange experience because until then I had always felt myself identified with my work rather than my status.

I made it a firm rule not to socialize with diplomats from communist countries for fear that, no matter how hard I tried to be discreet, they would elicit more information from me than I from them. In May 1981, at a reception given by the Embassy of Czechoslovakia, the Soviet ambassador, Anatoly Dobrynin, introduced me to Bessmertnykh, his first secretary, urging me to meet with him from time to time to "clarify" U.S. policies, but I did not act on this suggestion.

I was in Washington barely one month when an event occurred that threatened to put a sudden end to this interesting and agreeable life: to this day I cannot decide whether it was an accident or a deliberate provocation. On March 17, 1981, at Dick Allen's request, I gave an interview to a Reuters correspondent by the name of Jeffrey Antevil. An insignificant-looking young man, Antevil spent half an hour in my office, questioning me on a wide range of subjects bearing on foreign policy. I spoke freely, in part because I was accustomed to speaking freely and in part because I believed our interview to be off the record. I was unaware, however, of the various gradations that lie between "on" and "off" the record, never having heard of "background" and "deep background" briefings, each with its own elaborate conventions. On a couple of occasions, having said something that struck me as potentially embarrassing, I asked, "You will not attribute this to me, will you?" to which he nodded assent. By local custom, having posed that question, I automatically switched the interview from "off the record" to "deep background." Antevil, of course, realized my ignorance of these conventions, but he did not have the decency to alert me to the change of the ground rules, for he had a scoop on his hands.

The next day the bomb exploded. Reuters carried the text of an interview with a "high White House official" who was quoted as saying, among other things, that "détente was dead" and that the German foreign minister, Hans-Dietrich Genscher, lacked the gumption to stand up to Moscow. Worse still, the unnamed official said that Russia was in such deep crisis that it had but two alternatives: either carry out far-reaching internal reforms or else venture on an aggressive foreign policy that could lead to war. Before the day was over, I was identified as the author of these remarks. All three major television networks carried reports of my interview that evening as the main news story, and the following day the papers were full of it. The communist propaganda apparatus had a field day turning one of my statements on its head: whereas I had told Antevil that the *Soviet Union* had the option of reform or war, it reversed it to mean that unless the Soviet Union reformed, the *United States* would go to war against it. The British communist organ, *Morning Star,* carried an alarming article under a banner headline: REAGAN WAR THREAT HORRIFIES WEST. Even the *New York Times* columnist Anthony Lewis adopted this line, and when I remonstrated with the paper's editorial office, asking for a correction, I had a difficult time making them realize the difference between the two assertions.[30] Similar confusion prevailed in regard to my other statement, "détente is dead," which was perception not prescription. Yet even the London *Observer* could say in reference to it, "Only the vultures want détente to die."[31] Haig expressed "outrage" and personally apologized to Genscher for my disparaging remarks about him.* From these hysterical reactions one might have concluded that I, a university professor on temporary assignment to the White House, had it in my power to unleash a nuclear holocaust.

Soft-liners rejoiced for it seemed likely that I would be fired. Reagan was persuaded, however, most likely by Allen, that I had said nothing out of line, at any rate, about the USSR. On March 18, the White House released a statement that the "high U.S. official" was not authorized to speak for the administration. Yet two days later, the *Baltimore Sun* carried a report of unnamed U.S. officials saying that "statements by a high U.S. official that seemed to bury détente and the prospects of new arms talks with Moscow embarrassed the Reagan administration, but were very close to actual policies": the administration's unhappiness derived mostly from my remarks about the allies, especially Germany.[32]

This incident made me, in the words of the *Washington Post*'s social correspondent, the "man of the hour."[33] The furor eventually died down but it had its consequences. I came to be regarded even in the

---

*At any rate, publicly. Allen told me that privately Haig had said to him, laughing, "I wish I could have said some of these things!"

White House as an undisciplined intellectual rather than a team player: Herblock, the *Post*'s main cartoonist, depicted me as one of the loose canons on the deck of Reagan's ship of state. Being fifty-eight at the time, I was considerably older than the other members of the NSC staff and accustomed to speaking my mind. To feel muzzled because I was sufficiently highly positioned so that every word I uttered could be interpreted as representing the administration came very hard to me: the greatest relief I felt upon my return to academic life was that I could, once again, speak for myself.

Throughout my two years in Washington, the press, both domestic and foreign, was almost uniformly hostile to Reagan and his policies: in the capital city itself, we could count on support only from the *Washington Times*. The entire liberal establishment viewed the Soviet government as more responsible than our own—when it acted in an incontrovertibly aggressive manner, its behavior was customarily interpreted as a justified reaction to our belligerency. The communists, of course, exploited this attitude to the fullest.

To illustrate this atmosphere, I would like to cite one incident. In October 1981, I received an invitation from a Harvard group to participate, on Veterans Day, in a debate with a representative from the Soviet Embassy on U.S.-Soviet relations. I made preparations to go when suddenly word came from Cambridge that my invitation had been rescinded. One of the hosts, Professor George Kistiakovsky, a chemist once involved in the construction of the Hiroshima bomb but now a fanatical peacenik, told the *Harvard Crimson* that my "nonappearance" was due to my failure to obtain clearance from the White House. This was a lie, for no obstacles had been placed on my attendance. The truth was that he and the other organizers of the meeting preferred to hear a Soviet representative without troublesome counterarguments from a Harvard colleague who was an official of the duly elected U.S. administration.

The "experts" to a man opposed Reagan's Soviet policies, which they identified with me, as counterproductive. One of them, Robert Legvold of Columbia University, declared in late 1982: "Pipes is wrong in assuming that there is a clear-cut division between two camps [in the Soviet Union]. Any U.S. policy designed to assure that some non-existent group of 'moderates' will come to power is chimera." Even if such moderates were lurking in the wings, "it is conceivable that vigorous, sometimes bellicose anti-Soviet policies on the part of U.S. authorities could vindicate and strengthen their hard-line rivals. This is precisely what some Soviets hint might happen."[34] In fact, the very opposite happened:

before long, the allegedly nonexistent moderates, represented by Gorbachev, replaced the hard-liners.

It is amazing how similar were the criticisms of Reagan's Soviet policy in the Soviet and U.S. media. Underlying them were the same two assumptions: (1) the Soviet Union is here to stay and one could not hope from the outside to alter its system let alone destroy it, and (2) any attempts in this direction hardened Soviet attitudes as well as risked a confrontation that could lead to a nuclear war. Time proved both premises to be wrong, but constant repetition lent them the appearance of truisms and, as such, beyond dispute.

In June 1981, Allen took me and several other members of the NSC staff to New York to brief Richard Nixon on Reagan's foreign policy. It was customary for ex-presidents to receive periodically such briefings. Allen spent some ninety minutes with Nixon privately while the rest of us went for a stroll. The desultory conversation that preceded the dinner which Nixon offered us in his town house on East 65th Street was painful: the ex-president simply was incapable of small talk. I mostly remember him complaining of being bothered by people asking to be recommended for ambassadorships, a post he considered quite useless. He was astonished that someone with my views liked teaching at Harvard: "We used to say, let Harvard sleep," he said with a sweep of his hand. He asked whether we took time off to exercise. When my turn came to respond I said that I tried to swim as often as I could. Unfortunately, he pursued the question, asking, "Where?" I hesitated a second, gulped, and said "Watergate."

Once we sat down at the dinner table, however, Nixon came into his own and gave us something like a lecture. Its gist was that we should not press the Russians too hard but extract concessions from them with promises of material help which, since they were in deep economic trouble, would make them accommodating; we should begin laying the groundwork for a rapprochement with the USSR, as he had done in the mid-1960s vis-à-vis China. I sat on his left, and every now and then he would grab my arm for emphasis, demanding in a booming voice: "Isn't this right, professor?" As we were about to leave, he asked me how old I was. "Fifty-eight," I replied. "That's a good age. You've got many years ahead of you. Just don't become an ambassador." I must say that I left his house under the spell of a powerful personality and keen intellect, although the latter was confined entirely to politics.

On assuming my post in the NSC, I conceived the idea of holding, in the Old Executive Office Building, weekly informal seminarlike meetings of Soviet experts from the various branches of government to discuss matters of common concern. It was to involve nothing more than the sharing of information and ideas without any policy implications. In early March, I invited several members of State and Defense. As soon as word of my initiative reached the seventh floor of Foggy Bottom, alarm bells went off: the NSC was encroaching on State's turf. No counterarguments availed: Haig ordered these meetings either be moved to State or else proceed without State Department personnel. Faced with this ultimatum, I chose the latter alternative. Formatted as "brown-bag" lunches these seminars, which met occasionally, proved very informative.

Reagan

The new president was isolated from his NSC staff members much of the time by his wife and two close advisors, Michael Deaver and James Baker. Nancy Reagan was troubled by her husband's reputation as a primitive cold warrior. Something of a social climber, she aspired to acceptance by Washington society and opinion makers, who were overwhelmingly liberal and looked down on the two former movie actors occupying the White House. She wanted her husband to win a place in history by ending the Cold War, by which she meant accommodating himself to communism rather than getting rid of it.[35] I do not believe that she had any influence on Reagan's convictions, they were so firm. But she could and did influence his attitude toward personnel, that is, those responsible for giving him advice and implementing his policies. Reagan was a poor judge of people: he basically liked everyone, which was part of his charm but also a source of weakness for a politician must be able to distinguish friend from foe. Deaver and Baker cooperated with her, being equally anxious to restrain the president from giving vent to his deeply felt views. They shielded him as much as they could from Allen's NSC staff lest they reinforce his natural hard-line inclinations. Like Mrs. Reagan, Deaver, whose job was to manage the president's image, did all in his power to curb Reagan's anticommunist instincts. This is why during the two years I served on the NSC I was only once invited to a social occasion at the White House, namely, a dinner on January 31, 1982, for the Polish ambassador, Romuald Spasowski. It may well have been the result of Spasowski's request. There was fear, probably justified, that I would reinforce the president's anticommunism. After I had returned to Harvard, Nancy Reagan brought in, via social channels, other Russian experts—not necessarily soft-liners but people who had a more romantic view of Russia, which she found congenial. I suspect that such behind-the-scenes intrigues were not without effect on Reagan in the latter phases of his presidency.

Nancy Reagan, Deaver, and Baker keenly disliked Allen for his conservatism as well as his administrative ineptitude and were determined to remove him. A flimsy pretext was soon found. On November 3, 1981, a Japanese newspaper reported that Allen had accepted $1,000 from three women journalists who had interviewed Nancy Reagan for a Japanese magazine. The incident had taken place on Allen's first day in office. One of the journalists attempted to give the First Lady an envelope containing ten $100 bills as an honorarium for the interview. To save her embarrassment, Allen intercepted the envelope and gave it to his secretary to put away. Then he forgot all about it. The envelope was found later that year in his safe, and he was charged with accepting a bribe. Although the Department of Justice promptly cleared him of any wrongdoing, the charge stuck and after returning from forced administrative leave, he was denied his old job. It was disgraceful behavior on the part of Reagan and his people, reminiscent of Soviet practices which dictated that every high official relieved of his job be charged with some crime. Safire rightly labeled it a " lynching."

Reagan was remote: even his children complained they could never get close to him. His amiability served as a shield that protected him from more intimate relationships. He drew on his inexhaustible reservoir of anecdotes to avoid serious conversation. He was a lonely man—lonely by choice. He held a few strong convictions and they guided all his policies. They included the belief that America was God's chosen country and that it had to be restored to its position of world primacy from which it had been dislodged by years of defeatism and military weakness. Communism to him was an unmitigated evil that was doomed if the United States and its allies tried hard enough. He wanted at all costs to avoid war. He believed in small government, low taxes, and private initiative. It seems to me that everything else was to him a matter of indifference and this helped him attain a high degree of spiritual serenity. Nor did he much care how his objectives were realized: he was concerned with the "what," not the "how." On one occasion, Judge William Clark, Allen's successor, told the NSC staff that the White House wanted a certain thing done. When we asked how we were expected to do it, Clark responded, "The president believes that if you do the right thing, good politics will follow." This indifference to the means, to implementation, later got Reagan into trouble in the Iran-Contra affair. But it also saved him from getting bogged down in trivia.

Unquestionably, Reagan's political and economic ideas were in some respects simplistic: I once heard him say that one million Sears Roebuck catalogues distributed in the Soviet Union would bring the regime down. And yet it is equally incontrovertible that he was a very successful president who contributed substantially to the collapse of the Soviet Union and the dissolution of its empire, events of world historical importance. How did it happen that this man, regarded by the intelligentsia as an amiable duffer, grasped that the Soviet Union was in the throes of terminal illness, whereas nearly all the licensed physicians certified its robustness?

For one, he possessed to a high degree the imponderable quality of political judgment. He instinctively understood, as all great statesmen do, what matters and what does not, what is right and what wrong for his country. This quality cannot be taught: like perfect pitch, one is born with it.

But the explanation may also be that intellectuals who determine what is sophisticated and what primitive pay too much attention to the elegance of ideas, to their inner consistency, to their theoretical rather than practical utility. In so doing, they tend to lose sight of the real world. Why else would so many of them have promoted socialism and communism long after their failures had become apparent to everyone else? Why would they believe that by repeating, like a mantra, over and over the word "peace" they would prevent war? Why would they march by the tens of thousands on behalf of "nuclear freeze," a meaningless slogan? Intellectuals tend to be captivated by words, because words are their currency. Among my papers I found a note that I had jotted down in the 1970s at some conference: "To deal with [Soviet] Russia you must have a simple mind." I meant by this that the USSR was a crude system, based on force and the exploitation of fear yet camouflaged with noble ideals: these confused subtle intelligences but not the people living in the rough and tumble of the real, physical world.

Reagan was accused by his opponents of dozing off at cabinet meetings. I attended numerous sessions of the National Security Council and never saw him fall asleep. Once in a while he did seem confused, and in retrospect this may be ascribed to the onset of the Alzheimer's disease that would afflict him after he had left office. Most of the time he was clearheaded. True, he asked few questions and kept his own counsel. But I attribute this behavior to his strongly held convictions which nothing could sway: what his advisors said either affected details of implementation, to which he was indifferent, or else matters of principle, on which he was immovable. A colleague of mine was present at a meeting between Reagan and Helmut Schmidt which took place shortly before the inauguration. The German chancellor harangued Reagan for half an hour about the necessity of toning down his anticommunist rhetoric and reviving the policy of détente. Reagan listened politely. When Schmidt finished, instead of engaging him in a dialogue, he asked with a smile whether he had heard his favorite anecdote about Brezhnev and his automobile collection.* Schmidt was on the verge of apoplexy. But with his humorous digression Reagan was conveying: "Don't tell me what to do about the Soviet Union. My mind is quite made up."

At NSC sessions he was occasionally stumped as arguments flew back and fourth. The following are my impressions, as written down in my journal, of the first NSC meeting which I attended (October 16, 1981). (It dealt with proposed embargoes on to the Yamal gas pipeline equipment.)

> RR totally lost, out of his depth, uncomfortable. After making some commonsensical remarks did not speak for forty-five minutes or so; when he finally spoke up it was to sigh "Oh, boy!"—meaning "what am I to make of this mess?" He chewed vigorously on his jelly beans which, I suppose, are his equivalent of cigarettes. He did not listen attentively, looking away or staring at the papers in front of him—except when Jeane Kirkpatrick spoke up and he briefly engaged in a dialogue with her. He smiled understandingly when [Donald] Regan said he was "confused." All this—both the substance and human conflict—is above and beyond him. He has not enough of either knowledge or decisiveness to cut through the contradictory advice that is being offered to him. . . .
>
> Haig, sinister, aggressive, a kind of Iago (except that RR would not play Othello, ignoring him completely). After he had heard out everyone, Haig swept it all aside and said that these matters had been previously decided upon already. He constantly (and he alone) praised the president and acted as his spokesman. He alternately glared and leered, making everyone feel uncomfortable. No one was with him, not even the representative of [the] Commerce [Department] who shared his view on the need of extensive trade with the Eastern bloc. A loner who, however, does not bide his time but charges furiously without letup, especially, of course, at Dick Allen.
>
> Dick [Allen] was surprisingly good, quite in command of the facts and the argument. He pleaded, without success, for a broader East-West policy context into which to place decisions on specific trade licenses. He

---

*Brezhnev, who had a hoard of costly, mostly foreign-made, automobiles, once proudly showed it off to his mother. "Well, mother, what do you think?" he asked her. "It is fine, son," she replied, "very fine. But what happens if the Commies come and take it away?"

told Haig that as a person concerned with the allies he naturally wanted a more lax trade policy. Haig leaped right back—no, he wanted a more "effective" policy. I had a feeling that Dick spoke most of the time over Reagan's head; at any rate, RR did not listen attentively to him—though more attentively than when Haig exercised his powers, to no effect.

But Reagan understood remarkably well—intuitively rather than intellectually—the big issues. His fury at the imposition of martial law in Poland in December 1981 derived from the sense that it shattered the hope that communism could evolve peacefully into democracy. The assistance he extended to the Polish underground in 1982 later made it possible for Solidarity to survive and ultimately compel the communists to yield power to it. This showed a far deeper understanding of the situation than one could find in the Department of State, whose denizens, proud of their "realism," wrote off Poland as a total loss. The two members of his cabinet who shared his moral approach to foreign policy were Caspar Weinberger, the secretary of defense, and particularly Jeane Kirkpatrick, for which reason he always listened with special attention whenever she spoke up.

He had a curious weakness for a statesman in his position in that he could not distinguish between the humanitarian and the political. Thus at the height of the Polish crisis in December 1981, when he was mulling a virtual rupture of relations with the Soviet Union, he demurred at closing the Moscow embassy because that would mean abandoning a family of Russian Pentecostals who had taken refuge there. Later that month, he spoke to me privately with great relish of having found a way to bypass our embargo on flights from Poland to bring to the United States for surgery dozens of Polish children with heart problems. He was altogether incapable of thinking abstractly: his mind worked either emotionally or in reaction to individuals whom he could visualize. Thus at the NSC meeting of July 21, 1982, he made an economic concession of major symbolic value dependent on Moscow's willingness to release a Russian named Petrov who had been on a hunger strike for forty-nine days.

He had irresistible charm, which allowed him to say things that, coming from someone else, would have spelled disaster. Thus, on one occasion, a group of Polish politicians from the Midwest came to pay him a visit. We entertained them as best we could until Reagan dropped by. He spent a few minutes with the visitors. As he was about to leave, one of them said how delighted he and his colleagues were to see that he had recovered so quickly from the wounds of a would-be assassin: unfortunately, the recovery of His Holiness, the pope, proceeded much more slowly. To which Reagan replied that he owed his speedy recovery to a wife who "was watching over him." We were horrified by this remark but he got away with it: none of the Poles was offended by what could have been interpreted as an anti-Catholic slur.

Although I have said that he liked everyone, I believe Reagan from the outset did not like Alexander Haig, whom he had appointed at the suggestion of his advisors. Haig's aggressive bearing, his mocking expression, his superior airs visibly annoyed Reagan. At NSC meetings, my allotted seat was behind the vice president, directly across from Reagan, which enabled me to observe closely his facial expressions and body language. I could not help but notice that Reagan never directly addressed or responded to Haig, who sat on his right; he always tended to lean leftward, toward Weinberger. Haig would roll his eyes to express scorn for the foreign policy pronouncements of various people around the table (though not the president's), as if imploring heaven to witness his suffering. He had not even the grace to pretend that he was the executor of Reagan's will. This was his undoing. It was only a matter of time before he would be let go.

Toward the end of 1981, I was seriously considering quitting my NSC job and returning to Harvard. But the events which broke out in Poland in mid-December 1981 instantly caused me to change my mind.

The Polish Crisis

The one-month interval in December 1981 between Allen's forced leave and the appointment of Judge William Clark as his successor was the most eventful of my stay in Washington. For it was during this interregnum at the NSC that the Polish crisis erupted, affording me a unique opportunity to influence the course of events.

Ever since Reagan had assumed office, there was brewing in Poland a conflict between Solidarity, formally a trade union organization but in fact an anticommunist political movement representing virtually the entire nation, and the communist dictatorship. When Reagan moved into the White House, it appeared almost certain that Moscow would soon send Warsaw Pact armies into Poland, as it had in Czechoslovakia in 1968. In February and March 1981, a young colonel from the Pentagon Defense Intelligence Agency paid me frequent visits bearing satellite photographs that showed concentrations of Warsaw Pact troops and other preparations for invasion. Especially worrisome were arrangements for major Warsaw Pact exercises on Polish territory under the code name "Soiuz-81," scheduled for mid-March, which could easily turn into an offensive military operation. My own mind vacillated between the prospects: I had difficulty choosing between the scenario of a full-scale invasion and an internal crackdown. In mid-February, I wrote Allen: "Should the situation in Poland . . . continue to deteriorate from Moscow's point of view, the most likely response would be the declaration in Poland of a state of emergency." On March 18, I reiterated my impression that a Warsaw Pact invasion was not in the cards. But in early April I reversed myself, thinking invasion imminent.

In February 1981, State developed contingency plans in case of a Warsaw Pact attack, which in my judgment had no teeth. There was concern at the White House that our monitoring of events in Poland suffered from inadequate coordination. In late March, I was asked to find out from State what they were doing to keep an eye on Poland. The official at State whom I contacted responded that he would call me back with the information, but in a subsequent call he told me that the matter would be handled between Deputy Secretary of State Walter Stoessel and Allen. I put the matter out of my mind until early the next morning when Allen telephoned me at home to find out what I had done to enrage Haig. It transpired that Haig had called the president in white fury to protest my "meddling" in State's internal handling of the Polish crisis: he interpreted my request for information as evidence that I was telling State "to get out of Poland." One might have thought we were two different and hostile governments.

No invasion occurred. As became known later, the Polish authorities had persuaded Moscow that it would be better if they themselves took care of Solidarity: as early as August 1980, the Poles had set up a secret center to prepare for the imposition of martial law. By a stroke of good fortune, one of the key members of this secret center, Colonel Ryszard Kukliński, had offered his services to the CIA. A Polish patriot, Kukliński, dismayed by the indifference with which the world had reacted to the 1968 invasion of Czechoslovakia, decided to save Poland from a similar fate. To this end, he passed on to the CIA information, first on developments in the Soviet military and then on preparations for the imposition of martial law.

It remains to this day one of the unsolved mysteries of the Reagan presidency why this invaluable information was never acted upon. Reagan's Director of Central Intelligence, William Casey, passed on

Kukliński's data on the Soviet military to Defense and his own person-nel, but he restricted the distribution of the intelligence on General Jaruzelski's preparations to the president and his national security ad-visor. Not only did Kukliński's reports not reach my desk, but even Haig was kept in the dark! On one occasion Allen invited me to his office and without a word of explanation showed me one of Kukliński's reports (the author was not identified). I was appalled by the tone of a loyal "interna-tionalist" that Jaruzelski adopted in conversation with the intimate circle of his collaborators: the man clearly was no Polish patriot, as he would later claim, for to him the interests of world communism, as represented by the Soviet Union, loomed supreme. But having seen only a snippet of Kukliński's material and unaware of its broader context, I could draw no conclusions from it. Thus, like the rest of the administration, I was ignorant that throughout the year the Polish government, under relent-less Soviet pressure, was laying the groundwork for a military crack-down. I doubt whether in history there can be found another example of vital intelligence data being so scandalously neglected.

Although I continued to vacillate between the likelihood of an inva-sion and an internal crackdown, toward the end of September 1981 I urged Reagan to mention at his press conference the possibility of mar-tial law being imposed on Poland. The advice went unheeded. The atmo-sphere in the NSC was decidedly calm. The NSC meeting on Decem-ber 10, addressed the issue of loans to Poland; the staff meeting that afternoon dealt with Libya.

In the evening of Saturday, December 12, 1981, I received a call from the White House to report at once to the Situation Room. Reagan was away at Camp David. Present were Vice President Bush and several members of the NSC staff. I learned that news had come in that tanks had surrounded the headquarters of Solidarity in Warsaw and that all communications with Poland had been cut. No one quite knew what to make of these developments. I called a Polish official at the United Na-tions with whom I had been in contact, but he was also in the dark. I then telephoned the Polish ambassador, Romuald Spasowski, but he, too, had no news. (A few days later, he resigned and requested political asylum.) Later that night James Baker showed up, dressed in a tuxedo: he made the impression of someone detached and quite puzzled by our excitement.

When the Polish crisis erupted the White House had no national security advisor. This vacuum gave me a great deal of latitude since the acting advisor, Admiral James Nance, previously commander of an air-craft carrier, knew little of Eastern Europe.

On the morning of Sunday, December 13, a meeting was called in the office of Deputy Secretary of State William Clark. By now it was clear that a massive, well-planned operation had been flawlessly carried out, that the Solidarity leadership, convinced of its invincibility and hence neglecting precautions, had been arrested, and that Poland found herself under a military dictatorship. The State Department assured us that the Soviet Union was not involved in these events.

In the afternoon a meeting was held of a special emergency group on Poland under Bush's chairmanship to which I was not invited.

On December 17, the president read a statement on Poland, the bulk of which I had written, in which he called the imposition of martial law and the accompanying mass arrests a "gross violation of the Helsinki Pact" and pledged to help Poland overcome her present economic difficulties if her government restored civilian rule.

Since Poland did nothing to meet these conditions, the administration began to discuss punitive measures, first against the Polish and then against the Soviet government. These were the subject of four consecutive National Security Council meetings held on December 19, 21, 22, and 23 in an emotionally charged atmosphere inspired largely by Reagan's mounting fury at the communists. His mind went back to the 1930s when the democracies had failed to stop German and Japanese aggression: he felt, as he put it at the meeting of December 22, that this was "the last chance of a lifetime to go against this damned force." The rest of the cabinet fell in step, although with varying degrees of enthusiasm: Haig forever worried about the reaction of the NATO allies, while the cabinet officers responsible for the economy (Secretary of Commerce Malcolm Baldrige, Secretary of Agriculture John Block, and Secretary of the Treasury Donald Regan) fretted about the harm economic sanctions would inflict on the United States. Nevertheless, on Reagan's insistence, quite severe punitive measures were adopted, although they were nowhere as drastic as those he had initially contemplated.

The first of these meetings took place on December 19. The president was absent, so it turned into a Crisis Management Group chaired by Bush. Weinberger, Kirkpatrick, and, in some measure, Casey favored forceful measures against the Soviet Union as the instigator of the Polish crisis, while Regan, Baldrige, and Block wanted either "massive" punishment or none which, as Weinberger rightly observed, really meant none. Haig adopted a centrist position. During a break, when Jeane and I were chatting in the corner of the room, Haig approached us, as I noted in my journal, with a "screwed up" face, and said: "I shall give the two of you some nukes." We looked at each other in bewilderment.

The first regular NSC meeting on Poland took place on December 21. Admiral Nance chaired this as well as the subsequent meetings, but he hardly ever intervened. Reagan spoke eloquently and in great anger. The events in Poland, he said (wrongly, ignoring Hungary and Czechoslovakia) were the first time in sixty years that something like this had happened. The Soviets must be told that if they wished to continue normal relations with the West they had to restore freedom to Poland. Referring to Roosevelt's 1937 speech which had called for the "quarantine" of aggressor states, he said that we should isolate the Soviet Union by reducing allied diplomatic and economic relations with it to a minimum. If our allies refused to come along then we should reconsider our alliance: he even went so far as to say that we should be prepared to boycott countries that continued to trade with the Soviet Union. When, in response to this suggestion, Meese proposed a list of possible actions—cutting off all trade, airline, and telephone connections, as well as severing diplomatic and political relations—Reagan demurred saying that diplomatic relations should be maintained and urging that a "carrot" be offered Brezhnev by telling him how much better off his people would be if he changed his behavior. Haig, however, cautioned that the contemplated measures were, for the Soviet Union, a matter of life and death and a potential casus belli.

The meeting two days later, on December 23, began with a wrangle over the text of Reagan's proposed letter to Brezhnev. The letter existed in two versions: one drafted by me, the other by State. Although my version had been cleared by State, Haig insisted at a private meeting with Reagan before the NSC had convened that he sign the State version. Meese defused the dispute by proposing that the two versions be turned over to a working group so that no time be wasted on the matter. After the NSC meeting had adjourned, I walked up to Haig with the text of my draft and asked what objections he had to it, to which he responded "I have no trouble with it." He suggested some minor revisions which made it eminently clear that the issue was not *what* was said but *who* said it. In fact, quite inconsistently, during the NSC discussions, he demanded that we keep open the military option against the USSR, which no one, not even Weinberger, thought feasible.

The substantive part of the meeting resembled that of the previous day. Haig warned of German opposition to any political and economic sanctions against the USSR and the possibility of Europe breaking with us if we persisted in imposing them. To which Reagan responded that in this event we would "go it alone." Jeane Kirkpatrick supported the president by reminding the group that in the United Nations the allies often openly broke with the United States.

Reagan's letter to Brezhnev, dispatched on the afternoon of December 23, was an amalgam of the two versions, my opening paragraphs followed by State's draft. At Haig's insistence, for reasons which I failed to understand, we removed a sentence that denied Solidarity was a "counterrevolutionary" organization. The letter rejected claims that the events in Poland were an "internal matter" on the grounds that in the months preceding the imposition of martial law, the Soviet Union had "repeatedly intervened in Polish affairs" in violation of the Helsinki Final Act to which it was signatory. Unless the Soviet Union ceased to aid repression in Poland, "the United States will have no choice but to take concrete measures affecting the full range of our relationships."

The following day, Christmas Eve, overruling Deaver's objections, Reagan delivered an address in good measure based on a draft written by me and slightly revised by his principal speechwriter, Aram Bakshian. In it he recounted the outrages perpetrated in Poland and warned that if they did not cease, serious consequences would ensue. At the same time he announced a number of sanctions directed against Poland, such as discontinuing Export-Import Bank credit insurance, suspending Polish flights to the United States, and denying Polish vessels the right to fish in U.S. waters. Years later, at an international conference devoted to the December 1981 events, Jaruzelski revealed that these and subsequent sanctions had cost Poland $12 billion, a substantial sum for that country.

On Christmas morning I received a call that Brezhnev's response was beginning to come in over the telex machine. I rapidly translated it. As had been expected, Brezhnev charged Reagan with interference in internal Polish affairs and, pretending that the Polish crisis was over, urged him to address himself to "more serious" issues, such as disarmament. He ignored Reagan's explicit warnings of U.S. countermeasures, apparently under the impression that they were rhetoric intended for public consumption.

This response made sanctions against the USSR inevitable, and the following day I sat down with my colleague Norman Bailey, the head of the economic section of the NSC staff, to draw up an appropriate "menu." On Sunday, December 27, I met with Larry Eagleburger, the deputy secretary of state, and several other officials in his office at State:

dressed casually, he had the *1812 Overture* blaring from the stereo. We went over the list and quickly agreed on the punitive measures.

These measures were on the agenda of a Special Situation Group which met in the morning of December 28 under the chairmanship of Bush: it was the first SSG gathering I had been asked to attend. At this meeting, the unpredictable Haig adopted a very strong line, saying that Brezhnev's reply, being "harsh and uncompromising," required a firm response. He expressed disgust with German Foreign Minister Genscher who, echoing Brezhnev, declared publicly that we had no right to intervene in "internal Polish affairs." Next arose the question of declaring Poland in default on the $350 million loan that was coming due. Although a tempting option, it was rejected on the grounds that it would inflict serious harm on international banks, especially German ones. The issue was discussed at greater length at a meeting of the Special Situation Group on January 2, where representatives of Treasury and Commerce explained the interrelationship of global finance and described the devastating effects a Polish default would have on European economies, both East and West. I carried away the impression that western bankers were not greatly worried about these loans.*

Experience with these sanctions taught me why intellectuals in general and academics in particular have so little influence on policy. It so happened that shortly before I was confronted with the issue, I received an unsolicited manuscript of a book on sanctions. It contained a sophisticated discussion of the subject, distinguishing between "vertical" and "horizontal" sanctions, showing which worked, which did not, and why. I invited the author to visit me. After we had chatted for a while, I said, "Very well, I understand your ideas, now what do we do about them?" "DO?!" the man exclaimed in astonishment. "Yes, do. You see my desk? On the left is an in tray, on the right an out tray. My job is to move papers from the left to the right, not to discuss policies in the abstract." He was of no help whatever.

The sanctions against the USSR were announced the following day, December 29. They involved a wide range of commercial and scientific relations but not the arms control negotiations then marking time in Geneva. American firms were ordered to withdraw from all work on the Siberian pipeline. The sanctions inflicted losses on U.S. corporations (Caterpillar Tractor, General Electric, etc.) running into hundreds of

---

*A representative of the Chase Manhattan Bank told me in July 1981: "Of course, we don't expect repayment on our loans as long as they are 'productively employed,'" i.e., bring interest income.

millions of dollars. But as would emerge later, many questions were left unanswered: were the sanctions retroactive, that is, did they apply to signed contracts or only to future ones? did they also apply to the foreign subsidiaries of U.S. corporations and their licensees?

The sanctions which we imposed on the Soviet Union in December 1981 had a significance beyond economics in that they broke with the Yalta syndrome that had tacitly acknowledged Poland as lying within the Soviet sphere of influence. They represented a direct challenge to the legitimacy of the Communist bloc, which under détente had been regarded as beyond dispute and which our European allies continued to treat in this manner. But it must be conceded that they were not properly explained either to the American public or to our allies, creating the impression that in imposing them Reagan acted in a pique. Only sophisticated observers, like the editorial writers of the *Wall Street Journal*, grasped their rationale.

At the beginning of January 1982, the post of national security advisor was assumed by William P. Clark, a onetime judge on the California Supreme Court and a trusted friend of Reagan's, who the preceding year had served as Haig's deputy. Although he was not well versed in foreign affairs, he was an intelligent man and because he felt secure—due to both his closeness to Reagan and his lack of political ambition—in most ways he represented an improvement on Allen. Unlike Allen, he enjoyed direct access to the president: Meese was eliminated as intermediary.

I cannot give equal praise to Clark's deputy, Robert C. (Bud) McFarlane, a tight-lipped retired Marine colonel who came with him from State. Apparently because of his experience on the NSC dating back to the mid-1970s, Clark entrusted McFarlane with the day-to-day management of the NSC staff. He seemed to me unsuited for the job, and I never understood how he made a political career, which culminated in his succeeding Clark in October 1983 as national security advisor. Peggy Noonan, Reagan's speechwriter, described him as a "computer" who had "decided long ago, as young people sometimes do, that intelligent people speak in an incomprehensible manner."[36] A brave and resourceful officer, he brought to politics a military mindset, with its ingrained respect for the chain of command and the tendency to regard all independent thinking as insubordination. Since I did think independently and expressed my opinions, at any rate within the confines of the NSC, from the day he took office he chose to ignore me to the point of refusing to take or return my calls. If he communicated with me at all, it was through his assistant, Admiral John Poindexter. His loyalties were to the

Department of State: in early 1983, in a private communication to George Shultz, Haig's successor as secretary of state, he referred to the NSC staff as "having . . . many ideologues."[37]

Soon after taking over, Clark fired several NSC staffers. I think it likely that I too would have been let go except that the Reagan administration at the time came under attack from conservative Republicans for growing "soft," and my dismissal would have added fuel to these charges. In fact, rumors reached me that my replacement had already been picked but that Clark insisted on my staying.

One of the initial problems I had with Clark concerned press leaks which greatly bothered him. Because I had numerous contacts with the press, he seems to have suspected me of divulging inside information: this is how I explain his initial decision to exclude me from several high level meetings of direct concern to me. Eventually, however, I gained Clark's confidence and established a good working relationship with him. By the time I was ready to return to Harvard, he would try strenuously to persuade me to stay.

From my personal point of view, Clark's coming brought another advantage. As long as Allen was security advisor—from January to November 1981—I was not permitted in Reagan's presence. All my communications to the president passed through Allen, who either forwarded them to the Oval Office with his approval (and in his own name) or else returned them to me without action.

Clark, who knew little of foreign policy, had to rely on expert advice. Within two months of his arrival, I was asked to brief the president, and from then on I did so fairly frequently. In contrast to Allen, Clark put our names on the memos written for the president. During the briefings which took place in the Oval Office, I was surprised to see how little deference Deaver and Baker showed Reagan—they seemed to treat him rather like a grandfather whom one humors but does not take very seriously.*

Clark authorized the publication of an interview I had given to Strobe Talbott of *Time* nearly a year earlier. Allen had initially approved the interview, whose purpose it was to explain the rationale behind Reagan's Soviet policy, on condition that it be cleared by the NSC staff. Then, however, without a word of explanation, he changed his mind and vetoed publication. The updated interview appeared in March 1982.

There were many more staff meetings than under Allen, most of the

---

*They seemed to feel the need to tell Reagan amusing anecdotes, which they did so badly they did not elicit even a chuckle from him.

time chaired by McFarlane alone or jointly with Poindexter, but they were usually brief—ten to fifteen minutes—and perfunctory.

The first two or three months of the Clark administration were very trying for me: I felt ignored and once again contemplated quitting. In May 1982 I was ready to return to Harvard. Word got out and a note to this effect appeared in *Business Week*. Having learned of it, Clark invited me to meet with him to discuss my grievances. He was both surprised and disturbed by what I told him of the obstacles placed in my path by his assistants as well as by State—evidence that he was not running the day-to-day operations at the NSC. He promised to correct them. At a meeting we had a week later he urged me to stay, saying that I "represented a different point of view" which he needed. After his intervention, I received from Poindexter the text of a Haig-Gromyko "memcon" which I had long sought; some other grievances were satisfied too, but soon things fell into the accustomed groove.

The passions aroused by events in Poland cooled surprisingly quickly. At the NSC meeting of January 5, chaired, for the first time, by Clark, Haig reported on the adverse effects of sanctions, namely, that they were making the Poles almost entirely dependent on Moscow. He opposed choking off credits to Eastern Europe on the grounds that it would only serve to enhance Soviet dominance. He thought we should not criticize the allies for disagreeing with us because every time we did so we gave a windfall to the Soviets.

Weinberger, who was invariably sound on these matters, held the opposite view and so did the president. Their premise was that the additional burden Moscow had to bear in supporting the economies of its dependencies drained its own economy. In retrospect, this turned out to be the correct assessment.

Toward the end of January 1982, I was asked to fly to Chicago to deliver, in English and Polish, presidential greetings to a Solidarity Day rally. Late in the evening the day before the rally, I received a call in the Chicago hotel from the White House that the presidential message would be delivered by Haig. I objected and as a compromise it was agreed that I would read the Polish version. The rally, held on February 1 in the International Amphitheater, was attended by an enthusiastic crowd of several thousand Poles. Haig received a raucous ovation: when he finished his brief remarks, he stood in the limelight, sweating profusely, while the crowd chanted "Haig! Haig! Haig!" As I observed this spectacle, two thoughts crossed my mind: how would these cheering thousands react if they knew that Haig had opposed sanctions on Poland

and the Soviet Union and how unpolitic it was of Haig to usurp accolades due the president.

The problems with the sanctions were not over. At the NSC meeting on February 26 Clark raised the question whether the December 29 sanctions were retroactive and whether they applied also to subsidiaries and licensees of U.S. firms. This issue had caused confusion in several European countries where component parts of the Siberian pipeline were being manufactured under U.S. licenses. There was tremendous opposition to our measures, even from Margaret Thatcher: the Europeans felt that signed contracts had to be honored and that we were bullying them. Haig commented that we had, indeed, acted hastily: the sanctions were much more costly to Europe than to the United States. He urged that pipeline equipment be exempt from the sanctions and that we concentrate instead on credits, that is, make it more expensive for Moscow to obtain Western loans with which to purchase this equipment. Reagan conceded that he had been hasty and that Mrs. Thatcher had made him aware of this fact. He was, therefore, open to suggestions about subsidiaries and licensees. Weinberger persisted in an uncompromising position. He thought it silly to argue that the father (i.e., American corporations) could not export energy equipment to the Soviet Union while the sons (i.e., European subsidiaries and licensees) could. We should go the whole way and impose a total embargo on this machinery. Such measures would delay the completion of the Siberian pipeline, scheduled for 1984, by two years. But Baldrige, Block, and, surprisingly, Casey argued that the extraterritorial extension of the sanctions would not work and agreed with Haig that in fact the more effective device were credit restraints, which could be imposed with allied concurrence. It was agreed to withhold a decision on this matter until the return from a European tour of ex-Senator James Buckley who was to sound out our allies on the subject of credits and energy dependence.

Buckley reported to the NSC on March 25. At the time, there was general expectation that the sanctions imposed on the Soviet Union would be lifted: both the business community and diplomatic circles lobbied furiously for repeal. Inside the U.S. administration, State and Commerce favored repeal, while Defense and the NSC opposed it. Buckley tried to persuade the allies of the "idiocy" of subsidizing the Soviet arms buildup through cheap, government-guaranteed credits. He also argued in favor of developing further European gas resources (especially in Norway). But he met everywhere with failure: all the Europeans opposed our stand.

By now, the entire cabinet except for Weinberger rejected sanctions on pipeline equipment in favor of credit constraints on the grounds that there was no realistic way of delaying the completion of the Yamal pipeline and that efforts in this direction were futile, causing needless friction with our allies. Haig questioned the value of economic diplomacy in principle. Referring to unnamed "experts" on the Soviet Union whom he had consulted, he reported that in their opinion it was "crazy" to think we could "bust" the Soviet Union: to be sure, the country was in trouble but there was no way of changing its system by means of economic warfare. Haig's judgment and that of his "experts" was wrong on the face of it and proved so over time. For the purpose of economic warfare was not to "bust" the Soviet Union but to aggravate its already serious economic distress. To alleviate its economic problems, the USSR would have to shift its priorities from building up its military capabilities and supporting proxies abroad to reforming its economy, which would lead to fundamental changes in the way it ran its empire and thereby attenuate and possibly end the Cold War. Which is exactly what happened.

On May 21 I learned that State was lobbying for diluting the sanctions by exempting items contracted for before December 30, 1981 (which meant, among others, equipment for the Siberian pipeline) in exchange for European concessions on credits. The trouble with this proposal was that we had agreed to credit controls as compensation for not extending sanctions extraterritorially: now the same reward was offered for exempting pre–martial law contracts since no credit controls had been imposed.

Reagan vacillated, anxious to avoid confrontation with the allies and yet convinced that delaying the pipeline was both possible and desirable. The issue was placed on the agenda for the May 24 NSC meeting. Hoping to prevail on Reagan to stand firm, Norman Bailey urged me to draft a memorandum on the subject. I wrote it on May 22 and delivered it to Clark by hand; he, in turn, showed it to the president on the morning of May 24, shortly before the meeting of the NSC. My two-page letter pointed out that the dilution of sanctions, without any measurable progress in Poland toward meeting our conditions, would severely damage our international credibility. It would mean that we would not be able to use economic sanctions in the future as leverage to influence Soviet behavior. "The Soviet government," I wrote,

> will conclude that President Reagan has no staying power and that his anticommunism is . . . mainly rhetorical: such a perception will surely

have immense bearing on Soviet calculations in planning future aggression. . . . We have basically two and only two levers to use toward the Soviet Union: the economic and the military. If we drop the economic (as in effect, we will be doing if we follow State's advice) we will have no choice but to rely on the military one. In other words, as we abandon economic pressures in the face of Soviet aggression we will, of necessity, have to resort to military moves which will increase the likelihood of confrontation and conflict. . . . This would be particularly regrettable now that the Soviet Union faces an unprecedented economic crisis and is more than ever vulnerable to various economic pressures.

The arguments I presented apparently swayed Reagan. Clark told me personally that they had helped "tip the scales" in favor of extending the sanctions extraterritorially. An NSC colleague later described my letter as a "bombshell" that could precipitate Haig's resignation.

The NSC meeting on the morning of May 24 was to lay the groundwork for the economic summit scheduled to meet in Versailles in the middle of June. The question on the table was whether to rescind the sanctions, maintain them, or extend them. Haig, ever concerned with allied reactions, especially the French who were the most recalcitrant, proposed a compromise: let us be flexible on sanctions if the Europeans restrict the flow of credits to the Soviet Union and limit their reliance on Soviet energy by developing the North Sea deposits. Casey argued that unless something was done, in ten years Europe would depend on the Soviet Union for half its natural gas supplies: the USSR already obtained 80 percent of its hard currency earnings from energy exports.

The question arose of what to do about the pipeline rotors being built under U.S. licenses abroad, that is, whether to extend the sanctions extraterritorially. Baldrige supported Haig; Weinberger, opposed him. Having heard out the arguments, Reagan declared that when the sanctions had been imposed they were not extended extraterritorially because of the promise of credit controls. Now he was beginning to have doubts. He would make no decision on sanctions today. But with clear reference to my letter, he wondered why we were talking of lifting them considering nothing had changed for the better in Poland—martial law remained in force and Wałęsa still languished in jail. If we lifted the sanctions, we would lose all credibility. The proposed credit restraints were a reward not for lifting our sanctions but for not extending them extraterritorially. He failed to understand why we were considering lifting sanctions without being given any pledges on credits. Instead of developing Russian energy resources, the Europeans would do well to expand access to the Norwegian gas deposits. In any event, the Russians ought to pay hard cash for their purchases and not benefit from cheap credit—hence the need also for credit sanctions. The USSR was economically on the ropes: it was the time to "push" it.

Reagan came back from the Versailles meeting in mid-June thoroughly disappointed and angry with the lack of any decisive moves by the allies on credit restrictions. He was especially furious with the French (a nation he keenly disliked) who claimed that they had contracts with Moscow which prevented them from cooperating in such measures yet refused to show us the texts of these contracts.

At noontime, Friday, June 18, I received an urgent call to report to Judge Clark's office. He asked me to prepare for the NSC meeting scheduled for 1:15 that afternoon three options on the sanctions: rescinding them, maintaining them, and extending them extraterritorially. He added, in an aside, that I need not spend much time on the first two. I formulated the options with the help of a colleague, Roger Robinson, in thirty minutes, just in time for the NSC meeting. Clark told me to expect the president to "render judgment from the bench," something I had not known him to do previously. It meant his mind was made up.

The meeting took place as scheduled despite the fact that Haig was in New York talking to Gromyko—Clark had refused his request to postpone it on the grounds that NSC meetings were never rescheduled. Haig's place was taken by Deputy Secretary of State Larry Eagleburger. Casey reported that while the allies were paying lip service to the principle of credit controls, they offered nothing concrete. Although dubious that sanctions would significantly delay the completion of the Siberian pipeline, he felt that lifting them would convey the impression that the United States was "flabby." Eagleburger cautioned that if the sanctions were maintained the Europeans would refuse to cooperate on credits. Weinberger countered that we ought not to be guided entirely by allied feelings: President Mitterand had confirmed that credit interest would not be raised from 7½ percent to 12½. As concerned the alleged violation by the United States of sovereign rights of the allied countries, it should be obvious that we were not attempting to apply our laws abroad: General Electric had private contracts with European licensees, such as the French firm Alstom-Atlantique and the British John Brown, and had not only the right but the duty to enforce them. The law required U.S. firms to abstain from doing directly or indirectly what U.S. law forbade: the contracts signed by General Electric with Alstom-Atlantique explicitly stated that the French licensee was bound to observe the Export

Administration Act which President Reagan had invoked to prohibit trade on grounds of national security.[38] In other words, if foreign governments authorized their firms to sell pipeline equipment to the Soviet Union despite the U.S. ban, they and not Washington would be guilty of interference with the freedom of contract. The sanctions would substantially raise the costs of the pipeline construction to the Soviet Union. Regan stated that the French denied there had been any understanding on credits reached at Versailles.

Having heard the arguments pro and con, Reagan said the United States had to stand on principle even if it hurt our business interests. If conditions in Poland improved significantly, we would respond in kind. He concluded the meeting by saying: "I did not ask you to come here to be yes-men. There will be no penalties for dissent. But you will not change my mind. There is no consensus but I feel strongly that we are at a moment of decision in the world— a better world."*

On June 22 it was announced that the pipeline sanctions were extended to U.S. subsidiaries and licensees abroad because the situation in Poland had not improved—if they were not extended, U.S. firms would bear the brunt of the costs (which in fact, several of them did, having canceled equipment contracts for the Siberian pipeline) while their foreign partners and licensees would profit from business as usual.

Three days later Haig tendered his resignation and the president accepted it. Haig's resignation was directly caused by the decision to extend the sanctions extraterritorially—he opposed this action and had been excluded from the final decision-making—but other factors contributed as well. Apparently at Versailles Haig behaved in an offensive manner, to the point of insulting Nancy Reagan, something Reagan's White House never forgave. Clark returned from Versailles furious with him. Haig had offered to resign several times before and each time was dissuaded. He apparently counted on this happening again. But this time Reagan accepted his offer. As Reagan explains in his memoirs, he found Haig's petulance and insistence on being in charge of foreign policy unacceptable: "the only disagreement there was over whether I made policy or the Secretary of State did."[39] The secretaryship was offered the very same day to George Shultz, president of Bechtel Corporation, who knew less about foreign affairs than Haig but had a steadier personality.

I felt sanguine about Poland. Talking to State Department officials,

*The record of this meeting leaked and William Safire in his *New York Times* column of June 21, 1982, page A19, provided a detailed account of its proceedings.

who were ready to give her up as a lost cause, I reminded them that Poland had managed to sustain her national spirit during a century and a quarter of foreign occupation: she surely would do so again. In mid-June, I told Solidarity's representative abroad that "time worked for Solidarity": "they should be patient, refuse to be provoked, assert by symbolic gestures their existence, and the regime sooner or later will have to come to them." The strong moral support the Poles received from the United States helped sustain their morale and by the end of the decade forced the communists to surrender power.

Unfortunately, the truculent mood in the White House did not last long, for Reagan came under relentless pressure from several branches of his own administration, notably State and Commerce, as well as the allies. Shultz had greater influence with Reagan than Haig simply because he was a more reasonable and tactful person. However, being primarily an economist and a businessman, he lacked a deeper understanding for the whole ideological and political dimension of our relationship with the Soviet Union. Like most corporate executives, he tended to treat our conflict with it as a CEO might treat disagreements with his firm's labor union: that is, assume that the two parties shared a common interest in the enterprise and only haggled over the division of profits. But in dealing with the USSR there really was no room for compromise, except on minor issues of no consequence, because the Soviet Union acted on the principle that foreign relations were a zero-sum game. In his memoirs, Shultz describes how, on assuming office, he wanted to "to try to turn the relationship [with Soviet Union] around: away from confrontation and toward real problem solving."[40] He thought in those commonsensical terms, unaware that the real problem was the Soviet regime with its ideology and its *nomenklatura* and that one could not negotiate with it its own destruction. This had to happen despite itself.

To lend his conciliatory initiative the aura of expertise, Shultz on August 21, 1982, convened a "seminar" on the Soviet Union, chaired by Hal Sonnenfeldt, once a close associate of Kissinger's. The participants in this gathering were carefully screened, which meant that I was not invited: the NSC staff was represented by McFarlane.[41]

Shultz did not believe in sanctions and resolved to be rid of them, pushing Reagan in this direction on the grounds that they hurt the U.S. economy more than the Soviet. Reagan, worn out by the disputes over the sanctions and unwilling to ignore the advice of his new secretary of state, began to waver. At the NSC meeting of October 15, Shultz reported that he had gotten all kinds of promises from the allies on how they would reciprocate for the lifting of sanctions. As far as I could tell, these amounted mainly to strengthening COCOM, the ineffective organization responsible for controlling the export of strategic equipment to the communists, and authorizing a variety of "studies."

The next day Clark told the NSC staff that the situation in Poland had improved to the point where the sanctions could be lifted. The pipeline embargoes were rescinded on November 13–14, 1982. The allies gave nothing in return for this concession, not even of a face-saving nature, largely because of French malice. I felt despondent about this turn of events; it seemed all I had done since the beginning of the year had been in vain.

Honoring Soviet Dissidents

In April 1981, Senator Roger Jepsen of Indiana approached Dick Allen with a request that he arrange for Solzhenitsyn to meet the president. Allen turned the matter over to me. I felt that Kissinger's advice to Ford not to receive the Russian writer had been both morally and politically wrong: when Solzhenitsyn arrived in the United States in 1975 he was known as a heroic dissident and fighter for human rights, and he should have been honored as such. In the intervening years, however, he had made numerous political pronouncements which indicated that if he detested communism, he had no sympathy for democracy either. As known from the history of fascism and national socialism, anticommunism does not automatically translate into prodemocratic sentiments. An anticommunist in Russia, in the West Solzhenitsyn rapidly turned into an anti-Western Russian nationalist. His ideal was a benevolent theocratic autocracy which he believed to be rooted in Russian history but which existed only in his imagination. He aligned himself with the nationalist right of the Russian political spectrum although he denied such affiliation because he preferred to assume the pose of a prophet who stood above parties.

I might add that the Russian nationalist émigrés in this country were very unhappy with my NSC appointment. In April 1981, a group named "Congress of Russian Americans," with reference to Solzhenitsyn's opinion, called for a massive postcard campaign to be sent to the White House demanding my dismissal. Unfortunately for its initiators, it never got off the ground.

Initially I proposed that Reagan send Solzhenitsyn a congratulatory message on some suitable occasion in recognition of his accomplishments as a novelist and the author of the *Gulag Archipelago*. Allen was not satisfied with this suggestion and the issue remained in limbo for several months. In fall 1981, Allen came under renewed pressure and asked me to meet with NSC colleagues to provide a better recommendation. We met on October 9. Carnes Lord, who handled the media for the NSC, proposed that we invite Solzhenitsyn together with a group of Soviet dissidents of diverse political opinions, some Russian democrats and religious figures, others representing different ethnic groups. Such an encounter would honor all those opposing communism, not merely those doing so on nationalist grounds. I liked this solution and forwarded it to Allen. Allen approved it, but at the time he had other problems on his mind and took no action.

In March 1982, under steady prodding from Jepsen and Congressman Jack Kemp, Clark—by now Allen had left the NSC—agreed to host, on May 11, a lunch for a representative group of Soviet émigrés, Solzhenitsyn among them. Deaver, believing for some reason that the proposed gathering would embarrass the president suggested instead a lunch where Reagan would met a group of "ethnic Americans." When this did not fly, he ordered that no photo or statement be released concerning the lunch so as not to annoy our European allies and Moscow.

On April 6, the story leaked to the press, which forced me to communicate with Solzhenitsyn prematurely, advising him to expect an invitation. Communicating with Solzhenitsyn, however, was no simple matter, for the sage of Cavendish, Vermont, viewing himself as a head of state in exile, did not countenance direct access, even from the president of the country where he had found asylum. Inquiries revealed that a certain Orthodox priest in Washington knew how to reach him. Shortly after I had spoken with this priest, requesting a telephone audience with Solzhenitsyn, I received a call from Mrs. Solzhenitsyn. When I told her of the president's forthcoming luncheon invitation, she asked, warily, whether anyone else was invited and if so, who. But she refused to discuss the matter, demanding that the invitation be conveyed in writing. A few days later the Russian émigré press carried reports of the invitation, hinting that Solzhenitsyn was offended not to be invited alone. We put our heads together and came up with the idea that prior to the lunch, the president would grant Solzhenitsyn a fifteen-minute private meeting.

The message to Solzhenitsyn which I drafted on April 30 in the president's name went to McFarlane for clearance. I gave the matter no more thought until one of the president's staffers appeared in my office quite agitated to say that the invitation to Solzhenitsyn to the private meeting had never been sent because it got mislaid in McFarlane's office. Immediately a telegram containing the unsent letter of April 30 went out, but Solzhenitsyn was now doubly insulted and flatly refused to come. Instead, he sent the president an impertinent letter in which he blamed all kinds of dark forces for the incident, accused the United States of plotting a genocidal nuclear attack targeted on the Russian population, denied being either an "émigré" or a "dissident," and ended by saying that (presumably, unlike the president) he had no time for "symbolic encounters." However, he concluded, we would be glad to entertain Reagan in due course: "When you will no longer be president and will have full freedom of action, if you ever happen to be in Vermont I cordially invite you to come and visit me." He regretted that (for some unstated reason) he had no choice but to make his private letter public. I expected Reagan to react angrily. But having read it, he calmly remarked that its author apparently regarded the fellow-dissidents with whom he had been invited as traitors. It was a keen observation.

Indeed, the *Washington Post,* reporting on the incident, wrote that Solzhenitsyn "did not think it appropriate for him, a writer, to participate in what he described as a group of politicians and professional [!] émigrés."[42] Radio Liberty, directed at the time by an ardent admirer of Solzhenitsyn's, had the poor judgment to broadcast his letter, with its absurd accusations that the United States had a genocidal strategy vis-à-vis the Russian population, around the clock without commentary, at any rate until I objected. The Russian émigré press, apparently on instructions from Solzhenitsyn, blamed me personally for "sabotaging" its hero's encounter with the president. Twenty years later, in his recollections of his U.S. stay, Solzhenitsyn blamed me for this incident, accusing me of harboring "personal hatred" toward him because of the critical remarks that he had made several years earlier about my *Russia under the Old Regime.*[43] (As a matter of fact I had paid no attention to his criticism because it was obvious that due to his ignorance of English he could not read my book and for this reason concentrated on my use of caricatures, which, in his unfamiliarity with modern historical methods, he thought unseemly in a scholarly book.) The megalomania Solzhenitsyn displayed on this occasion was a harbinger of the failures he would suffer on his return to Russia twelve years later: his intolerance and prophetic posturing would alienate from him his own people and ultimately marginalize him.

The lunch—the first time an American president met with a group of Soviet dissidents—went well though not without minor hitches. Georgii Vins, a Baptist pastor, announced he would not take his place at the table if alcoholic beverages were served; they were removed. The representative of the Jewish minority and a prominent leader of the refuseniks, Mark Azbel, arrived dressed like a kibbutznik in blue jeans and a plaid sport shirt without a tie. I managed to procure him a tie. At the lunch, each guest spoke of the trials and tribulations of the group he or she represented. Reagan listened attentively and, in turn, tried to amuse the group with his favorite communist jokes: he was visibly disappointed when it turned out that they knew every one of them. He read a brief and innocuous speech which expressed the hope that freedom would be restored to the Soviet Union. When the lunch broke up, journalists hovering outside interviewed the participants. They also requested the text of Reagan's speech. When I tried to obtain it, I was told that it was not available for distribution. It was a particularly blatant example of his entourage "protecting" the president from himself. The U.S. press generally ignored the event. Moscow Radio wondered: "Perhaps Reagan finds pleasure in meeting people who, for American dollars, slander their former homeland."

Disturbed by the influence Solzhenitsyn and his like exerted on the U.S. government, which they succeeded in persuading that Soviet public opinion was dominated by Russian nationalists, I coaxed the appropriate authorities to subsidize at least one liberal, pro-Western periodical. The result was *Strana i mir* (*The Country and the World*), a monthly edited by Kronid Liubarskii from 1984 until 1992.

Lebanon

On June 6, 1982, the Israeli army invaded Lebanon with the intention—perfectly justified in my eyes—of destroying the large military force which the PLO had deployed there and of putting a stop to recurrent Palestinian attacks on Israel from Lebanese soil. There seem to have been some crossed signals between Jerusalem and Washington, the American government being under the impression that this was a limited incursion whereas Israel thought of it as major strategic initiative. George Bush was very angry at the Israelis for what he regarded as their deception: I was told by a high official in State that he wanted the United States to support a Security Council resolution condemning Israel for its invasion of Lebanon, an intention thwarted by Haig and State who, for once, were in favor of resolute military action on the part of our Israeli allies.

I became somewhat involved in these events because Moscow lost no time intervening on behalf of the Arabs. On the morning of June 9, a message arrived from Brezhnev demanding that the United States pressure Israel to stop its "large-scale aggression" and threatening Soviet involvement to protect its security in a region located "in direct proximity to its southern borders"(?!). In view of these threats and intelligence information that the Israeli and Syrian air forces were engaged in combat, a meeting took place of the Special Situation Group. There was general confusion but also a sense of alarm lest the conflict expand. Weinberger insisted on Washington taking firm steps to restrain the Israelis.

I helped draft Reagan's response to Brezhnev's letter; it went out in the afternoon. My contribution consisted of a polite reminder that the Soviet Union bore "no little responsibility for the current crisis in the Middle East by its failure to support the Camp David Accords and its readiness to furnish a steady supply of weapons to PLO forces in Lebanon" and that we expected it to exert a restraining "influence over PLO, Syria and [its] other friends in the area."

During these events I was repeatedly surprised by Bush's anti-Israeli attitude and his seeming lack of understanding for Israeli behavior.

NSDD 75

During the two years I spent in Washington, I worked intermittently on the draft of a general policy statement of the Reagan administration's policy toward the Soviet Union that in January 1983 resulted in the National Security Decision Directive (NSDD) 75. (The preceding, Carter administration, had produced no such document.) The final version of this directive contained clauses that ran counter to all the policy statements that had previously guided American policy toward Moscow in that it called for not merely punishing unacceptable Soviet behavior but for doing all in our power to avert such behavior by inducing changes in the nature of the Soviet regime on the premise that it was the source of Soviet behavior. Without taking undue credit, I believe I can claim this idea as my main contribution to the Reagan administration's foreign policy. It took a great deal of bureaucratic maneuvering to overcome entrenched ways of thinking, especially in the Department of State.

The consensus of the academic and the government communities concerning the Soviet Union and our policies toward it rested on three seemingly commonsensical and irrefutable propositions:

1. Like it or not, the Soviet Union was here to stay. By repulsing every internal and external challenge and overcoming the most formidable adversities since October 1917, it has demonstrated beyond any doubt its viability. Its triumphs could not have been achieved without popular support.

2. From this premise it followed that the noncommunist world had no choice but to accept the Soviet bloc such as it was and seek to reduce as much as possible the sources of friction with it. Failure to do so would make the USSR more combative and risk a nuclear holocaust. Friction was best reduced by summit meetings, arms control negotiations, and a broad spectrum of contacts between the citizens of the two societies. In the long run, such policies would produce genuine coexistence between communist and noncommunist societies which actually were not as dissimilar as their ideological differences might have suggested.

3. Such conciliatory measures had to be accompanied by a "containment" policy that required us by all means at our disposal, short of a direct military confrontation, to prevent Moscow from expanding its domain.

These convictions were reinforced by the belief, prevalent in the business community here and abroad since the 1920s, that trade made for peace. This faith inspired businessmen to promote the image of the Soviet Union as less menacing than commonly envisioned in order profit from trade with it, much of it carried on with government credit guarantees.

This entire complex of ideas was plainly unrealistic, as proven in 1991 by the swift collapse of the Soviet regime: a fact which revealed that it was neither stable nor popular, and that the entire political strategy based on the premise that it was both had been fundamentally mistaken. Nevertheless, from the 1960s until communism's demise, such notions enjoyed a virtual monopoly on respectable opinion in the United States and Western Europe.

Although they would indignantly deny it, those who held these views were thinking and behaving in a manner not very different from the British appeasers of Hitler. The latter, too, motivated by an understandable desire to prevent another war, attributed to the enemy rational and limited objectives. They too trusted him more than they trusted his opponents. They had the same faith in personal contacts with Nazi leaders and similarly dismissed anyone who disagreed with their tactics—

notably Winston Churchill—as war mongers. Until Reagan was sworn in, I believe that the atmosphere in the State Department vis-à-vis Moscow did not greatly differ from that which had prevailed in the British Foreign Office in the 1930s. And it remained much the same, although muted, throughout the eight years of his presidency.

The Russians skillfully exploited these attitudes. Publicly, they insisted we were all in the "same boat," fueled nuclear hysteria, and depicted themselves as a country that strove hard to catch up with the United States. In private negotiations with high U.S. officials, as I learned from reading the "memcons" of talks between the U.S. secretaries of state and their Soviet counterparts, they pursued a consistent line: the United States had no right to allow its relations with Moscow to be influenced by Moscow's global actions. These relations had to be strictly bilateral and focus on arms limitation talks. Gromyko, the Soviet minister of foreign affairs, steadfastly refused to discuss Soviet actions in Afghanistan, Poland, or Central America on the grounds that these were all "internal" matters of the countries concerned. Moscow adopted the same line in the presidential correspondence.

These tactics enjoyed considerable success: the Russians were exceedingly adroit, since Lenin's day, in exploiting the weaknesses of their adversaries. Over the long term, this was of a mixed benefit to them because it caused them to underestimate our strengths just as we tended to overestimate theirs. Our mistake, in the end, proved the less costly.

The reaction of the Sovietological community in and out of government to Reagan's rhetorical belligerence vis-à-vis Moscow was grounded in fear that it would unravel the whole fabric of cooperative arrangements laboriously woven under the détente policy, pushing relations between the two countries to the point of no return. Proponents of détente had become so accustomed to symbolic and largely meaningless summit meetings and arms control negotiations that Reagan's refusal in the first term to engage in either presaged in their view a complete collapse of the (imaginary) balance of power carefully constructed since Stalin's death. One month after the election of Reagan, Bernard Feld, an MIT professor and editor of the *Bulletin of the American Atomic Scientists,* reported that his publication had decided to move the hands on the Doomsday Clock featured on its cover from seven to four minutes to midnight, because, as "the year 1980 drew to a close, the world seemed to be moving unevenly but *inexorably* closer to nuclear disaster."[44] This meant that the folks who had given us the atomic bomb considered us but 0.0028 percent away from Armageddon: measured on the scale of one kilometer, a mere 2.8 centimeters.

The frightened noises made by these "experts" had no basis in reality. They had no clue what kind of people ran the Soviet Union, what motivated them, what their aspirations were. Read twenty years later, their *Bulletin* conveys the impression of having been written by a pack of hysterical ignoramuses who knew physics but little else. Ignorance of history and lack of imagination persuaded them that Soviet leaders were driven by paranoia caused by centuries of (alleged) invasions and that the main task of U.S. diplomacy was constantly to reassure them: hence the stress on summits and arms control negotiations as pacifiers. The more harshly one treated the Russians, the consensus held, the more obdurate and aggressive they became.

In June 1982 I had a visit from the Canadian ambassador to Moscow, Robert A. D. Ford, who articulated such conventional wisdom on this matter in the hope of convincing me that our policies toward the USSR were fundamentally flawed. "The best policy," he assured me, "would be to persuade the Soviet leadership that the United States does not desire the breakdown of the regime and the dissolution of its empire: this policy alone stands a chance of convincing Moscow to cut down its military expenditures and turn to its domestic problems."* Every sentence in this statement turned out to be wrong: it was mirror-imaging at its worst. I am not aware that either Ambassador Ford or any other diplomat holding such views ever retracted them or admitted to having been mistaken.

It is difficult today to understand the passions aroused by arms control negotiations. This was a direct result of the belief, actively fostered by Moscow, that in the nuclear age *all* that mattered was avoidance of war; hence, no difficulties should be raised over communist activities in any part of the world, the more so in that they did little more—so it was alleged—than support spontaneous local strivings for social justice and/or national self-determination. Arms control negotiations, Moscow insisted with the backing of Western liberal opinion, were the alpha and omega of East-West relations. Nothing else mattered. In reality, these negotiations were hollow rituals intended to reassure a frightened public that they reduced the threat of nuclear war, thus making it amenable to concessions to Moscow.

Viewed dispassionately, the whole position of the arms control lobby

---

*He reported on our conversation in his memoirs published in 1989: Pipes, he wrote "was convinced of the coming collapse of the Soviet economy and social system and certain that a little push on the part of the West was all that was needed to hasten the day. I argued that an economy the size of the Soviet . . . could not collapse in the classic Western sense." Robert A. D. Ford, *Our Man in Moscow* (Toronto, 1989), 326.

rested on a glaring contradiction. The same people who, in order to impede our military buildup, insisted that nuclear superiority was meaningless argued that it was vital to reduce nuclear arsenals. On the one hand they depicted nuclear superiority as futile because the two sides already possessed arsenals capable of destroying life on earth a hundred or more times over—the figure was bandied about quite loosely. At the same time they argued that stopping the growth of these arsenals made the world safer. How? Why should we feel safer when instead of facing destruction one hundred times over we were confronted with the prospect of "only" fiftyfold annihilation? Or, for that matter, tenfold? None of this made any sense, but millions of people were persuaded that arms control negotiations assured a more secure tomorrow.

In a debate in which he and I engaged in Chicago in 1980, Paul Warnke, a prominent Washington lawyer and onetime head of the Arms Control and Disarmament Agency, contended that unless SALT II was ratified, we faced the likelihood of World War III. In fact, the treaty was never ratified and no World War III ensued. Strobe Talbott, then a journalist working for *Time* and later deputy secretary of state under Clinton, published in 1984 *Deadly Gambits,* an attack on Reagan's refusal to resume arms control negotiations, which, as its title indicates, the author considered inviting a potential catastrophe.

The truth was the contrary of this accepted wisdom: the more secure Soviet leaders were, the more aggressively they behaved, and vice versa. The only time they were utterly accommodating to a foreign "capitalist" power was in 1940–41 when they feared that Hitler, having conquered continental Europe, would turn against them: to placate him, they showered him with food and strategic materials and even turned over to him German communists who had sought refuge in Moscow. It is true that in their relations with us they felt anxiety, but it had a different cause from that which conventional wisdom attributed to it: as long as the United States was free and prosperous they could not rest in peace because this freedom and prosperity was a permanent thorn in their side, challenging their authority at home. Hence no matter what we did, short of self-destruction, they felt threatened and acted aggressively, especially if they thought they could do so with impunity: in the words of George Kennan, they were hostile to us not for what we did but for what we were. Aggressiveness was imbedded in their system. Only when this system collapsed could there be peace, as indeed happened after 1991.

But at the time such thinking seemed positively inane. When the Reagan administration adopted the strategy of pushing the Soviet Union toward reform it ran into a wall of hostility in and out of government. Talbott wrote in 1984 as follows:

> Speaking privately, [some] Administration officials, especially professional diplomats and intelligence analysts with long experience in Soviet affairs not only disavowed the notion that the United States could manipulate Soviet internal politics, but they expressed confidence that the Soviets recognized such theorizing for what it was: idiosyncratic, extremist, and very much confined to the fringes of government.*

Talbott singled me out as the "principal theoretician" "of the controversial view about the vulnerability of the internal workings of the Soviet Union to external manipulation" and agreed with Soviet spokesmen that I was an "extremist."

It is true that Reagan's view of the Soviet regime, although in its fundamentals profoundly sound, was not fully thought out. He believed that the communist leaders, like all heads of state, cared for the well-being of their people and if they failed to bring them freedom and prosperity, it was because they were captives of a false ideology. At one NSC meeting (March 25, 1982) he wondered aloud whether the day would not come when the Soviet Union would find itself in such an economic predicament that we would be able to say to its government: "Have you learned your lesson? If you rejoin the civilized world we will help and do wonderful things for your people." He realized only later the vested interest that the Soviet ruling elite, the *nomenklatura,* had in keeping its population lean and hungry.

Yet, at the same time, he understood very well—intuitively rather than intellectually—the fundamental weakness of the Soviet regime. Just how he managed to do this I have never understood, but I think his strong moral sense played an important role because in dealing with totalitarian regimes the customary "realistic" or "pragmatic" criteria were of little use. Similarly, Churchill had grasped the nature of communism almost from the moment it came to power in Russia, as he did fifteen years later that of national socialism. Like Reagan's, his was virtually the only voice of courage in a chorus clamoring for accommodation.

Yet for all his virulent anticommunism, Reagan was quite willing quietly to negotiate with Moscow. He had a dread of nuclear war. He also felt he could appeal to the human side of Soviet leaders, believing

---

*Strobe Talbott, *The Russians and Reagan* (New York, 1984), 74–75. The title of this book sponsored by the Council of Foreign Relations is in itself revealing: the author was not so much concerned with what the U.S. president and his advisors thought of the Soviet Union, but what Soviet leaders said about them.

that they were, fundamentally, like us and only blinded by communist doctrine. In April 1981, while recuperating from the attempt on his life, he addressed a personal letter to Brezhnev intended to appeal to his human side. The letter was shown to the NSC staff and several others for vetting. Having read it, we looked at each other in dismay: it was so maudlin and so at odds with Reagan's public stance.[45] Reagan deliberately wrote it by hand to emphasize its personal nature and was disappointed to receive a typed answer which made him doubt that Brezhnev had ever seen it.[46]

Because Reagan knew what he wanted but could not articulate his feelings in terms that made sense to foreign policy professionals at home and abroad, I took it upon myself to do so on his behalf. My intention was to formulate the theoretical rationale of his Soviet policy in the hope that it would serve as the foundation of an official document. Within days of joining the NSC staff I asked Allen for authorization to draft a paper that would spell out the premises of the Reagan administration's policy toward the Soviet Union. Allen promptly agreed.

But the proposal at once ran into opposition from the Department of State, which disliked the idea of such a paper for it smacked of "ideology," its bugaboo. It feared the policy paper would serve to institutionalize Reagan's belligerent anticommunism, so far confined to rhetoric, and cause no end of trouble with our allies. But if it had to be done, it insisted on doing it on its own premises. Toward the end of February 1981, Haig commissioned Paul Wolfowitz to draft a "Soviet strategy paper." Wolfowitz, a student of Albert Wohlstetter and a onetime member of Team B, was a bright young specialist on military matters but in no sense versed in Soviet affairs.

In early March, State convened the first Senior Inter-Agency (SIG) meeting on the subject, which I attended along with Allen. The discussion, chaired by Under Secretary of State and former ambassador to Moscow Walter Stoessel, meandered aimlessly until an exasperated Allen asked: "Do you want a paper or a policy?" Later that month I received a copy of Wolfowitz's "East-West paper." It was predictable State Department boilerplate, the product, undoubtedly, of many hands. It spelled out how we were to react to Soviet aggression but avoided any suggestion of initiatives. I reported to Allen my reaction to it on March 30, 1981, as follows:

> None of this strikes me as bold, innovative, or likely to succeed. *We must put the Soviet Union on the defensive.* I cannot express the central idea of a Reagan Soviet policy more concisely. To do so, we must turn the tables on them and exploit their internal difficulties which are steadily worsening.

State is not capable of thinking in such terms. I propose that we duly comment on their paper and then shelve it in order to proceed with our own undertaking.

State, however, would not let go. Several more meetings took place, each chaired by a lower ranking official. In July, another SIG was convened under Stoessel to discuss the East-West paper. Some tougher language had been inserted into it to meet our objections, but it was still insipid. During the discussion I asked: "What do we hope to achieve with our policies?" This question produced general consternation: apparently in concentrating on the means, the drafters never considered the ends. No response was forthcoming. It never came and in the end the paper was shelved.

The absence of a document explaining the rationale behind our Soviet policy had a serious drawback. In the discussions with the allies which accompanied the various crises in our relations with Moscow, we never made clear what we were aiming at with our countermeasures. They were asked to cooperate but left in the dark about our objectives. They therefore tended to misinterpret our rhetoric and our moves as visceral anticommunism, dangerous as well as futile, devoid of any rationale, for which reason most of the time they refused to go along. Whenever I had the opportunity to explain our strategy to a European diplomat or journalist, the response was one of surprise that we really had a goal in mind. Reagan delivered stirring speeches against communism, but he never spelled out, unemotionally, the theoretical underpinnings of his policies.

In May 1981 I submitted to Allen the manuscript of my own paper, hoping he would forward it to the president. But Allen kept it on his desk without action for several months. In September 1981, he finally convened a small group to discuss it: the reaction was favorable, but when the meeting was over Allen told me that the president would have no time to read it. He submitted it to Reagan only around Thanksgiving 1981, days before departing on what turned out to be permanent leave.

This was accompanied by a most unpleasant incident that underscored Allen's insecurity. On November 8, 1981, following a staff meeting, I approached him to inquire about the president's forthcoming foreign policy speech. According to my journal for that day:

> Before I could say anything, he turned to [his assistant] Janet [Colson] and asked: "Did you tell him?" She shook her head. "Get that cover off!" (He was referring to my "Reagan Soviet Policy" memo that was to go to R[onald] R[eagan] on the cover of which I had given my name as author.

Such had been our understanding when I joined the staff—that all my papers for RR would carry my name.) I said something about our agreement, but he shot back: "Get that cover off! I have asked you to do so." . . . He added he'll see to it that RR knows who wrote it.

I have not been spoken to in this manner since my days as an army private. Such treatment considerably dampened my regret when shortly afterwards Allen was fired, the more so because I had no reason to believe that he had really informed Reagan who had authored the document.

Allen's outburst was probably prompted by the fact that by this time he and his NSC staff had come under increasing criticism from the media: it bore all the earmarks of being orchestrated from the White House. The attacks continued in the late summer and intensified toward the end of the year. *Newsweek* launched a brief but brutal assault on him in November 1981 when it reported that the NSC staff were stung by reports of their alleged incompetence: "all they're asking is for a *chance* to be incompetent."[47] A week later, on November 27, William Buckley's *National Review*, highly regarded by Reagan, took Allen to task for mismanaging the NSC and recommended that he be transferred to Commerce. It singled me out as the "leading light in the NSC firmament," adding that according to gossip I felt "underutilized and constrained, like a circus stallion required to run around a very small ring."[48] Some interpreted these words as Buckley's way of promoting me for Allen's post. It naturally made Allen very edgy. I was privately advised by a number of friends to contact Haig, presumably to see if I could switch to State but I ignored this advice. Still, I was dismayed by the situation and in July wrote in my journal: "The NSC is dead."

There were numerous signs of disarray at the NSC, of which the following will serve as an example. Early in November 1981, State sent me the draft of a proposed two-sentence message from Reagan to Brezhnev on the occasion of the forthcoming anniversary of the Bolshevik 1917 "revolution." The second sentence wished Brezhnev "prosperity." I removed this sentence and cleared only the innocuous first. To my astonishment, I learned soon afterwards that Admiral Nance, one of Allen's two administrative assistants, without consulting me, had cleared the State's text several days earlier. I contacted our Moscow embassy to stop it from being delivered, but it was too late.

In my paper I advanced four central propositions:

· Communism is inherently expansionist: its expansionism will subside only when the system either collapses or, at the very least, is thoroughly reformed.

- The Stalinist model . . . confronts at present a profound crisis caused by persistent economic failures and difficulties brought about by overexpansion.
- The successors of Brezhnev and his Stalinist associates are likely in time to split into "conservative" and "reformist" factions, the latter of which will press for modest economic and political democratization.
- It is in the interest of the United States to promote the reformist tendencies in the USSR by a *double-pronged* strategy: *encouraging proreform forces inside the USSR and raising for the Soviet Union the costs of its imperialism.**

Reagan wrote on the cover "very sound." The essay, passed on to Tony Dolan, one of the White House principal speechwriters, provided the theoretical basis of Reagan's famous London speech in June 1982.

My advice ran into the teeth of conventional U.S. Cold War policy toward the Soviet Union which applied behaviorist psychology by punishing Soviet aggression and rewarding good conduct but carefully avoided interfering with the regime itself. To me such a policy appeared futile because, as I have noted previously, it was the system that drove the Soviet Union to aggression. This being the case, we had to do all in our power to change the system, mainly by a policy of economic denial and a vigorous rearmament program. The former would require Moscow to reform its command economy; the latter would demonstrate to it the futility of attempting to gain military superiority over us.

The policy of containment, which remained one of the foundation stones of U.S.-Soviet policy, had long been overtaken by events. This policy recommended that we thwart Soviet territorial expansion in order to create internal pressures that would, in time, force change. It was an old-fashioned concept in that it viewed imperialism in traditional territorial terms, assuming that the Soviet Union, like Nazi Germany, expanded by military conquest. In reality, the communists had devised since 1917 a whole array of instruments of conquest, of which direct military action was only one and by no means the most important: the invasion of Afghanistan in 1979 was the first occasion since the failed assault on Poland in 1920 that the Soviet army was used in peacetime for the purpose of expansion. Their preferred method was to work from within by promoting political subversion and creating economic dependence. After 1949, when China was taken over by the communists, the containment policy lost its relevance. In the years that followed, Moscow leaped over our barriers and set up proxy regimes on every continent: there was Ethiopia, Angola, and Ghana in Africa; North Korea and

---

*It was only much later—in 1999—that I learned similar premises and similar policy recommendations had been articulated by Emmanuel Todd in *La chute finale* (Paris, 1976), translated into English and brought out by a small publishing house in 1979 as *The Final Fall*.

North Vietnam in Asia; Cuba, Chile, and Nicaragua in Central America. In none of these countries did Moscow establish hegemony by military conquest. As our unfortunate war in Vietnam demonstrated, it was impossible to stanch communist expansion by military means, for communism had metastasized globally. Hence, it was a hopeless undertaking to try to prevent its further spread at the periphery: one had to strike at the very heart of Soviet imperialism, its system.

But this point of view remained unarticulated because State pigeon-holed its own paper and ignored mine. On March 5, 1982, I wrote Clark that we could not hope to secure allied support for our harsh policies toward the Soviet bloc (which at that time included sanctions) unless we clearly spelled out their rationale. I quoted a recent Washington speech by French Minister of Commerce Michel Jobert, in which he said, "You are asking us to go with you on a journey but you are not telling us where you are heading and where we will end up." I suggested that to answer this legitimate concern we draft a National Security Decision Directive on the Soviet Union that would furnish the intellectual underpinning of a major speech on the subject which the president was deliver on his trip to Europe in June. Clark agreed to my drafting the Terms of Reference for such a document. My draft was ready on March 10, but my hope that an NSDD would be completed by the end of April proved unrealistic, largely due to the resistance of the Department of State. On March 23, Poindexter told me that my Terms of Reference draft would raise a "ruckus" at State. He suggested that we shelve it and instead dust off the State's own East-West paper of 1981, inserting some of my own ideas. Clark, eager to avoid conflict with State, agreed to this suggestion, but nothing came of it because the old paper was not capable of revision. In a note to Clark I wrote:

> The basic difference between State and myself is philosophical. State believes that we should be content with an attempt to influence Soviet *behavior* by proffering rewards to the USSR when it is peaceful and punishments when it is not. Following what I sense to be the President's belief, I, by contrast, argue that behavior is the consequence of the *system* and that our policies (such as the recent sanctions and credit restraints) aim at modifying the system as prerequisite of changed behavior (e.g., compelling the USSR to alter its economic structure). The most controversial item in the attached Terms of Reference is the following sentence: "[The Review] will proceed on the premise that Soviet international behavior is a response not only to external threats and opportunities but also to the internal imperatives of the Soviet political, economic, social and

ideological system." State may be expected to fight this proposition tooth and nail, although it seems to me to express the quintessence of the President's approach.

Even though no policy paper was completed in time for the president's trip, it was agreed that the president would deliver a major address on our Soviet policy during his forthcoming visit to England. At the end of April, State submitted the draft of the projected speech in the preparation of which I did not participate, and routed it to the NSC for approval, not through me but through another staff member. It was filled with typical cliché-ridden rhetoric. However I was gratified to see that its authors finally did accept, although in what they called a "reduced and moderated form," my principle that "the nature of the Soviet system affects its foreign policy." Even so, I refused to endorse the paper, submitting in its place my own draft. The president received both versions. He rejected State's text, asking instead that a new text be prepared by Tony Dolan, an outstanding White House speechwriter who drafted most of Reagan's speeches on communism. (It was he who would coin the expression "evil empire.") Dolan, in turn, asked me for suggestions. He incorporated from my draft one paragraph that explained, in Marxist terms, why the Soviet Union found itself in what the communists called a "revolutionary situation."

It was initially intended that the president address the House of Commons at Westminster, the seat of the Parliament, and such was the proposal of Prime Minister Thatcher. But local opposition prevented this—the English elite regarded Reagan as a dangerous simpleton—and he had to settle for the setting of the less prestigious Royal Gallery in the House of Lords. Although initially he had told us he would not agree to "second best," he took this mean-spirited rebuff in good humor. "In an ironic sense Karl Marx was right," Reagan said in the speech he delivered on June 8, 1982:

> We are witnessing today a great revolutionary crisis, a crisis where the demands of the economic order are conflicting directly with those of the political order. But the crisis is happening not in the free, non-Marxist West, but in the home of Marxism-Leninism, the Soviet Union. . . . What we see here is a political structure that no longer corresponds to its economic base, a society where productive forces are hampered by political ones. *

*I was subsequently told by Dolan that in the original text of his address, President Reagan gave me personal credit for this statement but his reference to me was removed at the request of an official of the State Department as well as a colleague on the NSC staff.

The London speech infuriated the Russians more than anything Reagan had said or done since taking office. They realized full well its implications: that the USSR was, in Marxist terms, facing inevitable collapse and hence was not a power whose interests had to be taken into account or with which it was worth the trouble to negotiate.* It provided the theoretical foundation for a speech Reagan had delivered at Notre Dame a year earlier, to which I had also contributed in which he had said that we would "transcend communism." The Russians correctly attributed the Marxist allusion in the London speech to me: a journalist who returned from Moscow shortly afterwards told me that my name had become a household word there and that I was considered, in my influence on Soviet policy, a counterpart of Brzezinski. Although the speech argued that the Soviet Union was destroying itself, official Soviet spokesmen, resorting to their customary "dialectic" reasoning, described it as a declaration of intent by the United States to destroy the Soviet Union. When I reported to Reagan on these reactions, he responded, "So we touched a nerve."

On July 13, 1982, we held a meeting at State to discuss my NSDD draft. Richard Burt, the assistant secretary for European affairs, confirmed to me privately that the State's bureaucracy really did not want such a policy paper.

By this time, with Haig gone, Clark was determined to assert the authority of the NSC in the making of foreign policy, and to this end he authorized its staff to draft decision directives. During the months that followed, there were intermittent discussions with State on the subject of the Soviet NSDD, but Clark liked my version and in the end it was accepted, with some modifications. By the beginning of November 1982, State, having yielded on the most controversial point of my position (attack the "system"), enabled us to proceeded with the drafting of what came to be known as NSDD 75. This document has now been declassified and published.[49] The key paragraph was the second one. It defined as one of the principal tasks of the United States in its relations with the USSR:

> To promote, within the narrow limits available to us, the process of change in the Soviet Union toward a more pluralistic political and eco-

---

*The text I inserted in the president's speech was no more than a loose paraphrase of a passage from Marx's introduction to the *Critique of Political Economy,* familiar to every educated Russian: "At a certain stage of their development, the material productive forces of society enter into conflict with the existing productive relations or . . . with the relations of property under which until now they had developed. From the form of development of productive forces they turn into their fetters. Then there follows an era of social revolution."

nomic system in which the power of the privileged elite is gradually reduced. The U.S. recognizes that Soviet aggressiveness has deep roots in the internal system, and that relations with the USSR should therefore take into account whether or not they help to strengthen the system and its capacity to engage in aggression."

Despite the timorous "within the narrow limits available to us," inserted on State's insistence, the formulation represented a great victory over State and the conventional wisdom of the Sovietological community.

However, State did manage to score a minor triumph. The original draft which I had submitted contained two sentences under the heading "Economic Policy." They called on us

> To induce the USSR to shift capital and resources from the defense sector to capital investments and consumer goods.
>
> To refrain from assisting the Soviet Union with developing natural resources with which to earn, at minimal cost to itself, hard currency.

State, Treasury, and Agriculture objected to both sentences, while Commerce objected only to the second. Why they did so was and remains a mystery to me since the sentences merely fleshed out the basic principle cited above.

Mark Palmer called from State to request—"demand" would be more accurate—that I remove these two points from the final text; but Clark, through Poindexter, instructed me to retain them. The text which I forwarded for discussion by the NSC, therefore, included the two controversial sentences. It seems, however, that sometime before the NSC meeting that morning, Shultz, who was out of town, had gotten in touch with Reagan and persuaded him to drop them.

The draft of NSDD 75 was the subject of discussion at a NSC meeting which Clark had graciously scheduled on December 16, the day before I was to leave the NSC. Over Weinberger's objections, Reagan insisted that the two controversial points be removed because they would leak ("I would read about them in the *Washington Post*"), giving the Russians propaganda ammunition. "We know what we will do— we don't have to spell it out," he added by way of explanation. This seemed strange reasoning since the entire document on the table "spelled out" what we would do. I believe the main reason for abandoning them was that they seemed to invoke the pipeline sanctions which had caused so much trouble and had been lifted only a few weeks before. Most of the meeting was devoted to clarifying and making more precise the wording on economic measures, with Reagan taking an active part. He insisted that he wanted nothing in the document that would "forego compromise and quiet diplomacy." At the end it was agreed that we could treat economic relations with Moscow on a case-by-case basis without formulating general principles, let alone advocate "economic warfare."

As the meeting drew to a close Reagan expressed thanks to me for having worked for him and regret that I was about to leave.

Later, privately, Clark asked my opinion who should take my place. I suggested Jack Matlock, our ambassador to Czechoslovakia, because I had been favorably impressed by his reporting from Moscow in early 1981 when he had served as deputy chief of mission there. Clark hesitated at first from fear that as a professional member of the Foreign Service, Matlock would be beholden to the Department of State, but I helped overcome these hesitations by pointing out that judging by his dispatches he did not reason like a typical diplomat. Matlock himself would have preferred to stay in Prague, but in the end he returned home and in June 1983 took over my job. He enjoyed the trust of Shultz and helped guide the administration to a less confrontational policy under Gorbachev until spring 1987 when he left the NSC to take over the U.S. Embassy in Moscow.

In addition to Matlock, the president and Shultz used as a source of information on the Soviet Union and a private channel to its leaders Ms. Suzanne Massie, a nostalgic admirer of old Russia, sponsored by Nancy Reagan. She assured the president that Russia was ready to respond to any encouraging steps from him. I believe that she also stressed the fact that the Russian people were religious. Such thoughts appealed to Reagan's sentimental side although there was little evidence for them.

The Final Months

In October 1982 I was given leave to travel to Europe to lecture and attend international conferences. I gave talks on "The Soviet Union in Crisis" in Bonn, Cologne, and Paris, meeting everywhere with lack of understanding and unconcealed hostility toward Reagan and his foreign policies. The Germans mouthed the Soviet line that the only alternative to détente was nuclear war. The French accused us of hypocrisy: they objected that we sold grain to Russia while trying to deny the Europeans the right to sell Russia technology for gas development. They seemed unable (or, more likely, unwilling) to understand that by selling Moscow grain we depleted its hard currency reserves whereas they, by developing

Russia's energy exports, augmented them.* Everywhere I met with complete misunderstanding, first, of the critical economic situation of the Soviet Union and, second, of the role that economics played in international politics. Since the audiences I addressed were made up of highly intelligent and well-informed individuals, I had to conclude that their incomprehension of what we were doing stemmed partly from resentment of America's hegemony and partly from the desire to profit from trade with the USSR while we bore the brunt of the expenses of containment. On my return home, I told some people that the allies, while married to us, carried on an extramarital affair with our adversary.

The only sensible advice on this issue came from my old friend Boris Souvarine, who, in October 1981, during what was to be my last visit with him before his death, told me: "Remember Pipes: they will do everything but go to war: they are blackmailers." These words etched themselves deeply in my mind.

On November 10, 1982, news came that the long-expected event had finally happened: the death of Brezhnev. At a hastily convened meeting in the Oval Office the discussion turned to the question of who should represent the United States at his funeral. Clark showed the president a list drawn up by Shultz which had him heading the delegation: Reagan took one look at it and said that it was a delegation fit for the funeral of the queen of England. He absolutely refused to go. Clark then said Shultz thought that if the president declined to attend, George Bush should lead the U.S. delegation. Reagan replied that this was not a good idea because the vice president was in Africa on a previously cancelled visit and it would be taken badly there if he left prematurely, adding, "Let George Shultz go." I interjected that this might not be a satisfactory solution because heads of state were certain to be in attendance, and hence the vice president would be a more appropriate leader of the U.S. delegation. Reagan gave it a moment's thought and then agreed: "OK, let Bush go." I was amused to read in the press the next day what subtle interpretations were given to this decision. But I did not find it amusing to learn that during his visit to Moscow Bush told Andropov that they had "something in common in our backgrounds."[50] Apparently he was under the impression that the KGB, which Andropov had directed, was, like the CIA, a mere intelligence-gathering organization.

---

*In the report of the Transition Team drafted on December 19, 1980, by Angelo Codevilla and myself, the point was clearly articulated: "Trade and loans that increase Western dependence on the Soviet Union shouuld be discouraged; economic relations that increase Soviet dependence on the West (in matters of consumables, for instance) should be promoted."

The remark, if meant seriously, was appalling; if intended as a joke, in poor taste.

Although the president would not go to Moscow for Brezhnev's funeral, he agreed to pay a visit to the Soviet Embassy to express his condolences. I was asked to draft a statement for him to inscribe in the condolence book. It was an excruciating task for I felt not the least sorrow over Brezhnev's death. I realized then how hard it is to put in words something one does not feel or believe. My wording was tortured: Reagan wisely rejected it in favor of something much better of his own.

Paving the way for his visit to the embassy on Sixteenth Street, I went to inspect the building with a group of Secret Service men. The stairs, lined with somber-looking embassy personnel, led to a room guarded by boys and girls in Pioneer uniforms. Dobrynin met us on the second floor and showed us the condolence book. I nodded and attempted to withdraw, but he thrust a pen in my hand and asked me to sign. I tried to refuse but he would not let me go. What could I do? I scribbled a completely illegible signature so that no future historian could accuse me of hypocrisy.

Once it became certain that Andropov would succeed Brezhnev, I wrote a memorandum (on November 17) in which I outlined what the new general secretary was likely to do: restore a sense of strong leadership; try to stem the psychological onslaught launched by President Reagan and his "interference in internal Soviet affairs"; stop or at least reduce internal corruption and consumerism; derail U.S. defense programs; and repress and isolate the Soviet dissident movement.

I was moved by the several lunches and dinners given in my honor by friends and associates on the eve of my departure: one acquaintance told me he had seen prima donnas retire with less fanfare. On December 14, at a farewell lunch given by the NSC, McFarlane generously praised me for "humility" and "hard work," adding that when Soviet subjects came up in the Oval Office, Reagan would often ask, "What does Dick Pipes think?"

As my departure approached, Clark offered to appoint me a consultant to the NSC, in which capacity, he hoped, I would write and lecture in support of Reagan's foreign policy. When I asked whether I could feel free to speak my mind, he responded, "Keep us out of trouble!"

Apparently this was something I had difficulty doing. Rowland Evans and Bob Novak, who had a weekly news program on CNN, asked me if I would give them an interview. I said, yes, I would, but only after I had officially severed my ties with the government, i.e., after December 17.

Unfortunately they said, the interview had to be taped in the morning of Friday, December 17, but this should cause me no problem because it would not be aired until the following day. On this condition I agreed. Novak's opening question concerned Soviet involvement in the attempt on the life of Pope John Paul II. I responded that given the virtually certain participation of the Bulgarian secret services, which the KGB controlled, it was not implausible to assume that the KGB had had a hand in it, although there was no hard evidence to this effect. In view of the fact that the man who had headed the KGB in March 1981 was now head of state, it was a serious charge. But by the time the interview would be aired I would be back in private life.

That afternoon, Clark gave a Christmas party at Blair House across from the White House. In the midst of the good cheer, Clark's secretary approached me to say that I was wanted on the phone. It was the *New York Times*. The caller said stories were circulating in town that I had accused Andropov of masterminding the attempt on the life of the pope. I was astonished by this news because I had been solemnly promised that the program would not be televised until the next day. It turned out that to arouse interest in it, CNN had called the *Times* and the *Post* to tell them its sensational contents. The following Monday, by which time I was out of range of their diplomatic artillery, the Soviet chargé, Bessmertnykh, lodged with the Department of State a formal protest, charging "an unbridled slanderous campaign" against Bulgaria and the Soviet Union. Eagleburger rejected the note, saying that "in his extensive experience in Soviet affairs, he had never seen a Soviet communication so intemperately worded."

There were only two occasions when I was employed as consultant, both in early 1983, following which my ties to the Reagan administration and Washington appreciably weakened.

Toward the end of January 1983, Vice President Bush's security advisor, Don Gregg, invited me to brief the vice president. We met in the afternoon of January 27. Our discussion concerned not Russia but the projected deployment in Europe of intermediate-range missiles, the Pershing II's, requested by our NATO partners as a means of balancing the SS-20's which the Russians had been emplacing for the past several years. Moscow launched a massive propaganda campaign in Europe to foil these deployments, using to this end large-scale public demonstrations which its agents organized and financed. Bush, who was about to depart for Europe, was worried sick over the prospect of confronting anti-American mobs. I did my best to assuage his fears, reminding him that, after all, the Europeans themselves had requested these deployments and that the mobs were manipulated by rent-a-crowd professionals. I do not know whether I persuaded him, for he still looked very troubled when I took my leave.

The other incident involved an encounter with Shultz. In early March 1983 Shultz had State produce a paper on "U.S.–Soviet Relations: Where Do We Want to Be and How Do We Get There?"[51] Ignoring NSDD 75, which was less than three months old, Shultz, hoping by means of this new paper to persuade the president that the time had come to change course in our dealings with Moscow, requested to see him. The meeting was set for March 10. Departing from customary procedure, either at the president's request or on his own initiative, Clark made it into a State-NSC confrontation. He invited me to attend.

Shultz left in his memoirs a distorted picture of this encounter to make it appear as if the president had agreed with his recommendation but was thwarted by Clark and the NSC staff, whose "prisoner" he allegedly was.[52] This interpretation is widely off the mark, as I can attest from my detailed notes of the meeting.

Present were fourteen persons.* Shultz opened with a warning that what he was about to say was extremely sensitive and would cause much harm if leaked. At this point Reagan, with a mischievous smile, pulled up the corner of the tablecloth and addressing an imaginary microphone planted by Andropov, said: "This goes for you, too, Iurii!" The secretary was not amused.

Before making his case, Shultz shot a look at me, saying, "I know everyone in this room but you." Clark informed him who I was, whereupon he proceeded to outline a series of initiatives we could take with Moscow, such as raising the issues of Afghanistan and Poland as well as proceeding with renegotiating various agreements that were due for renewal (transportation, atomic energy, fisheries, etc.). At a certain point he stopped and glaring at me, said, "Your taking notes makes me very nervous." Clark assured him that I had been a trustworthy member of the NSC staff for two years.

Reagan listened to Shultz's proposals with growing impatience, yawning, and at one point almost dozing off. When Shultz finished, he spoke his mind. "It seems to me," Reagan said, "that in previous years of détente we always took steps and got kicked in the teeth." Our attempts

---

*The president and the vice president, Shultz, Clark, Ed Meese, James Baker, Bud McFarlane, William Casey, Admiral Murphy, Arthur Hartman, John Lenczowski, Richard Burt, Larry Eagleburger, and myself.

to get the Russians to cooperate led nowhere. We should exercise caution in dealing with them and make no overt appeals. When they remove irritants in our relations, we will respond in kind. In other words, Reagan was saying, no initiatives of our own, only responses to Soviet positive initiatives.

Clark then turned to me, requesting my opinion. Addressing Shultz, who sat directly across from me, I asked whether he proposed to take these steps one by one or all at once. Shultz stared me straight in the eye but made no response. I repeated the question and again received no answer. I suppose he was offended that having addressed the president of the United States, he was subjected to questioning by an academic.

Reagan then stepped in once more. If the Russians allowed the Pentecostals holed up in our Moscow embassy to leave the country, we could agree to fishery negotiations. We would respond similarly if they released Anatoly Shcharansky from prison. Should such goodwill gestures be made, we would not "crow" but quietly reciprocate. At this point he articulated what for him was a rather novel idea and which, I must assume, I had planted in his mind: "I no longer believe they are doctrinaire Communists—they are an autocracy interested in preserving their privileges."

When the meeting, which lasted an hour, was about to break up, a defeated and visibly irritated Shultz muttered to himself but so that others could hear: "What I get is: eschew bilateral talks, be careful with Dobrynin, and 'bang away' at Cuba, Afghanistan, and the Pentecostals. Personally, I don't think this is good."

In May 1983, I was requested, on Casey's initiative and on behalf of PFIAB, to undertake an analysis of the CIA's track record of political forecasting on the USSR over the previous five to six years. I chose three case studies—Poland, Afghanistan, and the Brezhnev succession—and with the help of two assistants went through reams of raw data. The findings, reached one year later, were not favorable to the agency. They indicated that in each instance it either failed to predict events or else predicted them wrongly: the culprit in each case was the familiar combination of mirror-imaging and wishful thinking. This time, the findings did not leak.

I also sat during the 1980s on consulting groups that advised the CIA on Soviet military, political, and economic developments, including the Military Advisory Panel of the National Intelligence Council (1986–88), which dealt with the highly sensitive intelligence data.

In December 1987 I was invited to join the "Dole for President" team as head of its Soviet advisory group. The work proved frustrating because, unlike Reagan, Dole had no clear vision of what our policy toward the USSR ought to be. He had too many foreign policy advisors: a mistake that would be compounded in his next and final effort at winning the presidency.

Bush systematically eliminated from his staff all Reagan personnel with the notable exception of his friend James Baker. I did brief him at Camp David prior to the Malta summit with Gorbachev in November 1989 but in the company of two other specialists who held a much more benign view of Soviet Union intentions than I did. Otherwise, I had no further contacts with him.

With the election of Clinton my connections with Washington ceased altogether. I did receive once or twice early in his administration invitations to consult, but I interpreted them as window dressing and declined.

Reflections on Government Service

I left Washington with mixed feelings.

Intellectually, the greatest benefit I derived from the experience was to be able to observe at close range how political decisions are made at the highest level. Like most historians, I used to believe in powerful, invisible forces directing statesmen. Like most educated people, I thought that high politics resulted from a careful, inductive process by virtue of which all the information available to the government is conveyed upwards and there subjected to judicious analysis, with all the pros and cons weighed until a decision is reached.

Reality turned out to be quite different. For one, personalities play an enormous role in high politics: likes and dislikes as well as fears, anger, and hopes. Previously I had found it difficult to believe the claim of contemporaries that Nicholas II had dismissed his chief minister, Sergei Witte, because he could not abide his coarse manners. This seemed too flimsy a reason to lose the services of a devoted and talented official. But observing Reagan's reactions to Haig, I concluded that such personal feelings could indeed play a decisive role in politics. Haig's frenetic behavior, his assertiveness and arrogance, went against the grain of Reagan's easygoing, amiable nature. Similarly, Reagan's antipathy to and anger at the French played a large role in his controversial decision to extend extraterritorially our sanctions on Siberian pipeline equipment. These lessons etched themselves in my mind and affected the way I henceforth wrote history. It has amused me ever since to see how younger historians, without experience in politics, would brush such considerations aside as I, too, might have done before my Washington days.

Second, as concerns the process of decision-making, it is not the result of careful weighing of data and all the pros and cons. The information which the bureaucratic machine spews out is too voluminous, complicated, and contradictory for statesmen to absorb. Decisions are therefore usually made ad hoc, on the basis of intellectual predispositions and the mood of the moment. This held true not only of the Reagan administration but of all that I have studied, including the governments of Russia under the tsars and communists.

It is for this reason that anyone who has had experience with the way government works views skeptically theories that explain political behavior in a purposeful, rational manner, let alone in terms of conspiracies. In October 1982, I addressed the French Institute of International Relations (IFRI) in Paris. The discussion which followed my talk centered on the embargo Reagan had imposed on the sale of gas pipeline equipment to the Soviet Union. One young participant asserted in a tone brooking no contradiction that the true purpose of these sanctions was to "wreck European industry." I looked at him as if he were mad. I responded that not only was nothing like it ever intended by a country that had spent tens of billions to rebuild European industries after World War II, but that even if someone had conceived such a bizarre plan, there was no mechanism to implement it. Can one imagine convoking a meeting of the National Security Council to discuss "wrecking European industry"? The NSC meetings were usually convened to deal with urgent current questions, rarely long-term strategies, and never philosophical issues. But this most people find difficult to believe. They prefer sweeping historical explanations if they are educated, and conspiratorial ones if they are not.

Judging by the journal I kept during my two years in Washington, nine-tenths of government work is a waste of time: one simply spins wheels in place. Once in a while, however, at critical moments, there occur opportunities to act, and what one does then can make a difference. Such moments are exhilarating. And I certainly derived satisfaction from the knowledge that I had made some contribution to a foreign policy that helped bring down the Soviet Union, the most dangerous and dehumanizing force in the second half of the twentieth century. My view is that the USSR collapsed primarily from internal causes, that is, from the inability of the communists to establish on solid foundations a regime that violated everything we know of human nature and social relations. However, the determination of the United States to foil Soviet foreign policy ambitions played a major role in this process, and here two presidents made a particular contribution: Truman at the beginning of the Cold War and Reagan at its end. Reagan's ideological offensive and his military buildup rattled the Russians, robbing them of the confidence, acquired in the 1960s and 1970s, that they had the United States on the ropes. That loss of self-confidence was a major factor in the mistakes they committed in the late 1980s.

Personally, I realized that I was ill suited for work in a large organization. My sense of frustration, my repeated (though unconsummated) resolutions to quit, were mainly due to the fact that I had been accustomed since the age of fifteen to intense intellectual effort, day in and day out. When I sit down to write or rise to speak, I express my own thoughts and feelings, and I can do so at any time. I am sovereign: my subjects are hundreds of thousands of words in the English vocabulary which I can order about as I see fit. I scrutinize them and, if they do not please me, rearrange them. But in government, as in every large organization, one is on the receiving end, busy only when superiors throw work one's way. I found this very frustrating, the more so that work was often deliberately diverted from me by officials who disliked either me or my ideas. And, of course, all one says or writes has to be coordinated or "cleared." Even the president has his public statements subtly censored.

When I first arrived in Washington, some old-timers predicted that I would never leave. As for myself, however, I had no doubt that I would be back at Harvard in two years, come what may. My certainty derived not only from a deep-seated love of scholarship but also from lack of taste for power, the impulse that drives political ambition. Power provides psychic compensation: it impels a person who cannot rule himself to rule others. I do not deny that I enjoyed the attention I received while in the White House, but power, as such, held no attraction for me, and hence the kind of advice I received from Kissinger went in one ear and out the other. Why this should have been the case was made clear for me by Eric Hoffer, one of the wisest minds of twentieth-century America. In his diary he wrote as follows:

> The significant point is that people unfit for freedom—who cannot do much with it—are hungry for power. The desire for freedom is an attribute of a "have" type of self. It says: leave me alone and I shall grow, learn, and realize my capacities. The desire for power is basically an attribute of a "have-not" type of self. If Hitler had had the talents and temperament of a

genuine artist, if Stalin had had the capacity to become a first-rate theoretician, if Napoleon had had the makings of a great poet or philosopher—they would hardly have developed the all-consuming lust for absolute power. Freedom gives us a chance to realize our human and individual uniqueness . . . those who lack the capacity to achieve much in an atmosphere of freedom will clamor for power.[53]

It was freedom not power that I yearned for. And on the first day out of government, I jubilantly noted in my journal: "Fantastic! It is 9:20 A.M.—the time I got to my office every day—and I have just arrived at the Library of Congress. . . . The collar and leash that invisibly tugged at me are gone."

FOUR

Back at Harvard

Survival Is Not Enough

I returned to Harvard in February 1983 something of a celebrity. My classes were filled to overflowing: in 1987, the course on the Russian Revolution, which I had first offered in spring 1976, was among the university's ten courses with the largest enrollment. I was constantly interviewed by newspapers and television networks, both domestic and foreign. I traveled frequently to conferences and universities around the country to lecture on current affairs. My calendars for this and the following several years are crammed with such engagements. Not infrequently, I would leave for Europe on Wednesday night and return on Sunday afternoon, concentrating my teaching in the first three days of the week.

When I go over my diaries for the period I am amazed where I found the energy to travel so much and depressed that the vast majority of these conferences, interviews, and so on left so little residue in the mind. Were they a waste of time? On balance, probably not. The discussions of the internal situation in the Soviet Union, of our relations with that country, or of nuclear policy rarely changed mine or anyone else's mind. But they did establish a certain consensus: we agreed what to disagree about, in this manner narrowing and sharpening the debate. By contrast in a country like the Soviet Union where such discussions could not take place and where one disagreed over what to agree on, every person formed his private opinion on every subject under the sun, with the result that there were as many opinions as there were people: when freedom was finally restored, Russians found no common language such as is indispensable to the functioning of an effective democracy.

Public engagements loosened my attachment to the History Department. Departmental meetings devoted a great deal of time to problems of individual students, junior faculty, and especially tenure appointments. These were important matters, of course, but compared to the issues I had dealt with in Washington they seemed inconsequential, and I could not treat them quite as seriously as before. Increasingly, therefore, the center of my professional life shifted outside the university.

As I was preparing to leave Washington, Bill Safire, the *New York Times* columnist, urged me to write a "book." I think what he had in mind was a personal account of my two years in the White House. He recommended that I contact his literary agent, Morton Janklow. Janklow normally handled best-sellers which earned multimillion dollar advances, but as a favor to Safire he agreed to represent me. It was the first time that I employed the services of a literary agent. Janklow sold the rights to my book to Simon and Schuster, whose editor, Erwin Glickes, gave me advice that ended with the admonition: "Remember—lots of anecdotes!"

I felt, however, that I could not write what in the trade is known as a "kiss-and-tell" book, describing what I had seen and experienced, without betraying the trust placed in me. So instead I proceeded to write a serious book about the Soviet Union and the prospects of our relations with it, drawing on information I had acquired while in Washington though without reference to classified data. After rejecting various alternatives, I settled on the title *Survival Is Not Enough,* by which I meant that avoidance of a nuclear holocaust was not an adequate objective for our foreign policy.*

I wrote the book quickly because I knew exactly what I wanted to say and had a great amount of material at my disposal. I began to work on it in June 1983 and in February 1984 sent the manuscript to the publisher: it came out in October 1984. An excerpt from it appeared in the fall 1984 issue of *Foreign Affairs* under the title "Can the Soviet Union Reform?"

For the book's epigraph, I drew on the Roman historian Livy (Titus Livius): *quo timoris minus sit, eo minus ferme perculi esse* (Where there is less fear there is less danger).[1] As I had jotted down in my Washington notebook:

---

*Riding in an elevator at the time, I told a friend what title I had settled on for the book-in-progress. A middle-aged lady, who happened to share the elevator with us, overheard me. When my friend and I parted in front of the apartment house she approached me, saying: "You are so right! I am tired of just surviving: I do want more out of life." I wonder how many copies of *Survival Is Not Enough* were bought by readers with her problem. In 2002, one Seth Godin would "borrow" my title for a book dealing with "Change, Organizations, Evolution, Darwin, Management, Job Security, Memes and How to Thrive in a World Gone Nuts." *New York Times,* January 14, 2002, p. C3.

Ultimately, the issue will be decided by the determination of the competing parties. The question is whether the desire of the *nomenklatura* to hold on to and expand its power is greater or lesser than the will of the democracies to preserve their way of life. There probably would be no dispute about the outcome if nuclear weapons did not strike such terror into the hearts of Western peoples so as to sap their will to stand up. The issue, therefore, is fear and courage. Clausewitz, speaking of the battlefield, noted that "all war is directed against human courage" and that the main effect of conflict is to "kill the enemy's courage."[2]

In the introduction to my book, I justified adding yet another volume to the vast literature on U.S.-Soviet relations with the argument that this literature suffered from a serious flaw: it treated our relations "almost exclusively as problems confronting the United States, to be debated and decided upon by Americans. The Soviet regime, with its interests, ideology and political strategy, is regarded in this context as only tangentially involved." It was, indeed, a striking feature of the Sovietological literature that it never tired of discussing what we must do and hardly ever what we should demand of the Russians, except that they cause us no trouble. This attitude seemed to me both insular and arrogant. Furthermore, I continued, even in the massive literature on the Soviet Union itself, "the link between its internal order and international conduct is rarely established." This was wrong because the foreign policy of all countries is a function of their domestic policies: "The manner in which a government treats its own citizens obviously has great bearing on the way it will treat other nations. A regime that does not respect legal norms inside its borders is not likely to show respect for them abroad. If it wages war against its own people, it can hardly be expected to live at peace with the rest of the world."

Proceeding from these premises, I devoted much space to the internal workings of communist regimes and the ways these affected their conduct of foreign policy. Next I went on to describe the economic and political crises afflicting communist countries: crises which set a limit to their ambitions and threatened their authority. For all the appearance of solidity and permanence, I wrote, the USSR found itself in a "revolutionary situation" from which the only way out was far-reaching internal reform:

> a growing discrepancy is emerging between the global ambitions of the Communist elite and the means at its disposal . . . this elite is finding it increasingly difficult to pursue its global ambitions and to maintain intact the Stalinist system. While the Soviet regime is in no danger of imminent collapse, it cannot forever "muddle through" and will have to choose

before long between reducing its aspirations to worldwide hegemony and transforming its internal regime, and perhaps even find it necessary to do the one and the other.

"Before long" turned out to be six months, when Mikhail Gorbachev would assume office as head of the Soviet government and launch his perestroika. My recommendation was to let the Soviet Union "subvert itself": "If the Soviet regime wishes to realize its global ambitions, it must move toward the adoption of economic and social institutions that will ultimately subvert it."

It thus transpires that I did not expect the "imminent collapse" of the Soviet regime which, in fact, occurred seven years after my words had appeared in print. But then neither did Gorbachev. On assuming office, Gorbachev and his associates, conscious of the crisis confronting the Communist bloc, set themselves to reform the system by introducing greater legality, giving greater scope to private enterprise, and decentralizing the administration. "The basic task" before Soviet leaders, I had written in my book, "is to harness the creative forces of the country in public service, to bridge the gap between the pursuit of private goals— presently the sole objective of the vast majority of citizens in Communist countries, their leaders included—and the interests of the whole." This is what perestroika attempted but failed to accomplish.

Why did it fail? It seems to me because the reformers fell victim of their own propaganda (as well as the teachings of foreign Sovietologists), which saw their regime as much more stable and popular than it, in fact, was. When the reforms Gorbachev initiated ran into the resistance of the communist apparatus, he sought to overcome this resistance by appealing to the population at large and involving it in the political process, confident that the citizenry would back its program of in-system reforms. That proved a fatal error because the population, silenced for seventy years, took advantage of the newly gained freedom of speech and modest political rights not to reinforce the communist system but to tear loose from it. Thus, rather than follow the Chinese example and keep political power firmly in his hands while carrying out the reform program, Gorbachev relaxed the reins of communist authority and the coach soon careened out of control. No one could have foreseen such a development, if only because it was the result of decisions taken by a handful of people, without mass participation.*

---

*Iurii Andropov, the longtime head of the KGB and for a short time, following Brezhnev's death, general secretary of the Communist Party of the Soviet Union, did foresee the dangers of relaxing controls over opinion. As he told the head of East German intelligence ser-

The reviewers of *Survival Is Not Enough* interpreted my views each in their own way, but I was struck that Helmut Sonnenfeldt, once Kissinger's Soviet expert, wrote in the conclusion of his review that I had "come close to promising peace after the transformation of the Soviet system. On this score, [the author] is, as he says, neither hawk nor dove, just *very* optimistic."[3]

A History of the Russian Revolution

Unknowingly—for I learned of his literary habits only years later—I emulated Anthony Trollope in that as soon as I finished one book, I proceeded immediately to the next. This practice stemmed not from the desire to see myself in print but from a routine of daily life established when I was still in my teens that revolved around research and writing. As an athlete feels the constant need to exercise his body so I feel the need to exercise my mind, especially in the first half of the day when my energy is at its peak. In 1973 while in London on a year's leave, having finished *Russia under the Old Regime,* I decided to take time off from writing: after all, I reasoned, I had published enough books and articles to be able to afford a few months of leisure. The result was torment. I would rise in the morning and face a bleak, empty day. I would run down several times before lunch to buy English and foreign newspapers and read them from cover to cover. I would listen to radio and television news. Such forced idleness proved not only stressful, but it also robbed me of the pleasure of enjoying London in the afternoon and evening because, having accomplished nothing earlier in the day, I could not relax. After a week or two I gave up and went on to the next book, which was volume 2 of the Struve biography.

This time, having finished *Survival Is Not Enough,* I addressed the subject of the Russian Revolution. It turned out to be my most ambitious undertaking, one that would occupy me, on and off, for more than ten years. I conceived the book as a sequel to *Russia under the Old Regime* and initially intended to cover half a century—from 1878 to 1928. I remember Isaiah Berlin urging me to write such a book, possibly because he wanted a foil to E. H. Carr, with whom he had carried on a long dispute about historical "inevitability" and whom he personally despised.

---

vices: "Too many groups have suffered under the repression in our country. . . . If we open up all the valves at once, and people start to express their grievances, there will be an avalanche and we will have no means of stopping it." Markus Wolf, *Man Without a Face* (London, 1997), 218–19.

At the time, the only history of the Russian Revolution worthy of the name was the one published in 1935 by the *Christian Science Monitor*'s Moscow correspondent, William Henry Chamberlin. His two-volume work lacked a clear conception but it was fair-minded and based on thorough research in the sources then available. The same could not be said of Carr's *History of the Soviet Union,* the first three volumes of which, dealing with the revolution, came out in the early 1950s. Carr avoided altogether narrative history and personalities in favor of a dry catalogue of events, which for him consisted mainly of legislative acts: suffice it to say that he did not find the space to mention even once Nicholas II, the reigning tsar at the time the revolution broke out! His magnum opus, ultimately spread over fourteen volumes, was a reference work rather than a history. It further suffered from a pronounced antidemocratic bias and a determinism grounded in the belief that whatever happens is, by the mere virtue of happening, inevitable and hence beyond moral judgment—an attitude that in the 1930s had led him to write editorials in the London *Times* urging the appeasement of Nazi Germany.

Thus there was room for another study of this momentous event, and even before completing volume 2 of *Struve* (1979) I turned to the revolution. In 1975–76 I offered for the first time a lecture course on the subject: it proved too schematic, as one of the undergraduate students pointed out to me. It underwent many revisions before finally (spring term 1984) taking shape as a Core Course called Historical Study B-56, which attracted large enrollments and which I taught on alternate years until my retirement.

The Russian Revolution was the defining event of my generation. It has been argued that World War I had an even more decisive influence on the twentieth century, and, indeed, without it there probably would have been no revolution in Russia and even if there were, it would have taken a different, less violent course. But I am more persuaded by the argument that if not for the Bolshevik power seizure in 1917 Russia, the post–World War I world would have sooner or later returned to some kind of normalcy. The Nazis would have been unlikely to take over Germany had Hitler not had the communist prototype both to inspire him and provide him with a bogey to frighten the German people into granting him unlimited authority. Moscow also supplied him with help at the critical moment in his drive to power in the 1932 Reichstag elections. And without Nazism and Moscow's assent to Hitler's invasion of Poland, there would have been no World War II. As for the post–World War era, it was dominated by the Cold War, the offspring of October 1917. For all these reasons, the record of the Russian Revolution—its antecedents, progress, and consequences—holds paramount importance for the understanding of our age. For this reason, too, when I come to think of it, nearly all my scholarly work was directly or indirectly connected with that pivotal event.

It is sometimes said that a historian can adequately deal only with a subject for which he feels sympathy. This contention strikes me as untenable since it means that one cannot write about topics which evoke universal opprobrium: by its terms, only a Nazi could write a satisfactory biography of Hitler. In fact, historians often write inspired by hostility: Lytton Strachey, probably thinking of his own study of the Victorian era, has observed that a point of view "by no means implies sympathy. One might almost say that it implies the reverse. At any rate it is curious to observe how many instances there are of great historians who have been at daggers drawn with their subjects"—citing Gibbon and Michelet as examples.[4]

Chamberlin's history and the others then available—I ignore those published in the USSR since these were not scholarship but propaganda—reduced the revolution to the struggle for power in Russia, concentrating on political, military, and, to a lesser extent, social events. But the Bolshevik revolution was meant to be total, to remake everything, man himself very much included—in Trotsky's words, "to overturn the world." This audacious aspiration of the men who made the Russian Revolution was ignored in every account that I could find.

The problem was compounded by the emergence in the 1960s among the younger generation of American and British historians of a "revisionist" trend. It had several sources of inspiration, one of them being the French *Annales* school which rejected political history in favor of a stress on culture, both high and low, *mentalités,* and patterns of everyday life. The atmosphere of détente in which this kind of revisionism emerged and flourished also contributed to its spread inasmuch as depicting the Soviet government as a totalitarian dictatorship born of a coup d'état smacked of the Cold War.

Methodologically, the main sources of the revisionist school were Marx and Engels with their claim that the decisive forces in history are economics and the class relations resulting from them, all else—politics and culture included—being relegated to the "superstructure." In the words of the *Communist Manifesto*: "All history until now has been a history of class struggles." The statement is as wrongheaded as would be one claiming that all history was a history of political or ideological rivalries. In reality, anyone who immerses himself in the past quickly learns that history is shaped by many different forces, including accidents and personalities, each playing a decisive role at particular times and places but never universally. The main effect of the Marxist approach is to ignore politics and culture altogether or at least reduce them to a subordinate role.* History has to be written "from below." One wonders how the adherents of this school would explain the most devastating events of twentieth-century history—the two world wars. Could they seriously maintain that the masses were clamoring for hostilities in which they would perish by the tens of millions? Or that their daily habits had a greater impact on their lives than the decisions made on their behalf by a handful of statesmen and generals? And how would they explain that the collapse of the Soviet Union occurred without social violence? Indeed, no less an authority on this subject than Gorbachev asserted publicly that under the Soviet regime change could have come only "from above," never "from below."[5]

My quarrel with the revisionists, therefore, concerned not only the driving force behind historical events but the very notion that human events are everywhere and at all times determined by the same forces. I believe that history—the cumulative lives of many human beings—has no more meaning than does the life of a single individual; or if it does, then our being in its midst precludes us from grasping what it is. There is no "History"; there are only histories. Things happen and we are capable of understanding their immediate causes and significance. But we cannot fit this knowledge into a broader, all-embracing philosophy. I find the whole Hegelian philosophy of history and its various offshoots to be as absurd as they are pretentious.

My own historical methodology is deliberately eclectic. That is, I believe that various events are propelled by diverse forces: sometimes it is by accident, sometimes individuals make all the difference, on other occasions it is economic factors or ideology. The skill of the historian consists in determining at each point in his narrative which of these factors was decisive: he resorts to different methods much as the surgeon resorts to different instruments. No one cause ever explains everything. To believe otherwise is to assume an overarching scheme of human history for which I see no evidence. In my own historical writing, my central interest has always been to determine the mindset of the principal actors and then to demonstrate how it influenced their behavior.

I approach the sources with an open mind and expect them to guide

---

*Paradoxically, Lenin, the most successful of Marxist politicians, held no such illusions: "Politics," he wrote "must take precedence over economics. To argue otherwise is to forget the ABC of Marxism." V. I. Lenin, *Collected Works*, vol. 32 (London, n.d.), 83.

me. In the course of pursuing one's researches, an outline emerges in the mind that gradually fills with content. It is not unlike an artistic endeavor and equally satisfying. It requires a great deal of patience: the difference between genuine scholarship and its popular imitations lies in the willingness of the historian to ponder the subject from all sides, and this takes time. I find myself in great sympathy with the observation on this subject of the sixteenth-century Florentine historian Francesco Guicciardini, who wrote: "In my youth I believed that no amount of reflection would enable me to see more in a thing than I took in at a glance. But experience has shown me this opinion to be utterly false; and you may laugh at anyone who maintains the contrary. The longer we reflect, the clearer things grow and the better we understand them."[6]

True as this statement is, there are limits to the time one can allot to reflection: the alternative is creative sterility. I usually continue to carry on research until I find that the sources tend to repeat themselves and no new evidence emerges to alter significantly the picture formed in my mind, at which point I stop.

I usually receive praise for my exposition, though some readers find my style pedestrian because it strives at clarity and brevity.* I do not enjoy an elaborate, "rich" writing style because it suggests that the writer is more interested in displaying his eloquence than communicating substance. This is why I dislike such celebrated authors writing at the turn of the twentieth century as Marcel Proust, Henry James, and Walter Pater. I strive at the greatest economy of words. Lytton Strachey defined this stylistic model as "classical": "The object of all art is to make suggestions. The romantic artist attains that end by using a multitude of different stimuli, by calling up image after image, recollection after recollection, until the reader's mind is filled and held by a vivid and palpable evocation; the classic works by the contrary method of a fine economy, and, ignoring everything but what is essential, trusts, by means of the exact propriety of his presentation, to produce the required effect."[7]

Such clarity and economy of words as I manage to achieve is the result of two factors. One, that I know what I want to say, or, at any rate, that I do not attempt to write until I have arrived at a precise notion of what it is that I want to say. And second, I keep on revising my drafts until I achieve the desired clarity. I find that on each rereading, I detach

*One French "postmodernist," very likely a windbag eager to justify his incomprehensible verbiage, has declared "clear writing" to be a manifestation of "reactionary thinking." John M. Ellis, *Against Deconstruction* (Princeton, 1989), 10.

myself more from the content and come closer to the situation of the prospective reader.

I generally favor narrative history because, obviously, since events happen in time, chronology furnishes the framework of causation. But I like to combine the narrative with synthetic analyses to provide the setting within which events unfold.

I assume that whatever strikes me as interesting will similarly impress my reader. To explain my meaning, I can do no better than cite Thomas Carlyle who in a letter thus described his method of note-taking:

> You ask me how I proceed in taking Notes. . . . I would very gladly tell you all my methods if I had any; but really I have as it were none. I go into business with all the intelligence, patience, silence and other gifts and virtues that I have. . . . For this certainly turns out to be a truth: Only what you at last *have living* in your own memory and heart is worth putting down to be printed; this alone has much chance to get into the living heart and memory of other men. And here indeed, I believe, is the essence of all the rules I have ever been able to devise for myself.[8]

Until the emergence of the revisionist school, the literature on the Russian Revolution had emphasized a combination of political and social factors. Traditional historians were aware of the grievances of peasants and industrial workers, but they focused on politicians, both those in power and those in opposition. They saw October 1917 not as a popular uprising but as a coup d'état carried out by a small band of conspirators who exploited the anarchy that followed the collapse of tsarism. This collapse they interpreted as avoidable and caused by Russia's involvement in the world war and the political ineptitude of the tsarist regime, notably its mismanagement of the war effort; the ensuing anarchy, they attributed to the blunders of its successor, the Provisional Government. The Leninist and Stalinist regimes were seen as deriving their authority principally from the application of terror.

The revisionists challenged this entire interpretation head on. The collapse of tsarism, in their judgment was inevitable, whether or not Russia entered World War I, because of the mounting misery and unhappiness of the "masses." The Bolshevik power seizure was no less preordained: far from being a conspiratorial minority, the Bolsheviks in 1917 embodied the will of the common people, who pressured them to take power and form a government of soviets. If their democratic intentions were not realized and the Bolshevik regime soon turned into a dictatorship, the blame fell on the Russian "bourgeoisie" and its Western allies who, refusing to accept the new reality, resisted the communist regime by force of arms. Stalinism was explained as the result of collaboration between the regime and the population which for some reason cooperated in its own mistreatment. To understand what happened and why, the scholar's attention had to turn to the social forces, especially the working class which, as Marx and Engels had posited, formed the driving force of modern history. The entire scheme was, by and large, in accord with Soviet post-Stalinist historiography although without the latter's obligatory references to Marx, Engels, Lenin, and whoever happened to hold power in the USSR at the time of writing.

In implementing it, the revisionists wrote and had their students write monographs on various aspects of Russian social history in the early twentieth century, ignoring previous work. They subverted the traditional view without replacing it with one of their own because it proved impossible to write a general history of the Russian Revolution without paying proper attention to politics and ideology. Their accounts were, therefore, of necessity episodic.

The quality that always struck me in the adherents of this school was their total insensitivity to the moral outrages of communism—outrages so strikingly reflected in the contemporary sources and so central to the literature on national socialism. Determined to act scientifically, they eschewed moral judgments and disregarded individuals. They dealt entirely in abstractions—"social classes," "class conflicts," party slogans, statistics—turning a blind eye to the living realities of Bolshevik rule from the first day of its existence, so vividly depicted in the newspaper articles of Maxim Gorky and the diaries of Ivan Bunin. They wrote bloodless histories about a time that drowned in blood, a time of mass executions and pogroms carried out by the new dictatorship: what to the peoples of Russia was an unprecedented catastrophe was to them a noble if ultimately failed experiment. This attitude enabled them to avoid moralizing. But the revolution was not nature acting on nature, nor humans acting on nature, nor nature acting on humans, but humans acting on humans and as such crying out for judgment.

The revisionists were united not only by a common methodology: they also formed a party determined to impose control on the teaching of modern Russian history. In a manner which I believe was new to American academic life though familiar from the history of Bolshevism, they strove and largely succeeded in monopolizing the profession, ensuring that university chairs in that field across the country went to their adherents. This entailed ostracizing scholars known to hold different views.

They acted in the same spirit in their writings. In arguing their case, the revisionists did not bother to demonstrate where their predecessors had been wrong and then proceed to construct their own alternative interpretation: they simply ignored them. It was, therefore, droll to observe how indignant they waxed when their opponents, such as myself, turned the tables on them and largely ignored their work as well.

Such was the condition of the literature on the Russian Revolution in the late 1970s. The older works were mostly out of print and out-of-date; the more recent literature was monographic as well as monochromatic. So I took it upon myself to fill the void. The task, as I perceived it, was to expand vastly the scope of the subject both in terms of chronology and subject matter: to go back at least to the end of the nineteenth century and to include topics normally ignored—culture and religion, foreign policy and subversion, famines and epidemics, population shifts, terror. To deal with the revolution adequately, one had to attempt "grand history" as history had been written before it was reduced to social minutiae and trivia. In May 1977, I signed a contract with Alfred A. Knopf, a firm that subsequently published several of my books: it has been a very happy relationship, for Knopf brought out my books in an elegant format and showed impressive commercial skill in marketing them.

The quality of the Harvard libraries is such that, whatever the subject, I could always count on finding on their shelves nine-tenths of the materials I needed. What they lacked, I located at the Hoover Institution in Stanford, California, the New York Public Library, and, more rarely, London or Paris. The Soviet Union with its archives was, for all practical purposes, out of reach for me until 1992.

Work on the revolution proved emotionally draining. I felt constant outrage at the duplicity and brutality of the communists as well as the delusions of their opponents. Their behavior reminded me time and again of the Nazis. I was driven to despondency and had difficulty sleeping when studying the details of the Red Terror, which the existing historical literature either minimized or ignored. (Carr, for instance, dismissed it altogether from his multivolume history.) While working on the murder of the imperial family in Ekaterinburg, I wrote in a notebook: "The whole time acutely depressed. I smell a whiff of the Holocaust. The burned bodies at the Four Brothers and the smokestacks of Auschwitz."*

My researches were interrupted by my two years in Washington and

---

*"Four Brothers" was a site in the woods outside Ekaterinburg where the bodies of the eleven victims of the massacre, five of them children, were stripped, hacked up, and thrown on a bonfire.

the writing of *Survival Is Not Enough*. I returned to them in 1984. I had to slow down in the spring and summer of 1985 because during a visit to Venice in March of that year I fell ill with a potentially fatal disease of the immune system called dermatomyositis. I tried to ignore it, traveling and also delivering at Harvard in April 1985 three lectures on the Ekaterinburg tragedy. But I also spent much time in bed, sweating profusely and moving with difficulty. Fortunately, before the year was over, the disease went away, as the physician attending me had predicted it would.

I worked concurrently on two parts of the book—"The Agony of the Imperial Regime," dealing with the years 1899–1917, and "The Bolsheviks Conquer Russia," covering 1917–19. In early 1989 I delivered the manuscripts to Knopf. I had intended the two parts to appear as separate volumes, but Knopf decided, for commercial reasons, to market them as a single volume called *The Russian Revolution*. It appeared in October 1990. By that time I was at work on the third and concluding part of the history, which would have been called *Russia under the New Regime* but for the fact that in late 1991 the Soviet Union dissolved, giving way to a democratic regime, and the title could have been misunderstood to mean the Russia of Boris Yeltsin. So I renamed it *Russia under the Bolshevik Regime*. It came out in 1994.

On completing the history, numbering 1,500 pages, I understood what George Chapman meant when three and a half centuries earlier, having finished his translation of Homer, he exclaimed: "The work that I was born to do is done."

I had a foretaste of the reaction I would receive from the revisionists at a conference on the Russian Revolution held at the University of Jerusalem in January 1988. I delivered my paper, a general assessment of the revolution, on the conference's last day. Nearly everything I said aroused indignation. The audience consisting of professional historians of the revolution was especially offended by my assertion that the Bolshevik regime exerted a major influence on Nazism both in positive and negative terms: positively because it provided the Nazis with the model of a one-party dictatorship, and negatively by enabling them to frighten the German population with the specter of communism. These rather commonplace and, to me, self-evident propositions provoked the audience to white fury. One participant declared me to be a very courageous man to draw such parallels: I replied that what I had said required not courage, since nothing threatened me, but knowledge.* An Israeli

---

*I might have cited Max Beerbohm who professed surprise how "few people have the courage of their opinion. . . . I do not see where 'courage' comes in. I do not understand why a

professor shouted from the floor: "Whom did you want to win the war: the Nazis or the Soviets?" Such was the level of the discourse.*

The organizers of the conference claimed afterwards that due to the failure of the recording apparatus they had no text of my talk and thus were unable to include it in a volume of its proceedings. Fortunately, a member of the audience, the editor of a Russian émigré publication, did tape and publish it in his journal. Alexander Yakovlev, the principal architect of perestroika, told me that he had read it on a trip to Israel, liked it, and showed it to Gorbachev.

The Soviet Union Opens Up: Sakharov

As soon as Gorbachev was appointed general secretary, I began to receive calls and visits from Soviet journalists who solicited my opinions on various matters concerning their country and reported them faithfully, without the customary abuse. The first to publish me (December 1986) was the *Moscow News*, followed, in July 1989, by *Izvestiia*. In early 1991, the Soviet magazine *Polis* even reprinted, with minor (though not insignificant) omissions, an excerpt from my *Russian Revolution* describing the Bolshevik dissolution of the Constituent Assembly.

In April 1990, I had arranged for the translation into Russian of *The Russian Revolution*. The publisher, Kniga, had in the past specialized in facsimile editions of rare and illustrated old books but had recently shifted to current topics. The contract called for a printing of a minimum of 50,000 copies by June 1992. It reflected the changing mood in Russia as the euphoria wore off that Kniga first postponed publication by a year and then unilaterally cancelled the contract because it had decided to concentrate on business literature instead of history and politics: in 1991, it changed its name to Kniga i Bizness. I found with some difficulty another publisher, Rosspen, which brought out *The Russian Revolution* in two volumes in 1994 in a printing of 5,000 copies and *Russia under the Bolshevik Regime* three years later in a printing of 2,000.

---

man should hesitate to say, as best he can, just what he thinks and feels. He has nothing to fear, nowadays. No one will suggest the erection of a stake for him to be burned at. . . . So far from being angry, people admire and respect you for your 'courage.' You gain a cheap reputation for a quality to which, as likely as not, you have no real claim. It is as a though a soldier in battle were accounted a hero for charging up to the muzzles of guns which he knew to be unloaded." Cited in David Cecil's *Max* (New York, 1985), 172–73.

*Harry Shukman of Oxford University, one of the participants, referring to this conference, described in 1996 how "most of us sat in shocked silence when Pipes presented Lenin and his 'achievement' as the conscious model for Hitler's regime. . . . Why we were shocked then, and why—I would guess—most of us would now accept Pipes's view is a simple function of the collapse of the Soviet Union." *Times Higher Education Supplement*, November 22, 1996, 22.

The progressive shrinkage of the editions can be accounted by two causes. One was the breakdown of the book distribution network which compelled Russian publishers to deal directly with retailers. This resulted in a great contraction of the market: for all practical purposes, new books were available only in Moscow and St. Petersburg. The other factor was the rapid loss of interest by Russians in serious nonfiction, especially the history of their own country: their reaction was not unlike that of the Germans in the years immediately following World War II when they turned their backs on the whole Nazi era. In Moscow, the bulk of the retail book trade spilled onto the sidewalks, where books were arrayed on the ground or on portable tables: most of the wares consisted of escapist literature (detective stories, romantic novels, pornography) or practical manuals (foreign language dictionaries, books on accounting, Dale Carnegie's *How to Win Friends and Influence People*). History fared poorly unless romanticized or sensationalized.

I also arranged with the book-publishing arm of the newspaper *Nezavisimaia Gazeta* for the republication of *Russia under the Old Regime* in Russian, a version which I had first brought out in 1980 at my own expense in the United States. It appeared in June 1993. A few years later, the deputy mayor of Moscow invited me for a chat: he showed me a copy of this book, marked up from beginning to end in pencils of varying colors, one of which stood for full agreement, another for partial agreement, and so on. Although, as expected, keenly disliked by the nationalists, the book made an impact, being rather widely read, especially by university students.

And yet, despite these favorable signs of a thaw, I remained deeply suspicious of Gorbachev and his reform plans. The new Soviet leader made no secret that he remained a committed communist and that he intended to reinvigorate the system rather than abolish or even substantially change it. On December 1, 1987, I wrote a highly critical review of his new book, *Perestroika*, in the *Wall Street Journal*—apparently the only unfavorable review the book received in the U.S. press. In retrospect, it appears to have been too harsh but in view of past disappointments with Soviet promises of change, my suspicions were not unwarranted.

One week after the appearance of the review, on December 9, I met Gorbachev at a lunch given in his honor by Secretary of State Shultz at the Department of State. As I was passing along the guest line to be introduced to him, my name was called out. Gorbachev at once reacted: "Oh, Mr. Pipes, you did not like my book, did you?" "I am afraid I didn't." "Well, you are an academic. You wanted me to outline a systematic program. But I am in politics."* We chatted in Russian. Shultz who stood by Gorbachev's side looked terribly worried by this exchange, incomprehensible to him: his expression suggested fear lest I unleash World War III. Fifteen years later, during Gorbachev's visit to Harvard, I admitted to him that I had been wrong in dismissing his pledge of perestroika.

Regardless of my suspicion of Gorbachev's intentions, I believed the Soviet Union was nearing its end. At a gathering of Russian specialists convened by the CIA in August 1987 I said the USSR was "unraveling."

The thaw continued.

An unusual experience occurred to me in June 1988 during a visit to Moscow. I had met there a Russian dissident economist by the name of Lev Timofeev, recently released from prison, who two months earlier had founded an institution grandly called "Independent University," although it had neither facilities nor faculty. He invited me to address this group on a subject of my choice. I suggested "Russia's past and the Soviet present." I delivered the lecture in a vacant apartment in an outlying suburb of Moscow. The main room as well as the kitchen were crammed: some in the audience had tape recorders.

In my talk I stressed the roots of communism in Russian history, a subject had aroused the ire of Solzhenitsyn. During the discussion period, the audience divided into two factions: Slavophiles (many identifiable by their flowing beards) and Westerners. The former espoused the familiar idealized picture of prerevolutionary Russia; the latter held a more realistic view. The atmosphere was exhilarating: one had the feeling of witnessing the birth of a new and free Russia.

After the lecture we adjourned to Timofeev's apartment, at the opposite end of Moscow, where we had dinner in the company of several prominent dissidents. One of them was Sergei Kovalëv, who would inherit the mantle of Sakharov as defender of human rights in Russia. Kovalëv, a scientist, had recently been released from prison and promised a job, but he was told the promise was contingent on his refusing to attend the reception for dissidents which Ronald Reagan intended to give at the American Embassy the following month. Kovalëv ignored the

---

*It was an unconscious echo of the words that Catherine II spoke to Diderot two centuries earlier: "Monsieur Diderot, I have listened with great pleasure to everything that your brilliant spirit has inspired in you. . . . You forget in your reform plans the difference in our two positions: you write on paper which suffers everything; it is all smooth, simple and presents an obstacle neither to your imagination nor to your pen, whereas I, poor Empress, work on the human skin which is far more irritable and delicate." Maurice Tourneux, *Diderot et Catherine II* (Paris, 1899), 81.

warning and was punished. I asked him whether he would have attended the lunch had he known that the authorities would carry out their threat. He thought for a moment and said yes, he would have. He and the other dissidents exuded calm courage, so different from the posturing of Western radicals who paid no price for their disagreement with government policy. They were among the most admirable people I have ever met. I may add that none of these heroes in the least resembled swashbucklers like Errol Flynn or John Wayne: they were quiet and introspective persons whose courage was revealed only by the look in their eyes—confident and candid. Their bravery came from within, from deeply held ethical convictions.

The most admirable of them, Andrei Sakharov, visited Boston late in 1988. He had been allowed to leave the country, for the first time ever, as a member of the directing board of a bogus organization called "International Foundation for Human Survival and Development," sponsored jointly by American and Soviet institutions. The sponsors hoped that Sakharov's presence would lend them credibility and help raise money. Sakharov agreed to join but not without qualms for he realized he was being used.*

On November 18, 1988, the organizers held a meeting at the American Academy of Arts and Sciences in Cambridge where Sakharov was the featured speaker. In his speech, however, instead, of promoting the International Foundation, he voiced reservations about its makeup and purpose: he told the audience, about 90 percent of whom were liberals, that he had doubts about belonging to an organization consisting solely of persons "friendly to the Soviet Union" and of a "left-wing persuasion." He even wondered aloud whether it deserved financial support (much of which, so far, had come from Armand Hammer). I watched Jerome Wiesner, the former president of MIT and one of the foundation's directors, who was sitting next to Sakharov, bury his face in his hands in embarrassment; his Soviet counterpart (I believe he was Evgeny Velikhov of the Soviet Academy of Sciences) sat nearby, stony-faced. When not long afterwards Wiesner suffered a heart attack, some people blamed it on Sakharov. To me, his behavior displayed superhuman civil courage.

A couple of weeks later, Sakharov's stepdaughter, Tanya Yankelevich, invited me to a private reception in honor of Sakharov at her home in Newton. On the morning of that day, I received a call from the BBC

---

*I later learned from one of the participants, that at the organizing meeting in Moscow, to general consternation, Sakharov had proposed me as member of the foundation's board. Needless to say, his suggestion was ignored.

asking me whether I expected to meet Sakharov and, if so, what I would say to him. "I would ask him: 'What do you think is the future of the Soviet Union?'" I replied. They promised to call me the next day to learn his response.

The moment I was introduced to Sakharov, and before I could say anything, he asked: "What do you think is the future of the Soviet Union?" I was flabbergasted. We conversed for a while. He wondered aloud whether he was being manipulated by joining the board of the International Foundation. I thought he was, but the price he paid was minimal whereas the reward was great. But his conscience clearly troubled him. He seemed to have no idea how famous and important he was: his modesty was overwhelming because there was in it not one iota of false humility.

In June 1990, I attended in Moscow a conference on the "Origins of the Cold War," organized by the Soviet Ministry of Foreign Affairs. In the paper I delivered, I placed the blame for the Cold War exclusively on the Soviet Union, its ideology and interests which required unremitting tension with the West. The discussion was polite and the Soviet delegation launched no attacks on me. All this was without precedent.

In February 1991, I was surprised to receive an invitation from the Soviet Embassy to attend in Moscow the following month a colloquium on "Lenin and the Twentieth Century." It was an extraordinary meeting at which, in the presence of communist officials and foreign visitors, in the heart of the Soviet Union's capital city and in a hotel once reserved for the exclusive use of the *nomenklatura,* I was able to present a paper that portrayed Stalin as Lenin's faithful disciple.

Two months later Sakharov's widow, Elena Bonner, organized a conference in Moscow in memory of her husband who had died two years before. Its high point was a celebration on May 21 in the Big Hall of the Moscow Conservatory where speakers recalled his achievements and outstanding musicians performed in his honor. In the loge on one side of the auditorium sat Gorbachev, while Yeltsin sat opposite. Gorbachev had to listen to bitter denunciations of himself by the speakers, including Elena Bonner. It was, I thought to myself, possibly a unique instance in history of a Russian head of state exposing himself to public censure.

During the intermission, I wandered into the lobby. In the middle of it stood Yeltsin surrounded by a crowd, being interviewed for television. The interview over and the lights turned off, he was left standing alone. I walked up to him and without a word of introduction said: "You know, Mr. Yeltsin, if you are elected president of Russia next month, you will be the first head of state in your country's history to be chosen by the people." "If I am elected," he said, somewhat startled. "Because Kerensky was never elected," I continued, "and neither was any other head of government before or since." He nodded. The next day I ran into Lane Kirkland, the head of the CIO/AFL, who had come to Moscow for the Sakharov celebrations. He told me he had met with Yeltsin that morning. "What did he say?" I asked. "He said that if elected president next month, he will be the first head of state in Russia," and so on. Thus I had given a brief lesson in Russia's history to her first genuine president.

From Moscow I proceeded to Tbilisi where I had been invited by the government of Georgia, which had proclaimed independence the previous month.

I had long maintained ties with the Georgian community in Paris where the leaders of independent Georgia resettled after their country was overrun by the communists in 1921. I felt a special sympathy for Georgians because of their charm and affability. In 1951 I visited their colony at Leuville near Paris and met—was received in audience would be more accurate—Noi Zhordaniia, the deposed head of their government who even in dire poverty managed to maintain presidential dignity. I established especially warm relations with Noe Tsintsadze, once a minister in the Zhordaniia cabinet and in emigration a successful businessman. It was he who fist told me the Georgian community's apprehensions about the security of their national archive which had been evacuated to Paris in 1921 and faced constant danger of being seized, first by the Nazis, then by the communists. Tsintsadze wondered whether Harvard would be interested in acquiring this collection. Harvard agreed and by 1959 was ready to sign a contract, but then some difficulties arose in the Georgian émigré community and the negotiations dragged on for years. The archive was finally transferred to Harvard's rare book library, Houghton, in 1974, where the frail paper was subjected to chemical treatment, catalogued, and microfilmed. The agreement called for it to be returned to Tbilisi in thirty years with Harvard retaining microfilm copies.

I spent a week in Tbilisi, observing the presidential elections which were won by Zviad Gamzakhurdia, a poet and courageous dissident. I met with Gamzakhurdia privately both before and after his electoral victory. He struck me as a painfully shy man for he never looked one in the eye and gave the impression of being deeply depressed. He asked me what he had to do to gain the friendship of Washington, which under Bush and Baker ostentatiously snubbed him. I suggested he conduct a

To Richard Pipes
With best wishes,

Ronald Reagan

Shaking hands with Ronald Reagan, July 1981.

Richard V. Allen, 1981.

At my desk in the Old Executive Office Building, 1982.

With the NSC staff: third from left, Lt. Commander Dennis Blair; second from right, Paula Dobriansky, 1982.

Irene with President Reagan, January 1982.

Lunch for Soviet dissidents in the White House, May 1982: introducing
the Russian émigré writer Andrei Sinyavsky to President Reagan; on
extreme left, Alexander Haig.

To Richard Pipes
With best wishes

Briefing Vice President George Bush, July 1983.

With Andrei Sakharov. Boston, 1988.

Family in Chesham, 1990.

Moscow, September 1991: the entrance to the old Central Committee
headquarters shortly after the failure of the Communist coup.

World Economic Forum, Davos,
January 1992.

Receiving honorary doctorate in Cieszyn, May 1994.

Lecturing on Struve in his birthplace, the Ural city
of Perm, February 2003. Photo by Oleg Nachinkin.

consistent democratic policy. He responded that he had already done so. But then, in self-defense, he called my attention to the protesters picketing the entrance to the presidential building. "Would President Bush tolerate such protests in front of the White House?" he asked. The question revealed the depth of his political naivete. I attended the victory banquet in his honor but the victory proved short-lived. In January 1992, under circumstances which remain obscure to this day, Gamzakhurdia was deposed and forced to flee; two years later he was found dead, the victim of either suicide or, more likely, assassination.

In summer 1997, the Georgian archive was returned to Tbilisi, the capital of independent Georgia. I visited Georgia shortly afterwards and was for a week guest of the government which appointed me honorary consul of Georgia as well as honorary citizen. These honors were bestowed on me by Gamzakhurdia's successor, Eduard Shevardnadze.

The Soviet Union Betrays the Sovietologists

During the night of August 18–19, 1991, I was awakened by a phone call from a news agency alerting me to some unusual happenings in the Soviet Union, including the rumored arrest of Gorbachev. What all this meant was unclear. Things became clearer the following day when we learned that a putsch had taken place in Moscow and a state of emergency proclaimed. Gorbachev was under house arrest in the Crimea. These developments did not surprise me: in November of the preceding year I had written an Op-Ed page article for the *New York Times* in which I predicted the likelihood of a putsch by the military.* But the rapidity with which the putsch collapsed caught all of us by surprise: in the end it was due to the courage of a single individual—Boris Yeltsin.

The *New York Times* called that morning requesting an Op-Ed page article on these events. I dashed it off in a few hours and it appeared the following day, August 20. In it I forecast the demise of Gorbachev's political career. As it happened, he stayed in office for another four months, resigning on Christmas Day, but after August de facto power passed into the hands of Yeltsin.

In December 1991, the Soviet Union fell apart into its constituent

---

*The *Times* sat on it for a month. When it finally agreed to print it, I had an argument with the copy editor who was unsympathetic to my point of view and tried to have me change my predictions; I stood my ground and the article appeared as I had written it. He had his revenge, however, by providing it with a completely misleading heading: "Soviet Army Coup? Not Likely." *New York Times*, November 20, 1990, p. A21.

republics: the events of 1917–18 were repeating themselves. Inevitable as this event was, it is now known that it unfolded in a most haphazard manner.* In late 1991, the leaders of Russia, the Ukraine, and Belorussia concluded that the Union led only a paper existence: Georgia had declared her sovereignty in April 1991, Azerbaijan and the three Baltic republics in August of that year, and the Ukraine held a referendum on December 1, in which 90.6 percent of the population expressed themselves in favor of independence. In the Soviet Union where political symbols often meant more than hard reality they signified that the Union had, in fact, ceased to exist.

The Union's leaders now faced the question how to give this fact legal expression in order to forestall the kind of civil war that was tearing apart Yugoslavia. Gorbachev had proposed a confederate arrangement, but this proposal was rejected because on closer scrutiny it differed from the old unitary state only in name. At this point Yeltsin; Leonid Kravchuk, the president of the Ukraine; and Stanislaus Shushkevich of Belorussia agreed to meet in Belorussia, in the seclusion of the Białowieża Forest, without Gorbachev, to resolve the issue. They proceeded on the assumption that the Union was dead. After long discussions among themselves and with the help of legal experts they proclaimed the dissolution of the Soviet Union and granted each of its constituent republics full sovereignty.† As a consequence, not only did the Soviet Union disappear from the map but along with it, the old Russian empire: four centuries of expansion were wiped out, and Russia reverted to her borders as of c. 1600.

These developments were unanticipated and misunderstood in the West to such an extent that in August 1991 President Bush, on a visit to Kiev, took it upon himself to warn the Ukrainians against seeking independence! The United States had a tradition of opposing separatism among the non-Russian peoples of the USSR from fear of anarchy, civil war, and Soviet nuclear weapons falling in wrong hands. But reality triumphed over wishful thinking, and in time Washington concluded that the breakup of the Russian empire was actually a positive development.

The Sovietological community was stunned by the collapse of communism and the dissolution of the Soviet empire, for it had stuck

*The following account is based on the recollections of the then chairman of the Belorussian Supreme Soviet, Stanislaus Shushkevich, as recorded in an interview with the Warsaw daily, *Rzeczpospolita* (Supplement "+Plus-Minus"), May 30–31, 1998, pp. 13, 19.

†Shushkevich dismisses as a "complete lie" the story circulating in the West that at the time this decision was taken Yeltsin was so inebriated he fell off his chair. All participants in these historic deliberations, he insists, were perfectly sober.

through thick and thin to the belief that, no matter what challenges the Soviet regime faced, it had both the will and the means to overcome them. If the Sovietologists had failed to anticipate the future, it was not for want of trying: rather, it was due to genuine incompetence. They studied their object as scientists would, ignoring everything imponderable, such as political traditions and culture of a country a thousand years old. Growing up in a society where laws were observed and property respected, they could not conceive of one where neither was the case. Lacking in imagination, they attributed to all alien phenomena features with which they were familiar, justifying the procedure with reference to pseudoscientific social "models." Deliberately suppressing emotions, they felt no sympathy for the victims of the communist experiment: but as Aldous Huxley had observed, "Nobody understands what he does not feel."[9] They claimed to be scientists yet they never tested their theories against the facts and even after the events of 1991 had proven their analyses incorrect, they did not bother to find out what had gone wrong in order to avoid repeating their mistakes. They shut their ears to any alternative point of view. They pretended to be disinterested, yet they had a considerable stake in depicting the Soviet Union as a powerful yet reasonable rival in order both to encourage the flow of scholarly subsidies from the government and foundations and to secure Soviet cooperation in their researches. I do not believe that ever in history has so much money been lavished on the study of a foreign country with such appalling results. Yet its practitioners went on with their pseudoscientific work without a word of explanation or apology.*

But these failures were not confined to the community of Russian and Soviet specialists: they rested on misconceptions shared by the entire intelligentsia, especially those who engaged in academic work, which in varying degrees sympathized with the communist experiment. It was baffling that the common man—the proverbial New York taxi driver—had a better understanding of communism than most university professors. Why this should have been the case has puzzled me for a long time. One clue to the riddle came from a report by the U.S. Department of Justice in February 1995 which, having investigated patterns of financial deception, arrived at the startling conclusion that "people with more education are more frequently victims of fraud than those with less education."[10] Much the same seems to hold true of ideological fraud.

*Similar incompetence, similarly aggravated by vicious treatment of dissenters from the consensus, is said to have prevailed among Sinologists: see Richard Walker in *The National Interest* 53 (fall 1998): 94–101.

I have often been asked, both before and after the collapse of the Soviet Union, how someone with my views on communism and the USSR could survive at "liberal Harvard." My answer, only partly playful, was as follows: Imagine yourself living five hundred ago, in the fifteenth century. The vast majority of people believe that the earth is flat. You, through your studies and observations, have concluded that it is round. Now no matter how idiosyncratic, indeed, how inane, your view may strike others, you know that sooner or later it will be vindicated. So you patiently wait for time to do its work.

It turned out that I was far from alone in my disgust of what was happening to the historical profession. Others, too, resented its growing trendiness and preoccupation with the trivial. In November 1994, during a conference of the National Association of Scholars, an organization dedicated to the preservation of scholarly standards, I proposed the creation of an historical society that would function separately from the American Historical Association, which had become captive of special interest groups. My proposal produced no immediate reaction and seemed to have fallen on deaf ears. But two and a half years later several scholars headed by Eugene Genovese acted on the suggestion, and, having raised the necessary funding and obtained the patronage of Boston University, organized The Historical Society.

In Liberated Russia

In early September 1991, days after the failed putsch, I visited Moscow on a flying trip to attend a meeting of the World Economic Forum. The atmosphere in the capital city was electrifying. People, especially intellectuals, walked in a daze, as if unable to believe they were not dreaming. On a stroll through the center of the city I saw the pedestal of the monument to Felix Dzerzhinsky, the founder of the Soviet secret police, which had recently been toppled, smeared with anticommunist graffiti. Nearby, on Staraia Ploshchad', in front of the headquarters of the Central Committee, its doors shut, a single militiaman paced nervously back and forth. A young man who observed this scene asked me, with a smile full of wonder: "Did you ever expect in your lifetime to see this?" Russians were drunk with freedom; they would soon learn its costs.

I returned to what was now the Russian Federal Republic in May 1992 to explore the possibilities of doing research in the Central Party Archive, once hermetically closed to all except reliable party hacks but now, thanks to Yeltsin, open to all scholars. The surprising decision of Russia's new rulers to give public access to the most secret depositories of the Communist Party was motivated less by respect for historical truth than by the desire of Yeltzin to discredit the communists, his principal rivals. The archives containing state secrets—those of the Ministries of Foreign Affairs and Defense, for example, as well as the security and intelligence services—remained off limits almost as much as before.

The Central Party Archive—clumsily renamed Russian Center for the Preservation and Study of Contemporary History—contains the original documents of all the founders of communism from Marx and Engels through Lenin and Stalin, as well as its minor figures and the various party institutions, including the Communist International. How important this archive was to the historian becomes clear when one learns that it held over 3,000 unpublished Lenin documents. All its materials were maintained in excellent condition, as befitted holy scriptures.

Yale University Press had signed a contract with this archival depository which gave it exclusive English-language rights to publish its holdings in a series called "Annals of Communism." The editor of this series, Jonathan Brent, approached me with a proposal that I edit from the secret part of the Lenin archive a selection of Lenin documents. I enthusiastically agreed.

I spent in Moscow one week, living comfortably in a private apartment consisting of two rooms, kitchen, and bath for which I paid $125 a week. To illustrate the absurdity of the Russian economy, the landlady told me that her monthly rent was equivalent of the price of an ordinary ball point pen. I returned in June 1992, this time for a two-week stay, to carry out research on the secret Lenin correspondence.

I jotted down the following impressions of the new Russia: "People much more content than I had expected and stores far better stocked. No interest in anything except their own sphere. Church bells ringing! Incredible 'shopping rows' near Pushkin street—like an anthill. But freedom in the air." By "shopping rows" I meant street vendors, male and female, young and old, lined up shoulder to shoulder on both sides of a street, displaying for sale to customers who walked between them one or two items: a blouse, a home-knit sweater, a handheld calculator. The militia, at a loss how to cope with this unfamiliar problem, would from time to time disperse these hawkers, but they instantly re-formed.

The contract with Moscow stipulated that the book would come out simultaneously in Russian and English. But this proved impracticable because the archival staff apparently found it psychologically impossible to treat Lenin with any degree of objectivity. Documents from the secret Lenin archive were delivered to me slowly and erratically: it was like pulling teeth. The staff, consisting of persons picked not only for their professional skills as archivists but also their commitment to the Communist cause, was polite but clearly uneasy handing materials on the most secret aspects of the regime to foreigners: I excused their behavior with the thought of archivists in the Vatican being asked to serve representatives of the Soviet Society of the Godless. Nevertheless, I made steady progress. The book, called *The Unknown Lenin*, came out in October 1996; the Russian edition, with slanted editorial comments and some omissions, appeared three years later.

This particular book, as well as the previously published two volumes on the Russian Revolution, had as one of their objectives to demolish the widely believed distinction between the "good" Lenin and the "bad" Stalin, by demonstrating that the main elements of what came to be known as Stalinism were imbedded in and derived from Leninism. The distinction between the two dictators was quite deliberately promoted by the post-1953 Soviet regime in order to place the blame for all the deprivations and atrocities that the country had suffered under communism on Stalin, who allegedly hijacked the socialist revolution. This interpretation found a friendly reception among the left throughout the world because it made it possible to admire communism without bearing the burden of Stalinism. It had no basis in fact. Although Lenin toward the end of his life, when in the throes of paranoia, quarreled with Stalin (as he did with nearly every other one of his associates), it was he who had promoted Stalin to the top posts in the party. Vyacheslav Molotov, who worked closely with both Soviet leaders for some forty years, when asked, in his retirement, who of the two was "the more severe" replied: "Of course, Lenin. I recall how he scolded Stalin for his softness and liberalism. 'What kind of a dictatorship do we have? We have mushy (*kisel'naia*) authority, not a dictatorship!'"[11] The only other historian to advance this argument was the late Dmitry Volkogonov. Neither of us had much success because the reputation of Lenin as an idealist who had to resort to cruelties against his will remained well ensconced in Russia as well as abroad.

While I was working in the archives, the newly established Constitutional Court was preparing to try a double suit: of the government against the Communist Party, which it had outlawed, and of the Communist Party against the government for outlawing it. A friend active in "Memorial," an organization dedicated to preserving the remembrance of the victims of communism, suggested to the court that it invite me to testify as an expert. On July 1, 1992, a government car drove me at breakneck speed to Arkhangelskoe, once an estate of Russia's richest family, the Yusupovs, subsequently the country residence of Trotsky, and finally a museum. There I met with two justices of the Constitutional Court and Sergei Shakhrai, Yeltsin's principal legal advisor. The question they posed to me was whether as a historian I could support the government's case that the Communist Party was never a political party in the commonly accepted meaning of the term but rather a "mechanism for seizing power." I responded without hesitation that I could. I was then invited to prepare a deposition for use by government lawyers at the trial.

The trial, which had opened in May 1992 and then recessed, resumed on the morning of July 7 in a modest room on Ilinka Street. Outside, the militia had to hold back a handful of communist demonstrators gathered to protest the proceedings. One had a sense of something of great historic importance happening: as he escorted me to the court room, my friend from "Memorial" said that he had waited all his life for this moment. On one side of the room sat government representatives, on the other, the communists. On the wall behind the benches of the judges, all of them former members of the Communist Party, hung two emblems: the hammer and sickle, and the Russian national tricolor—an incongruous combination that accurately symbolized half-liberated Russia.

The court consisted of thirteen judges. In his introductory remarks, Valery Zorkin, the chief justice, mentioned me as one of the experts engaged by the court to testify on the matter before it. On hearing this, one of the communists leaped to his feet to protest: "Why do we need an American? Why not a Chinaman?" Zorkin dismissed the complaint on the grounds that the court had the right to engage as expert anyone it chose. The first day, the communists presented their case: listening to them one might have concluded that the Communist Party which had ruled Russia and her dependencies with an iron hand for over seventy years was a philanthropic organization, financed entirely from dues paid by its members and dedicated solely to the glory and well-being of its citizens. There was a great deal of procedural wrangling. The communists behaved as if they were still in power, strutting about and treating representatives of the new government with unconcealed contempt: they resembled an ex-champion shadow-boxing, unaware that he had been dethroned.

I had expected to testify in person, to read the statement in which I argued that from the very first day in power the Communist Party had established a political monopoly and used the state to pursue its private objectives. But as no one could tell me when I would be called upon to do so, I handed in my deposition and departed for London. It seems there were over one hundred such depositions, only fourteen delivered orally, three-quarters of them submitted by Communists who declared Yeltsin's decree unlawful and the Communist Party of the Soviet Union a "constitutional" party![12] In the end, the trial turned out to be a disappointment, with the court issuing an inconclusive verdict that neither exonerated nor condemned the Communist Party. While it sat in session, the Communists managed to steal for their personal benefit a good part of the wealth accumulated by their party over the years. The trial proved a turning point that refused to turn.

By February 1993, the ruble had declined to the point where I received 800 rubles for one dollar. A pack of Camels, which in May 1992 had cost 70 rubles, now cost 350. The ruble kept falling, ultimately sinking to the level of 6,000 for one U.S. dollar. As a result, the 14,000-ruble advance which the publisher had deposited on a bank account he had opened in my name in Moscow in 1992 for the translation rights to *Russia under the Old Regime,* and which at the time could have bought a modest country lodge, now sufficed for just two slices of pizza.

Early in 1994, I received notice that the University of Silesia in Poland wished to bestow on me an honorary doctorate. It was to be conferred by the university's branch in Cieszyn, my birthplace. I had hoped mother would accompany me but her heart and kidneys were rapidly deteriorating. On the evening of Sunday, May 1, 1994, at my request, she described to me in detail the layout of the apartment where I had been born over seventy years ago, for though her body was failing, her mind was clear and her memory reliable. Since she was not feeling well, I called an ambulance to take her to the hospital. I stayed with her until the doctor advised me to leave. I called her the following morning. She said she felt fine and wished to go home. We agreed that I would pick her up before noon. But an hour later the hospital doctor called to say that she had died while eating breakfast. She was 92. My mother dreaded more than anything else being moved to a nursing home or being artificially kept alive: she made me promise I would not allow her to be subjected to such treatment. So she left this world the way she would have wanted to. In her last years she bore a striking resemblance to the English Queen Mother who lived to be 101.

Everyone who knew her considered her an extraordinary person: she had both young and older friends to the end. She had a wonderful sense of humor, never complained, and took life as it came. I most appreciated her tolerance toward me when I was a youth, allowing me to go through the difficult stages of growing up almost without a word of reproof. I sorely missed her as time went on.

I traveled to Cieszyn later that month. Unlike their American counterparts, Polish universities do not award honorary degrees wholesale but individually. The occasion was very solemn: there was a choir singing "Gaudeamus igitur"; there were testimonials from government officials and sister universities; there were more flowers than in an average florist shop. I was happy to revisit my birthplace for the first time in fifty-five years. It is a charming, partly Renaissance, partly Baroque town that has emerged unscathed from World War II—save for the synagogue which the Germans burned down on September 13, 1939, immediately on occupation. I visited the two-story building where I was born and found my parents' apartment exactly as mother had described it.

The mayor of the town also bestowed on me the city's honorary citizenship. When I asked what this honor meant in practice, he replied that if I ever found myself in need, I could turn to him or his successors for help. To which a Polish journalist present added, sotto voce, "and vice versa."

In Russia, in the meantime, the euphoria was beginning to wear off. I believe many Russians thought that as soon as they had discarded communism and declared themselves free-market democrats they would wallow in riches: indeed, Yeltsin as much as promised them this on coming to power. Instead, they found that with the collapse of communism the entire social services safety net which they took for granted had vanished and they were on their own in an unfamiliar and bewildering world. They did not resort to violence: they were too fatigued for that and anyway they had lost faith in violence as a solution to anything. They simply withdrew into their private worlds. Polls showed that a good proportion—nearly one-third—felt they had been better off under communism; yet when asked whether they wished communism to return, most of this group replied they did not.

I have written of tsarist Russia that the true religion of her people was fatalism. Communism changed nothing in this respect: if anything, it made Russians feel still more powerless. Centuries of life under a harsh and capricious climate and an equally harsh and capricious government have taught them to submit to fate. At the first sign of trouble they withdraw like turtles into their shells and wait for the danger to pass.

Their great strength lies in their ability to survive even under the most adverse conditions; their great weakness is their unwillingness to rebel against adversity. They simply take misfortune in stride; they are much better down than up. If they no longer can take it, they drink themselves into a stupor.

Two incidents etched in my memory illustrate this quality. They are trivial but nevertheless characteristic. In 1975, when working in the Public Library in Moscow, I needed a page copied and went to the window where orders were filled. The woman behind the glass grille looked at my request form and told me that since I worked in Hall No. 1—"the Professors' Reading Room"—I had to wait till 2 P.M. to file my order. It was 1:45 P.M. and no one was waiting. "Could you not take it ahead of time?" "No." As 2 P.M. approached, a line formed behind me. The woman continued to sit, immobile, with her hands folded. Promptly at two o'clock she rose to her feet, posted a notice on the window "Out to tea," and walked away. I was furious and looked behind me for sympathy. I found none. The other readers stood impassively as if what had just transpired was in the nature of things and only a fool would make a fuss.*

On another occasion, a subway train I was riding in approached the station. "*Ostorozhno, dver' otkryvaetsia*" (Careful, the door is opening), the recorded message warned over the loudspeaker. The train came to a full stop but the doors remained locked. In the United States under such circumstances, the passengers trying to get out and those trying to get in would probably attempt to pry the doors open or, at the very least, pound on them; in Israel, they might demolish the car. Here, all stood motionless and resigned. "*Ostorozhno, dver' zakryvaetsia*" (Careful, the door is closing), the loudspeaker intoned, and the train moved on with its captive crew to the next station.

---

*I subsequently read in Dostoevsky's *Diary of a Writer,* published a century earlier, a description of the behavior of a typical low-level tsarist official that matches my experience and indicates that its roots lie in precommunist Russia: "He acts haughtily and arrogantly, like Jupiter. This is especially noticeable in the smallest insects, like those who sit and dispense public information, take your money and issue tickets, etc. Look at him, he is occupied with work, he is 'busy,': the public gathers, forms a queue, every one eager to get his information, answer, receipt, ticket. And he pays to them not the slightest attention. You finally reach the head of the line, you stand, you talk—he does not listen, he does not look at you, he has turned his head and talks to an official behind him, he takes a sheet of paper and does something with it, although you are quite prepared to suspect that he does this only for show, that he has no need whatever to do anything with it. But you are prepared to wait and—abruptly he gets up and leaves. Suddenly the clock resounds and the office closes—beat it, public!" Dostoevsky explained this kind of behavior by the petty officials' desire to avenge themselves for being nobodies. *Polnoe Sobranie Sochinenii,* vol. 23 (Leningrad, 1981), 75.

Under the new regime they grumbled but did nothing. Especially disappointing was the behavior of the intelligentsia: they could not rid themselves of the legacy of opposition to the government, even to a democratic government, because Russian history had accustomed them to define themselves by resistance rather than involvement. In April 1992, by which time Russia was a democracy, I attended a conference at Rutgers University where I delivered a paper on Sakharov. During the discussion period, Tatyana Tolstaya, a brilliant Russian essayist, asked me what role I thought Russian dissidents ought to play in the new Russia. The question astonished me: I replied that in a democracy there was no room for dissidents, and that those who had once belonged to that group ought now to devote all their energies to constructive political work. But such obvious advice was not heeded. Most of the dissidents, so brave under the totalitarian regime, now retired from public life to sulk, abandoning politics to the old Soviet *nomenklatura*.

The democratic regime gave Russians more freedom and opportunity than they have had since 1917. Yet it failed to reconstruct the apparatus of government, root out pervasive corruption, and install the rule of law. As a result, it soon became dependent on the West for financial support in the form of periodic injections of loans and credits. By the end of the 1990s Russia turned into a Third World country living off the sale of raw materials, mostly energy, and foreign aid. It was a discouraging spectacle. I had expected Russia to recover more rapidly. Apparently, for all my reputation as a "cold warrior," I had underestimated the damage that seven decades of communist rule had inflicted on the country and the psyche of its people.

Reception of *The Russian Revolution*

The Russian Revolution met with two quite different reactions. The daily press and general periodicals, both in the United States and Britain, greeted it enthusiastically, praising the book for its sweep and style. It also had a warm reception from the public at large. I received numerous fan letters. One lady wrote that she found the book so fascinating that she had spent a sleepless night reading it; another confided that, for some unspecified reason, my description of the murder of the imperial family made her understand better her own marriage. The book sold well: well enough to have the profession declare it a "popular" work. The fact that, having been brought out by a trade publisher, it sold in the five figures, rather than the low four figures usually earned by university press books, did not endear it to academics. Hostile critics made certain to inform their readers that I had served in the Reagan administration, signaling in this way that anyone who had worked for such a nonintellectual cold warrior president was obviously a nonintellectual cold warrior himself and hence not to be taken seriously.

The specialist publications either ignored it or criticized it for being "biased" and "angry": the revisionist reviewers condemned as unscholarly my temerity in passing judgment on an epic historic event. Committed to the principle that history was "made from below," they criticized my downplaying the role of the workers and peasants during the revolutionary upheaval, particularly in the Bolshevik coup. But what they found most galling was that I did not take seriously their own work: they seemed more concerned with my treatment of them than with my treatment of the subject.* I plead guilty to the charge. I had three reasons. One, that if I wanted their interpretation of events, I preferred to go to the original source, namely, Soviet historical literature, whose representatives at least had access to the archives. Second, the book was long enough—nearly one thousand pages—without being burdened with scholarly controversies of interest only to the specialist. And third, and most important, I do not like to engage in academic polemics, in which so many scholars delight, because it diverts me from the subject at hand. I found support for this attitude in the introduction to his magisterial, five-volume work of the mid-nineteenth-century German theologian Richard Rothe: "I have virtually abstained from anti-critical polemic, with the exception of a very few cases when the weight of either valid arguments or the name of the critic seemed to prompt different behavior. Whenever my critics are unable to shake my conviction with their objection, then I gladly leave them with their opinion, because my critical inclination in scholarship is to criticize my own thoughts, not those of others."[13]

As for expressing judgment of historical events, I felt no need to apologize for it since, as I wrote above, I was dealing not with inevitable

---

*A particularly truculent English revisionist historian, Edward Acton, in his review of my *Russian Revolution,* criticized me for overlooking the work of this school and failing even to list it in my bibliography. (In fact, although I rarely polemicized with them, in the text and notes I made quite a few references to revisionist publications.) "Perhaps he saw that to acknowledge them would be to undermine the very foundations of his own interpretation," he speculated (*Revolutionary Russia,* June 1992, 107). Yet in a massive volume of the subject, wrtten by dozens of contributors, which he coedited (*Critical Companion to the Russian Revolution 1914–1921,* Bloomington, Ind., 1997), none of the scores of bibliographies listed a single one of my works let alone referred to them in the text.

natural phenomena but with the consequences of deliberate human actions that, as such, were open to moral condemnation. In dealing with Nazism, historians do not hesitate to damn it, and properly so: why make an exception for communism which claimed even more human lives? I recalled the words of Aristotle who wrote in the *Nichomachean Ethics* that there were situations in which "inirascibility" was unacceptable: "For those who are not angry at things they should be angry at are deemed fools," he wrote. I also followed the opinion of Lord Acton who felt strongly that the historian must take a moral stand: not to do so when dealing with historical crimes is to become an accomplice. "To commit murder," he wrote, "is the mark of a moment, exceptional. To defend it is constant, and shows a more perverted conscience."[14]

The book was translated into several foreign languages beside Russian, but, with the exception of Poland, it had a much smaller impact abroad than in the English-speaking world. In France and Italy the study of Russian history had long been the preserve of communists and fellow-travelers who, as could have been expected, disliked my interpretation and paid little attention to it: the French paperback edition, which Presses Universitaires priced at 278 French francs ($48), elicited virtually no reaction and soon went out of print.

In Germany the situation was different. Here, the three volumes brought out by Rowohlt, the country's largest publisher, were widely reviewed but with an animus that astonished me by its virulence and uniformity. I had not a single favorable German review: it was as if the reviewers were marching in lockstep, responding to some command from above. Some accused me of ignoring social problems, others of Russophobia. To certain German reviewers the book read too well—like a *krimi* or detective story, in the words of one—to be truly "scientific." I concluded that this rejection had less to do with my work than with German's own troubled past. Because Nazism, at any rate in its propaganda, had been fanatically anticommunist, any condemnation of communism brought to mind Nazism, touching a raw nerve. This held especially true of the historical profession whose practitioners were among the most zealous Nazis: disassociating themselves from anticommunism, was for them a form of self-defense.* I found confirmation of this

---

*Volker Ullrich writing in *Die Zeit* (no. 37, September 3, 1998, p. 35) called German historians "Hitler's willing guild" who dreamt of a Nazi-dominated and Jew-free Europe. Few of them lost their chairs after the war. Two influential historians of the postwar era in West Germany, Theodor Schieder and Werner Conze, turned out to have been among the intellectual forerunners of the program to "cleanse" Eastern Europe of Jews.

hypothesis in the reaction of one German journalist to a book that recounted the horrors of the Soviet Gulag: "Was Goebbels then right?" he asked himself, obviously deeply troubled.

The dissolution of the Soviet Union dealt a fatal blow to revisionism. Psychologically, this trend had derived its self-confidence from the fact that the communist regime had succeeded, time and again, in overcoming every challenge to its authority, not only managing to survive for over seven decades but rising to become America's rival superpower. From these facts the revisionists deduced—again, psychologically rather than logically—that it enjoyed solid mass support. Extrapolating further into the past, they posited that it had come into existence on a wave of popular revolution, as its rulers claimed. Its sudden collapse, without even token resistance, revealed that these claims had been hollow, that the regime was rotten to the core and enjoyed the shallowest backing. This knocked out the foundations of the revisionist interpretation and compelled its adherents if not to revise their revisions then at least shift toward a more realistic position.

I addressed myself to the deeper causes of communism's failure in two lectures which I gave at the invitation of the Nobel Peace Institute in Oslo in spring 1993.[15] On this occasion, I approached the subject from a philosophical perspective, inquiring how one could expect a regime to survive which violated everything known to be true of human nature. One could do so only by denying the existence of human nature and attributing human behavior exclusively to the environment and hence interpreting such behavior as infinitely malleable. This notion, however, rooted in the philosophy of the Enlightenment and reinforced by modern behaviorist psychology, is refuted by everything known of human beings from anthropology and history. There are certain aspects of human behavior that can be found everywhere and at all times, among them the belief in the supernatural and the desire to acquire property, to speak one's mind, and to live in families, all of which the Bolsheviks were determined to uproot. Convinced that there was no such thing as human nature but only externally conditioned human behavior, they set themselves to transform radically the entire social environment in order to create a "new man." They failed as they were bound to fail because their very premise was faulty. I concluded my lectures with warnings that the Western democracies showed evidence of committing some of the same errors by restricting property rights and limiting, through social pressure ("political correctness"), the freedom of speech.

The Problem of Property

By the time I delivered these lectures I was engrossed in a new undertaking, a book on the history of property. My interest in this subject was by no means new. I first became aware of the relationship between political power and property when living in Paris in 1956–57. I was struck that Western historians generally paid no attention to the role that property played in the development of European civilization because they simply took property for granted. But to the historian of the non-European world, property rights appear as something singular because they are so uncommon outside of the West. I first applied this hypothesis eighteen years later in *Russia under the Old Regime*. The question which I posed in this book: "why in Russia—unlike the rest of Europe to which Russia belongs by virtue of her location, race and religion—society has proven unable to impose on political authority any kind of effective restraints" seemed best answered by the fact that Russia (i.e., the Moscow state), during the decisive stage of formation of statehood (fifteenth to seventeenth centuries), lacked the institution of private ownership inasmuch as all the land, the main source of productive wealth, was claimed by the crown. I now meant to put to a test the thesis that property is critical to the development of democratic institutions as well as human rights.

After I had written in four and a half months a digest of my two books on the revolution called *A Concise History of the Russian Revolution* (it came out in 1995 and was translated into half a dozen foreign languages), I turned my attention to the historical role of property. This was a neglected theme: most of the (small) existing listerature concentrated on the contribution that property rights made to economic progress. It was exhilarating to leave the familiar territory of Russian history and contemplate such exotic subjects as Christian attitudes to property, the nature of utopias, and acquisitiveness among primitive peoples, children, and animals.

The book, *Property and Freedom*, completed in the winter of 1997–98, consisted of five chapters. The first dealt with the idea of property from Plato to the present, the second with the institution of property. Chapters 3 and 4 contrasted England and Russia, demonstrating how the early development of landed property in England enabled her population to impose checks on royal authority whereas in Russia its absence led to the rise of autocracy. The final and most controversial chapter argued that the modern welfare state, although it did not challenge the principle of private property directly, displayed some of the same antiproprietary and therefore antilibertarian traits as the premodern, absolutist one.

I tackled the new subject with enthusiasm. It was not that I had grown weary of Russia and her history, but I found that after half a century of intense work on this subject further research brought diminishing returns: it was hard for me to say something new. Since scholarship entails as much learning as teaching, I missed the excitement of acquiring fresh knowledge. I found it in dealing with property: anthropology, ethnography, psychology, the history of law and institutions opened up to me new and exciting prospects. It was thrilling to learn about the acquisitive habits of a fish called the three-spined stickleback, of possessiveness among toddlers, of attitudes toward ownership among Negritoes of Southeast Asia and Eskimoes, of the concept of property in seventeenth-century England.

The book, published in May 1999, had a predictable reception. Socialists and liberals dismissed it; conservatives loved it. The reviews thus reflected not the quality of the scholarship or the writing but the political sentiments of the reviewers.

I followed it with a brief—44,000 word—history of Communism, which traced both the ideal of a propertyless society since ancient times and attempts at its implementation in modern Russia and the rest of the world. It appeared in fall 2001 in a series called "Modern Library Chronicles."

This done, I was at a loss what to do next. Montaigne, one of my intellectual mentors, advised that on reaching old age, one give up study, but I was not inclined to follow his advice because my mind would not rest and my energies were still considerable. The question was whether to tackle something small that could be completed in a year or so, or a major study that would take years. I tended in favor of the small solution until I read Lord Acton's recollections of his last meeting with Leopold von Ranke. The German scholar was then in his early eighties, half-blind and ailing, and Acton was convinced that the next he would hear of him would be in an obituary. But at age eighty-four, Ranke launched on a history of the world, and he completed one volume a year until his death nine years later. That settled it. Encouraged by his example, I ventured in late 2001 on an intellectual history of Russia which I expect will take me four or five years to finish.

Retirement

In seed time learn, in harvest teach,
in winter enjoy.
　　WILLIAM BLAKE, "Proverbs of Hell"

I v mire startsu uteshenie,
Priroda, mudrost' i pokoi.
And old age finds consolation
In nature, wisdom, and tranquility.
　　PUSHKIN, "Ruslan i Liudmila"

It is easier to begin an autobiography than to end it, since life trails off without clear signposts.

The great watershed of professional person's late life is retirement. Harvard traditionally required its tenured faculty to retire at age sixty-six. On rare occasions, the president of the university would visit a professor in person and invite him to stay on a few years longer. Subsequently, the rules were somewhat relaxed: on reaching sixty-six, every professor had the choice of teaching full time for two more years or half-time for another four. The age of seventy was the absolute limit of active service. In 1983, however, Congress passed a law which forbade mandatory retirement on grounds of age: universities were exempt from its provisions for ten years. This meant that as of July 1, 1993, Harvard could no longer require a professor who had reached the age of seventy to retire. By a stroke of good fortune, having been born on July 11, 1923, I qualified under the new rule by eleven days. The decision to retire was mine: as far as the law was concerned, I could teach as long as I wanted.

I did not rush into retirement and continued to teach past my seventieth birthday. I finally resolved to quit for several reasons. One was that as I grew older I found my energy waning. I recall Samuel Butler writing somewhere that aging meant growing steadily more tired. Full-time teaching drained me of the energy to write and do the other things that I liked. There was the alternative of teaching half-time. But apart from the fact that the university—rightly, in my opinion—did not approve of a half-time faculty, one of my colleagues, speaking from personal experience, warned me that it meant, in effect, a full teaching load at half salary.

Second, teaching the same courses for forty years became something of a chore. Although most years I reworked one or more of the lectures, the basic structure of the courses and their thrust remained the same. Teaching simply ceased to be exciting: it was more like acting than thinking aloud, especially in large classes.

Finally, there was my disappointment with the department's refusal in May 1995 to promote to tenure an excellent young specialist on twentieth-century Russian history. I had strongly endorsed him because I believed he did the most original work on the early Soviet period in the country, in a variety of ways revising (in the positive sense of the word) the prevailing view of that period. I was outraged by this decision not because my judgment was overruled but because the department did not even bother to read any of his work and rejected him in an offhand manner on the negative recommendation of a small committee inspired more by political than scholarly considerations, namely, the feeling that the candidate was "too passionate" in his views of communism and in his criticism of scholars of the revisionist school. This verdict and, even more, the manner in which it was reached convinced me that my days in the department were over: it was no longer a cohesive body which treated departmental interests as the supreme good, but an agglomeration of individuals who pursued their private concerns and careers. As a result, its reputation declined precipitously: traditionally in the first or second place in the national rankings compiled by *US News and World Report,* by the end of the 1990s it had sunk to sixth or seventh place.

I resolved to quit while on a walk in Chesham on a sunny summer day in 1995. I lay down in a meadow, looked at the sky, and suddenly felt that the time had come: I wanted to be as free and unencumbered as the clouds above me. I waited on communicating this decision to the dean and departmental chairman until October 27, the anniversary of our departure from Warsaw—the first watershed of my life. I gave my final classes in the academic year 1995–96 and became professor emeritus as of July 1, 1996. The department gave me a nice farewell dinner. It generously invited to it all my ex-graduate students: some attended in person while the others sent letters. Of course, on such occasions, comments are by their very nature favorable. But since nearly all praised me for the freedom that I gave my students both in the choice of dissertation subjects and their treatment of them, I felt they were more than perfunctory.

One of my better qualities is the ability to close, without regrets, one chapter of my life and proceed to the next. This quality eases the pangs of aging even as it robs us of the consolation of nostalgia. Still, after nearly fifty years of university teaching I was surprised how little I missed it. What I missed the most was contact with young people and the opportunity of testing my ideas on them.

The first year of my retirement did not differ from the sabbaticals and leaves of absence which I had taken routinely every four years. But by the time the second year came around and I had no students to teach, the change struck home. I realized that with no formal duties I had to organize my days very carefully or else risk wasting them: the various academic obligations had provided something of a framework of daily life. The framework gone, I had to create my own. In practice, this meant writing at home mornings and in the afternoons doing research in the library. I was pleasantly surprised how much I could accomplish freed of my previous obligations.

I also gained time because Russia attracted less interest than during the Cold War. There were fewer lecture invitations and less media interest. Furthermore, whereas before specialists like me had been the only authorities on Russia, now there appeared on the scene English-speaking Russians prepared to lecture and write on the subject with the authority of insiders. I did not mind being less in demand, partly because my interests had shifted somewhat, and partly because I found liberated Russia a discouraging subject.

Among the encouraging developments in post-Communist Russia have been my relations with the Moscow School of Political Studies, an institution dedicated to the spread of democratic ideas and practices. Its founder and director, Lena Nemirovskaya, is a marvelously resourceful and energetic promoter of Western values, conducting frequent seminars attended by young Russian politicians, journalists, and scholars. Her husband, Yuri Senokossov, directs a publishing enterprise that translates Western works, most of which are distributed free of charge to participants, libraries, and educational institutions. I have been attending their seminars annually since 1999 and have had several of my books translated by them.

We are not trained to grow old, a process someone has described as not for the faint of heart. The surprise lies not in physical infirmity which is obvious to the eye, but in the psychological realm where changes occur that those who undergo them prefer not to discuss and others not to notice. The strange experience is that in contrast to one's youth, when one senses constant change in oneself while the environment seems to remain the same, now one remains the same while the environment seems in constant flux. Having reached seventy, one migrates imperceptibly and unwittingly into another world. The people you had known gradually die out and you find yourself among strangers. These strangers think differently and behave differently. In time, you begin to feel like a foreigner in your native land even if the physical surroundings remain the same. It came as a shock to me, for instance, in the year 2000 to wander into a shopping mall near Washington, D.C., and realize that among the hundreds of milling people, I was the only one wearing a jacket and a tie: a Frenchman must have felt like this during the post-Napoleonic Restoration era if he ventured in public dressed in knee breeches and a powdered wig. Recalling the time when, as a college student, I had worked for 35 cents an hour, I found it bizarre to have to pay $3.65 for a scoop of ice cream. Students whom one had taught as undergraduates sent announcements of their retirement! And how was one to react to young girls bandying casually four-letter words that in one's youth even a Marine sergeant would have been embarrassed to utter in the presence of ladies? Adjustment to such changes is difficult and breeds a sense of isolation as well as uselessness.

Concluding Thoughts

At this point it is appropriate to end this account of my life. Have I learned anything in the years I had been granted? A thing or two.

Concerning myself, reviewing the nearly eighty years I have lived through, I am driven to the conclusion that more than power or money or fame, I cherish my independence, the uncompromising right to be myself in word and deed. I consider my beliefs and opinions to be as much of me as my body: they are *me* in the literal if nonphysical sense of the word. I do not much care whether someone agrees with me or not: however, I furiously resent anyone objecting to my holding these beliefs and opinions because I regard such pressure as an assault on my very being. Insistence on this right has often gotten me in trouble because society at large and the smaller groups to which one belongs by virtue of one's occupation, organization, religion, and so on demand conformity. But I have never regretted being true to myself.

More generally, I have learned that human beings are utterly unpredictable, that one can neither anticipate what they will do nor understand why they will do it. This is the reason I am highly skeptical of attempts to grasp human behavior either individually through psychology or en masse through political science or sociology. Science investigates phenomena that act in an undeviating, predictable manner whereas human beings act randomly and erratically. It seems to me that gardening (along with history) provides a much better preparation for politics. The gardener knows that plants can be regimented only so far and no further: that if forced to grow in an unsuitable soil or climate they wither and die. Cultivation thus involves cooperation between humans and plants, not commands, such as are possible with inert matter. No wonder that, according to his daughter, Stalin hated gardening.

For those of us fortunate enough to be able to choose our future—and we are a small minority of the earth's population—it is important to decide early in life what we want to do and then do it. I believe that no extraneous consideration, least of all money, should deflect one from his purpose.

We must have commitments—to people, to jobs, to beliefs, to places. I find distressing the trend among today's younger generation to remain free of all commitments, to float permanently in search of self-gratification. The good life is never attained in this manner.

The sentiments of George Sand, which I read somewhere and made a note of, reflect my own philosophy of life: "One is happy as a result of one's own efforts, once one knows the necessary ingredients of happiness: simple tastes, a certain degree of courage, self-denial to a point, love of work, and above all, a clear conscience."

As to the purpose of life, if the question makes any sense, I must conclude that in view of the fact that the fear of death and the love of our offspring are our most powerful emotions, its only objectives seem to be survival and procreation. The world appears to have been so arranged that all creation wishes to perpetuate itself, though why and to what end is concealed from us.*

Do we remain the same from childhood to old age? Reading some of the things I had written as a youth I am often perplexed by sentiments that are quite alien to me today. When we are young, for instance, we care terribly for the approval of our peers. In my freshman year in college I was "rushed" by four of the five fraternities on the campus. Pleased as I was by these signs of popularity, it troubled me that one of them did not want me. Today, I care much less what anyone thinks of me, knowing that hostility is as often as not due to something extraneous to me: envy, prejudice, misunderstanding. My expectations of life, my likes and dislikes, my fears and hopes were very different then from what they are now.

---

*My conviction has been strengthened when I learned that there exist species of moths that live only three days, during which they do nothing—they do not even eat—but only seek to mate in order to produce offspring that will live three days, doing nothing but seeking to procreate.

And yet . . . To answer the question I posed at the beginning of this book—am I the same that I always was?—I can do no better than cite the reflections of the French nineteenth-century literary critic, Sainte-Beuve:

> I have arrived, perhaps by way of secretly excusing my own idleness, perhaps by a deeper feeling of the principle that all comes to the same, at the conclusion that whatever I do or do not, working in the study at continuous labor, scattering myself in articles, spreading myself about in society, giving my time away to troublesome callers, to poor people, to *rendez-vous* in the street, no matter to whom or to what, I cease not to do one and the same thing, to read one and the same book, the infinite book of the world and of life, that no one ever finishes, in which the wisest read farthest; I read then at all the pages which present themselves, in broken fragments, backwards, what matters it? I never cease going on. The greater the medley, the more frequent the interruption, the more I get on with this book in which one is never beyond the middle; but the profit is to have had it open before one at all sorts of different pages.[16]

As concerns death, when one thinks of it, it is as much of a miracle as birth, if not more, because we can do nothing about it except perhaps postpone it for a while. Walking on Brattle Street in Cambridge to my father's funeral at the Mt. Auburn Cemetery on a lovely spring day in 1973 I felt a strange sense of religious exaltation not unlike that I had experienced on the birth of my first son. Anyone over a certain age knows he lives under a suspended sentence of death. Unwittingly, one begins in one's mind to bid farewell to one's friends and most cherished possessions—the summer house, the books and works of art, family photo albums—and wonder who will own them after one is gone and what they will do with them.

When death does come, my regrets will be those of Praxilla of Sicyon, the Greek poetess of the fifth century B.C.:

> Loveliest of what I leave behind is the sunlight,
> And loveliest after that the shining stars, and the moon's face,
> But also cucumbers that are ripe, and pears and apples.

Notes

CHAPTER 1. POLAND, ITALY, AMERICA

1. Apoloniusz Zawilski, *Bitwy polskiego września,* II (Warsaw, 1972), 248n. They also destroyed 191 tanks and 421 planes.

2. New York and London, 1895, p. x.

3. *"Nichts is wahr, Alles is erlaubt,"* in *Genealogy of Morals,* part iii, no. 24 (*Werke,* vii, Leipzig, 1910, 469).

4. Cited by A. L. Rowse in *The Use of History* (London, 1946), 54.

5. Henry Festing Jones, *Samuel Butler,* II (London, 1919), 306.

6. The story is told in Richard C. Lucas, *Eagles East* (Tallahassee, Fla., 1970).

7. *Frankfurter Allgemeine Zeitung,* Magazine, September 11, 1981.

CHAPTER 2. HARVARD

1. Isaiah Berlin, *The Proper Study of Mankind: An Anthology of Essays* (London, 1997), 535.

2. Michael Ignatieff, *Isaiah Berlin: A Life* (New York, 1999), 71.

3. *Foreign Affairs,* April 1951, 360.

4. *The Privilege Was Mine* (New York, 1959), 31.

5. Sergei Khrushchev, *Nikita Khrushchev* (University Park, Pa., 2000), 220.

6. In Richard Crossman, ed., *The God That Failed* (New York, 1940), 178.

7. A. P. Chekhov, letter of October 4, 1888, to A. Pleshcheev, in his *Sobranie sochinenii,* VI (Moscow, 1955), 489.

8. Book 5, chap. 8.

9. In George R. Urban, ed., *Stalinism* (London, 1982), 350.

10. *Foreign Affairs,* July 1947, 581.

11. F. M. Dostoevskii, *Polnoe Sobranie Sochinenii,* VI (Leningrad, 1973), part 3, chap. 1, 155. See also his essay on "Vranyo," ibid., vol. XXI (Leningrad, 1980), 117–25, esp. 119.

12. I. S. Turgenev, *Polnoe Sobranie Sochinenii,* V (Moscow-Leningrad, 1963), 198.

13. Martin Gilbert, *Shcharansky, Hero of Our Time* (New York, 1986), 244.

14. Natan Sharansky, *Fear No Evil* (New York, 1998), 202.

15. *Financial Times,* September 26–27, 1998, p. iii. The survey was organized by Durex, an international manufacturer of condoms.

CHAPTER 3. WASHINGTON

1. *Encounter* 35, no. 4 (October 1970): 11.

2. Gerald K. Haines and Robert E. Leggett, eds., *CIA's Analysis of the Soviet Union, 1947–1991: A Documentary Collection,* Center for the Study of Intelligence, Central Intelligence Agency (Washington, D.C., 2001), 256.

3. "Watchdogging Intelligence," in *Seminar on Command, Control, Communications, and Intelligence* (Incidental Papers, Center for Information Policy Research, Harvard University, 1980), 179–80.

4. "Why the Soviet Union Thinks It Could Fight and Win a Nuclear War," *Commentary* 82, no. 4 (October 1986): 25–39.

5. *National Intelligence Estimate 11-3/8-76,* 18.

6. *New York Times,* January 19, 1997, p. A22.

7. David Callahan, *Dangerous Capabilities* (New York, 1990), 380.

8. A sanitized version of this report was declassified and released on February 16, 1978.

9. *New York Times,* February 17, 1978, p. A6.

10. *Insight,* June 23, 1986, 15.

11. *New York Times,* November 23, 1978, pp. A1 and A6.

12. Reprinted in Charles Tyroler II, ed., *Alerting America: The Papers of the Committee on the Present Danger* (Washington, D.C.: Pergamon Press, 1984), 10–15.

13. *Washington Post,* August 29, 1977, p. 5A.

14. Richard Burt in the *New York Times,* February 10, 1979, p. 5. See further Zbigniew Brzezinski, *Power and Principle* (New York, 1983), 455–59.

15. *New York Review of Books,* May 3, 1979, p. 45.

16. *Izvestiia,* no. 179, June 27, 1988, p. 3.

17. William E. Odom, *The Collapse of the Soviet Military* (New Haven, 1998), 67, 70.

18. *Wprost* (Warsaw), no. 25, June 23, 2001, pp. 82–84.

19. *Wall Street Journal,* December 24, 1980, p. 3.

20. Peggy Noonan, *What I Saw at the Revolution* (New York, 1990), 212.

21. *Washington Post,* May 25, 1981, pp. A1 and A12.

22. *Baltimore Sun,* July 12, 1982, p. A3.

23. Supreme Headquarters Allied Powers Europe.

24. December 24, 1980, pp. A1 and A3.

25. *Pravda,* February 18, 1981.

26. *National Journal,* July 17, 1982, p. 1247.

27. *Die Zeit,* March 26, 1982, p. 10, cited in *Frankfurter Allgemeine Zeitung* of May 19, 1982, p. 8.

28. Strobe Talbott, *The Russians and Reagan* (New York, 1984), 131.

29. *The Soviet Economic Predicament and East-West Relations.* Sov 82–10001.

30. *New York Times,* November 10, 1981, p. A22.

31. *Observer,* March 22, 1981.

32. *Baltimore Sun,* March 20, 1981, p. A4.

33. March 24, 1981, p. B4.

34. Quoted by Strobe Talbott in *Time,* November 22, 1982, p. 31.

35. Michael K. Deaver, *Behind the Scenes* (New York, 1987), 126–27, 39.

36. Noonan, *What I Saw*, 90, 224.

37. George P. Shultz, *Turmoil and Triumph* (New York, 1993), 162.

38. See the *Wall Street Journal* editorial of July 23, 1982, "Breach of Contract."

39. Ronald Reagan, *An American Life* (New York, 1999), 362.

40. Shultz, *Turmoil and Triumph*, 159.

41. Ibid., 121–22.

42. May 11, 1982, p. A6.

43. *Novyi Mir*, no. 9/905, September 2000, 176–79; My response: ibid., no. 3/911, March 2001, 222–24.

44. *Bulletin of the American Atomic Scientists*, January 1981, 1. Emphasis added.

45. The letter, in edited form, is reproduced in Reagan's memoirs, *An American Life*, 554–55.

46. Ibid., 555.

47. *Newsweek*, November 16, 1981, 31.

48. Page 1, 391.

49. It first appeared as an appendix to Robert McFarlane's memoirs, *Special Trust* (New York, 1994), 372–80.

50. Shultz, *Turmoil and Triumph*, 126.

51. Ibid., 265–66.

52. Ibid., 267–68.

53. *Between the Devil and the Dragon* (New York, 1982), 388.

CHAPTER 4. BACK AT HARVARD

1. *History of Rome*, book 22, chap. 5.

2. *On War*, book 4, chaps. 10 and 11.

3. *New York Times Sunday Book Review*, November 18, 1984, p. 12.

4. "Macaulay," in *Literary Essays* (New York, 1939), 195.

5. In a lecture at Harvard University on November 11, 2002.

6. Francesco Guicciardini, *Ricordi* (New York, 1949), 45, 47.

7. "Madame de Deffand," in *Books and Characters: French and English* (New York, 1922), 102.

8. *New Letters of Thomas Carlyle*, II (London and New York, 1904), 10–11.

9. *Point Counter Point* (New York, 1928), chap. 21, 292.

10. Associated Press Report of February 8, 1995.

11. *Sto sorok besed s Molotovym: Iz dnevnika F. Chueva* (Moscow, 1991), 184.

12. F. M. Rudinskii, *"Delo KPSS" v. Konstitutsionnom Sude* (Moscow, 1999), 109.

13. Richard Rothe, *Theologische Ethik*, 2d ed., I (Wittenberg, 1869), xi.

14. Cited in Gertrude Himmelfarb, *Victorian Minds* (New York, 1968), 177.

15. They were published jointly in 1994 by Oxford University Press and the Scandinavian University Press under the title *Communism: The Vanished Specter*.

16. C. A. Sainte-Beuve, *Monday-Chats*, ed. William Matthews (Chicago, 1877), xliv–xlv.

Index